Jungle Child

Jungle Child

By NORAH BURKE

With 32 Photographs by Aileen Burke

NEW YORK

W · W · NORTON & COMPANY · INC·

PRINTED IN THE UNITED STATES OF AMERICA
FOR THE PUBLISHERS BY THE VAIL-BALLOU PRESS

Contents

5

Illustrations

Between pages 120 and 121

Jungle Child

ONE

My Father and My Mother

Along the foothills of the Himalayas lie forests where wild elephants and tigers and panthers and all the other creatures of the Indian jungle live. My father was a Forest Officer in that area, moving camp every few days as he toured his district, sometimes a hundred miles or more from civilisation, and we children and my mother went with him.

We travelled from camp to camp on elephants, the baby in a laundry basket tied to an elephant's back, and the tents and luggage on a string of camels. The thought of a train journey was far more thrilling to us children at the time than any journey by elephant; and when we were at railhead we used to go down to the station and just sit in a train before it left, to see what it felt like.

I first opened my conscious eyes upon tents and trees and wild animals, and we imagined the whole of the earth was like that. Around us lay the world as it left the hand of the Creator—river and forest and hill, unhurt by Man, and peopled by majestic creatures who have accompanied Man out of the Dawn of Time.

11

Every few days we moved to a new camp, and there were new rivers to fish, and huge fish to be caught, and turtles and tortoises too; There were pythons, and crocodiles in the great clear rivers, and quicksands. Parrot and peacock and jungle fowl decorated the wilderness. After a tiger was skinned and the naked carcass thrown out of the camp, scores of vultures formed and dropped out of the empty blue air and stripped the bones clean. Spotted deer and monkeys were everywhere. But of course, though we saw wild animals around us, we saw their tracks more often. As every camp was near water, there were always rivers and fishing, and the sand of the dried-up riverbeds was printed with footsteps, some of them as we reached them still wet, or the grass beginning to stand up again after being pressed down.

Everywhere the monkeys watched us. My brother and I used to play Grandmother's Footsteps with them, by turning our backs and making them so curious about what we were doing that they'd creep up behind us to see. Then we'd look around, and they'd skitter back to the beginning again.

They and we were inhabitants of the jungle together. There was nothing between us children and the newborn world. Civilisation did not insulate us. The original life of sun and fishing and grass huts in the woodland was ours. To be in the forest with wild animals, dangerous and not-dangerous, was simply the way one lived. There was no other. The trees, the faded plains dotted with thorn and bamboo and ant castles, the bright powerful rivers, and all the complexity of creation were there to be learned. The voice of bird and tiger patterned the day and the night. If you looked close at a peacock feather you had found in the jungle, you discovered that it was made like a fern, and then brushed with gold. Moths had feathers all over them. A shed snakeskin was inside-out, and even the contact lens over the eyeball had come off. There were a million-million things to find out.

The root of events which have profoundly influenced our lives may go back a hundred years or more, before even our parents were born. For me it lies in the nineteenth century, when my grandfather chose Indian Railways for his career.

This was my mother's father. I never met him and she herself hardly knew him either, because he was in India all the time she was being brought up in England, and he died there. He was a civil engineer, and his sons followed him into Indian Railways. Because they were out there when my mother grew up, she went to India too, and so met my father.

A different train of events took him East. Born the second child but eldest son of a family of ten, he lived with them in our home of Auberies in East Anglia, to which he was the heir. That was the golden age of the stately homes of England, before the first world war. Auberies, a long grey house, set among its cedars and lawns, and its two thousand acres of farmland, shared in the splendour, patriarchal and feudal. Here my father grew up. He became fond of shooting and fishing and an isolated life. When the time came for him to choose his work, his parents bought him a book describing various careers for boys, and he decided to enter the Indian Forest Service, which would give him all these things. From Eton he went to Cooper's Hill to learn forestry, and so to India and the jungle.

The earliest pictures of my mother, Aileen Marion Wrench, show a little girl with a sweet, serious face. Her hair is drawn back tight, her forehead is high, and her eyes large and dark. Black woollen stockings cover her little legs and disappear under the skirt of her wool dress, which is trimmed with rows of braid. She has a big mouth, the kind which is now so much admired, and which is essential for film stars. But in those days a rosebud mouth was the thing, and Aileen Wrench had the nickname Mouthy among all the brothers and friends and cousins among whom she was brought up.

For her mother died when she was five. This little gentle sensitive child, not ready yet for the cold winds of life, was led in at the age of five to take farewell of her mother lying dead among lilies and candles, with her hands folded upon a Bible.

The Wrench children were now left orphans, their mother dead, and their father away in India. India was much further away in those days than it is now, the climate made it impossible to keep children out there, and there was education to consider. Consequently parents often said goodbye to their children for five years or even ten, and such dreadful partings were the common prospect for all parents in India at that time. Mine also had to go through it in their turn.

The Wrench children were brought up in Bedford by a widowed aunt, Jessie Bocquet, who was trying to raise her own family of four big boys on an almost invisible income. By filling her house with such children as the Wrenches, and others belonging to parents in India, she was able to do so.

In these quite happy but rather school-like surroundings, with no parents, my mother grew up.

What were the prospects for a girl of good family when she left school in those days, at the beginning of this century? Women's emancipation had not yet occurred. It is hard for us now to realise that there were *no jobs whatever* open to such girls. They had to live at home until married. Only governessing offered a chance, in conditions described by the Brontës; and this one occupation was already crowded ten times over with the daughters of the clergy and of other such families. When a friend of the Wrenches advertised for a governess, the postman came staggering along the street, carrying a huge extra mailbag stuffed to the brim with letters answering the advertisement.

Mother's father died in India, just as she was about to go out to him. Her brother Tom wrote and suggested she should come out to India after all. He and Jack and other friends and relations were already there, so she decided to go.

It was really difficult to get together the necessary clothes. Plenty of dresses would be needed for the very social life of India at that time—for the balls, dances, theatricals, picnics, riding, tennis, gymkhanas, and the myriad other entertainments of an Indian station.

It is hard for us now to realise the complications of such a wardrobe. At that period (1904–1906) there were no such things as ready-made dresses. All had to fit perfectly, and were therefore made for you. This meant that there were no cheap frocks. The first ready-made things came in a little later and were complete except for the back seam, which was left open for you to put your own hooks and eyes in to get a perfect fit, and you aimed for a twenty-inch waist. The zip fastener, of course, was not to appear for many years yet.

Dresses were sumptuous and needed plenty of space in a trunk. The skirt had to go out at the hem, and to *rustle,* with lots of frilly petticoat underneath. If you could afford it, you had a taffeta petticoat, much pleated and frilled at the hem. These petticoats fastened at the waist with long tapes which crossed over to tie in front. They were heavily inserted and tucked. Evening dresses—and some day dresses too—were longer at the back and trailed on the ground. On dance dresses there was a loop of ribbon to put your arm through to hold this long part up while dancing. Indeed, most smart dresses needed to be held up at the back. Off-the-shoulder and bertha necklines were the thing. One of the dance dresses my mother took to India was of string-coloured lace and washable, perhaps the only one we should now consider practical at all.

The blouses were never plain, but a mass of tucks and lace, like the baby-clothes of the period. My mother had one with eighty tucks down the front, all done by hand, and each tuck the width of a pin. Lace insertions in a garment scandalised the older ladies, who called such things "pneumonia blouses."

The underclothes were equally complicated. Besides the petticoats and the frilly drawers and the corsets, there were camisoles, with tucks and lace and threaded with pink-and-blue baby ribbon. Broderie anglaise, torchon lace, and every kind of hand embroidery appeared on all underclothes.

No silk stockings, of course. They were very rare—almost unheard-of—though my mother had a pair for her wedding, and they cost a pound, which I suppose would mean at least five pounds now. A girl she knew announced that she would marry only a man who could buy her silk stockings. Even then the silk was only halfway up the leg. It was rather dashing to wear brown stockings with brown shoes, since most people wore black. Not till much later was it possible to have petunia stockings to wear with a petunia gown.

It must have been difficult enough to pack all these frills and flounces to go to India, but what of the hats? All were large and beautiful, massed with muslin or valenciennes lace, perhaps, or with black ribbon and flowers, or with blue ostrich feathers. The hatpins were huge and gorgeous, the size of a ping-pong ball maybe, and they might be made of gilt or braid. Girls in India even rode in topees piled high with white muslin.

Women wore gloves for absolutely everything. Evening ones were supposed to cover the elbows, but a girl who was not well-off might have to make do with shorter ones. Gloves were worn so tight that when you went to buy them there was a pad on the counter on which to rest your elbow, while the shop assistant, using French chalk, worked the glove onto your hand. This operation might take five minutes.

Then there were fans for dancing, especially in India in the hot weather when it was customary for the gentleman to fan the lady. He probably did it badly, waving away in the wrong direction, but he had to do it! There were fans made of sequins or black lace, and painted ones, or perhaps white ostrich feathers mounted on mother-of-pearl.

You had to have sunshades with long handles, hand-painted possibly, or frilled with lace. Two or three stoles of marabout or clipped ostrich feather were necessary as well.

But there was absolutely *no* make-up of any kind whatever, not even powder: the slightest addition to the face was the sign of a loose woman.

Nor were there any handbags as we know them. All skirts had pockets. The first "handbags" were reticules attached by a silver chain to the belt.

The getting together of such a wardrobe took both time and money, but it was accomplished, and my mother sailed for India.

She was a girl of nineteen, slim and beautiful, with jet-black hair and brown eyes, and a face that reflected a sweet, good, and gentle nature, already well-tested by life.

In the meantime, at Auberies, only sixty miles from Bedford, Redmond St. George Burke had grown up.

My grandparents at Auberies lived a life which is now a museum piece. People paid afternoon calls in carriages, and left their calling cards. They played tennis and croquet. They gave house parties and garden parties and balls. An indoor staff of ten or twenty, under a housekeeper, ran the house, and had their own Servants' Dance too, as well as other amenities. Large farm and garden staffs—I don't know how many—kept the beautiful gardens and grounds in order, and ran the Home Farm from which home-made hams, milk, eggs, chickens, cheeses, butter, cream, brawn and other things were supplied to the house. From the garden came every kind of vegetable, new-grown and freshly picked, as well as forced strawberries, peaches, grapes, melons, and nectarines.

Auberies stands upon a rise of land, looking across a park, with those tall ancestral trees, down to the lake. An ancient oak in the park has been known for two hundred years as the Gainsborough Oak, because Gainsborough once painted it. In the time of my grandparents, the grounds were in excellent condition. Smooth lawns flowed like silk from cedar to cedar. Herbaceous borders blazed with colour under the grey walls of the house. Bedding-out beds flamed first with wallflowers, and then perhaps with antirrhinum.

Inside the house, behind cool green shutters that could be drawn against sun or snow if needed, the drawing room, the billiard room, the library and dining room, as well as other rooms reposed in all their polished beauty. There were rooms for everything, from pantries and larders, and boot and lamp rooms to housekeeper's room and servants' hall. The gun room was full of guns and rifles, the storeroom was packed with jams and preserves. There were nursery and schoolroom, ruled by nurse and governess, there were family bedrooms and staff bedrooms, as well as best bedrooms. All the double bedrooms had gigantic four-poster beds and gigantic furniture; and each of course had its own dressing room so that husband and wife need not dress together but could retain the romance and manners of separation.

There were all these rooms but there wasn't a proper bathroom in the place. Each bedroom and dressing room had instead its hip bath which would be set out upon its turkish towel in front of the coal fire, and filled by house-maids with brass cans. Every room had, of course, its marble-topped cane-backed washstand with its set of matching china.

And all this enormous house was heated by coal fires in each room, and lit by oil lamps. It was bitterly cold in winter, and every night the ladies in their bare evening dresses were thankful for a gauze scarf over the shoulders as they went down to dinner.

In the dining room, the great mahogany table could be extended, with extra leaves put into it so that at least twenty-four people could sit down to it, if desired. The spare leaves did not get polished so much as the rest of the table and always looked different, but this flaw did not matter much because all would be covered with a table-cloth of pure white damask linen, heavy and glimmering with the polish of starch and the design in the linen, and brought fresh from among the lavender in the linen cup-board. Table napkins were clean for every meal and folded into intricate designs by butler or footman. And among all this gleaming napery was laid the heavy silver, glittering and engraved with the Burke cat and coat of arms, and the motto on a garter. Great silver candelabra lit the room and sent a drift of candle smoke across it.

Splendid food came to this table. Not the adulterated and ersatz things we eat nowadays, but pure natural food, grown and prepared upon the estate. Even bought butter was absolutely unheard of, let alone margarine. There was a cellar full of cobwebby bottles of port, burgundy, claret, hock, champagne. In any vintage year, wine was laid down for the years to come. Some of those bottles lying there at that time were waiting for my wedding.

It was a great day for any member of the family when,

having progressed from nursery meals to schoolroom meals, he was at last promoted to coming down to dinner in the dining room. A great but also an alarming day. In all the grown-up splendour of dinner jackets and evening dresses and jewels, he had to be sure he made no mistake at table. The family played a trick on the two youngest daughters the night they first came down. When the finger bowls were handed round for dessert, everyone lifted them and drank. The anxious girls hastily followed suit.

The Auberies estate, like any other at that time, was almost completely self-contained. Besides farm and garden and dairy and saw-shed and so on, they also had their own laundry, to deal with so much table linen.

And all this peaceful prosperous beauty, shared alike by Master and Man, providing work for both, and supporting them both from birth to death in dignity and honour and security, and *home to them both*, was part of the incomparable fabric of England, now thrown away. The stately homes. Rich in peace and in rewards, as well as in labour and duty for all, both high and low. A few years ago, when one of our old men lay dying in hospital, he whispered to my mother while his tears flowed, "I shall never see Auberies again."

I did meet my grandfather, Walter St. George Burke, at Auberies when I was about three or four years old, but I don't remember him. We returned to India, and he died before I saw him again. He was a strict and, I believe, a fierce old man. People quaked in his presence. His family had to be punctual at meals, neither one minute early nor one minute late. The bedrooms were some distance from the dining room, and in order to escape censure, it was apparently necessary to wait, ready, at the door of your room for the dinner gong, and race downstairs the moment it began to ring.

He was aloof and remote. It was said that he did not

even know how many children there were behind the gate in the nursery passage. Even my father had practically never seen the private stairs leading to Grandfather's dressing room until he returned from India as master of Auberies himself. Then those stairs became *his* stairs, and in due course my own boys were not really supposed to use them either. One of them, peeping like a mouse up the forbidden staircase, as his ancestors had done before him, whispered "Not for boys!"

On Sundays, my grandparents led their whole large family and all the staff—except two left behind to cook the Sunday lunch—to Bulmer village church for morning service. The Burkes owned the chancel, and their hereditary pews were nearer to the Altar even than those of the choir. Here, when the sermon began, Grandfather would bring out his large gold watch and open it and set it before him. At the end of fifteen minutes precisely, he closed it with a loud snap that echoed through the little church and that indicated it was now time the sermon came to an end. It did so.

My brother Harry, a baby, once toddled up to this terrifying old man and, before anyone could stop him, removed his walking stick. All present held their breath, but the baby got away with it where anyone else would have lost his life.

I remember only one thing about Grandfather Burke. I had been given a blue cushion which squealed when you sat on it. I was delighted, and played the joke on everyone.

"I shall ask Grandfather to sit on it," I planned.

Everyone spoke at once, "Oh no! I shouldn't do that."

Grandmother Burke, whom my own babies later christened not Great Granny but Gran-Gran, was a tiny woman, very beautiful in her day; and in her old age witty, clever, and vivacious always. Original and unafraid. It was she who, as an old lady, placed all her silver in a basket each night at the top of the stairs so that if a burglar wanted it he could get it without disturbing her. It was she who refused help on her travels as an old lady to the Riviera because "if you have anyone with you, you've only got to look after their luggage." And she again who, in Hitler's war, never went to any air-raid shelter but removed a large picture over her bed in case it fell on her as she slept. "Home is where you are," she used to say, peaceful and wise. And again, "Don't apologise to me, Norah, because your babies are playing with mud and sitting on the wet ground. Do you think I'd have raised ten if I'd minded them sitting on grass?"

She really was tiny, hardly five foot, and looked much too small to have borne ten splendid sons and daughters.

Most of these babies were born in the Blue Room at Auberies, in the great four-poster bed. It was not her own bedroom but the room where "Gran-Gran used to have her babies because she could look out at the cedars." And, no doubt, at the red squirrels which sometimes played there. On an old estate account: "New ewer for the Blue Room." When you washed at that washstand, blue roses wobbled underneath the water, in the flowered china bowl.

Gran-Gran had one great secret, never revealed till all her family were grown up. *She always knew when anyone had fallen in the pond*. No matter what they did to conceal this frequent occurrence, she always knew. They could appear before her, dry as a bone, and she knew at once. "It was because you had changed your clothes," she told her grown-up family. "Nothing else would have made you change of your own accord."

My father grew up at Auberies to be very like grandfather Burke. He was blunt and severe, but also the most generous man I have ever met. He gave and gave, and hated to be thanked. His heart was vulnerable inside a rugged exterior though he never admitted it. He was also what was once described to me by an astonished onlooker as "unnecessarily honest."

He disliked flowers, hated music, and declared that if there were harps in heaven he would rather go to hell. Nor was he a social man. He did not care for lots of people and parties, but preferred a lonely life away from towns, and latterly became rather a hermit.

All these things influenced him in his choice of a career. Besides, he was a really outstandingly brilliant shot, and tough, too. Even after he was seventy, he was prepared to take sandwiches and lie in a snowy ditch all day, waiting for pigeons, with a white mask over his face so they should not see him against the snow. He devised many ingenious traps for marauding wild animals in India and for rats and other vermin in England. Once he even disguised himself as a cow, in order to stalk rabbits. On that occasion, every rabbit fled. But everything else he did was a great success, for he was the most thorough, efficient, and conscientious person I have ever known, and the tidiest person in the world.

He and my mother met at Gorakpur in India, and they became engaged.

They were a handsome pair, he with the magnificent big thick moustaches of the period, and she dark and pretty, her black hair combed up high into the fashionable tall roll over the forehead and flattened as much as possible at the back, as fashion dictated, with all the little loose ends caught into a slide of real tortoise shell that you could test with a flame to prove it wasn't celluloid. At dances one always put a rose or a velvet bow or some such thing into the hair as well as the slide.

With the low necks of those evening dresses, this hairdo must have been most graceful and effective. In the daytime, though, collars covered the whole throat right up to the ears, and were held up on little bone supports which dug into the neck. My father gave my mother a pair of these collar-supports, made of gold.

Gorakpur at that time (1905–1906) was very gay with concerts, tennis, gymkhanas, and all the rest. Bridge was just beginning to come in, and soon took precedence over all other card games. I can't imagine my father feeling at all comfortable among all the music and dancing. He was a man's man and an outdoor man, not a dancer at all, and it must have seemed as if he would never get married. A woman-hater. Gorakpur was particularly musical at that time, and they put on several Gilbert and Sullivan operas. Since there was no radio, people everywhere made their own music, and a lady would be asked to "bring your music" to a dinner party, however weak in performance she might be. Everyone thus had to think and give instead of just sitting and receiving.

Though all the houses of English people in India were called bungalows, this did not mean they were small. Each had a large staff of Indian servants as was the custom, and entertained lavishly.

In this endless round of parties, there was a great deal of drawing-room music, but the regimental band—if there were a regiment in the place—provided the music for balls. The dances were nearly all waltzes, two out of three, with a few polkas and barn dances, and probably one lancers in the evening. Sir Roger de Coverley was not popular with the girls because the men tried to whirl them off their feet, and it became rather rough.

Of course, it was not the done thing for a girl to dance more than twice in a single evening with the same man. That would have been compromising. So you arrived rather early, in time to get your programme full. There were always programmes at every dance, which was why every house had a collection of those tiny programme-pencils on string left over and kept them in case they might be useful.

To sustain you through the evening there were the most wonderful refreshments, which included ices—a feat in those days. For men there was whiskey to drink; the ladies drank nothing but such things as iced lemonade or ginger beer.

Conveyances at that time were usually horses, the carrying-chairs called dandies with four jampanees in the memsahib's livery to carry them, or dogcarts called tum-tums. You could hire a ticca-gharry or tonga. A few smart people had carriages. The first cars appeared in India about 1906. You sat up high, with no windscreen, and had to tie a veil down over your hat and under your chin to keep the hat on. Beetles sometimes hit your face. There were paraffin head-lamps.

But how romantic those times must have been. For instance, how exciting to dance with a man three times in one evening and set the whole station talking. How exciting to learn his Christian name! The night my mother got engaged, she lay awake, thinking, thinking. She was trying to remember his name.

My parents were married in Gorakpur, and had a camping honeymoon in the jungle. My father introduced my mother to his elephants and to the wild life she was thenceforth to lead.

Close to them, just over there beyond the trees, lay the blue hills of Nepal, the unknown land, into which at that time no one might enter, and where the last Indian rhinos live. One day my father took his bride on an elephant over the border into forbidden jungle. I thus went to Nepal before I was born.

For my parents were now to be blessed with young immediately. This was absolute damnation. Not a baby already! But perhaps, they consoled themselves, the child would at least be a boy.

TWO

We Lived in Magic

I was born in John Bunyan's town on August 2, 1907, at Brighton House, Bedford, my parents having returned to England for the event.

It was not in those days considered necessary for a mother to have any medical advice prior to the birth unless she felt ill, and my mother never set eyes on the doctor who attended her until things were already well-advanced. The nurse sent for him when she considered it time to do so.

Someone gave Mother a book called *Baby's Record*, arranged by the Reverend R. I. Woodhouse, M. A., in which she was able to record that the baby's eyes were "deep blue" and the hair "light brown." This charming little book "as used by the Royal Mother of the Future King of England" has places for the weight, length, and *breadth* of the child. I see that at seven years old I weighed "42 lbs. with clothes."

I was christened Norah Aileen at St. Leonard's Church, Bedford, by the Reverend V. Wyatt, and I received a "christening robe and £5 in the bank from Mrs. Bocquet." This was Aunt Jessie, one of my godmothers. I was given also a brooch and a necklace.

How different are the first solid foods with which we now feed our babies, and how much earlier they are given. I was having "oatmeal water and cow's milk" at one year old. Also rice in chicken broth. "Pish-pash," my Indian nurse called it.

There are "First Outing," "First Short Clothes," and "First Big Bump on Forehead." I am pleased to see that, at 2½ when playing tag with someone aged 1¾ I "made a point of not catching Margaret *too* often." But this is offset by "Loves new clothes."

I first went to Auberies when I was a month old, and six weeks later we sailed for India. My first sentence was a mixture of English and Hindustani; these two languages came to me together.

I survived whooping cough at six months, but it left me a skinny baby: "*State of Health*: poor, because she is so thin."

Then there is "Norah first learnt her alphabet at 4 years 2 months old," and "From 10½ years onwards she began writing stories, and this was her chief hobby." This last entry was made a year or two after I was ten, and was not quite correct. I was writing from the age of eight. Owing to the difficulties of lessons in the jungle in a moving home, I could not really write fluently till then, but I was so anxious to learn to write that I used to rescue old papers from the wastepaper basket and trace over what others had written, although I could not understand it. The moment I could really write, at eight, I began to produce stories. The first did not tax my staying powers. This is it:

Once upon a tim ther was a litle girl called Norah who wanted a puppy for her birthda and her mummy said she wold see when the tim came.

At least it showed observation.

My father had a typewriter for the office side of his work.

It travelled around in camp with us, and on it I later learned to type.

"Use all your fingers," he taught me, "not just the first two," and though my hands were not yet big enough, he showed me which finger to use on which letter. I still type the way he showed me then.

His disappointment in the birth of a daughter had by that time been tempered by the arrival of my brother Harry St. George Burke. My father loved boys, whom he could teach to shoot and fish, and he wanted an heir for Auberies. It did not now matter that the first child had been a girl. In fact, he had long ago become quite fond of her. She too was mad on fishing and climbing trees, and on wild animals, and he was keenly interested in her stories, advising and encouraging her.

"The best thing about being a writer," he told me, "is that you can take your work with you wherever you go; all you need is pen and paper. It will be a satisfaction to you all your life, and if you are successful you will make a lot of money."

So began our life in the jungle. Somewhere here, I mean. It had, of course, begun earlier, but that does not count. Everything that happens before consciousness dawns is history, not life. To me the world began when I did.

Some time about 1909 an Indian jungli woman walked across a strip of sand to the river, and she bent and filled her gurrah with water to carry home. This nameless incident, performed every day by countless millions of women all over India, became for me my first remembered thing in life.

The things we first remember are very curious. For me it could have been an elephant or a ship or a doll or a new dress, or playing on a verandah under the care of a man armed with a spear because there was a man-eater in the district. No. I remember this woman filling her vessel with

water for cooking. Similarly my mother's first recollection is
standing with her mother on an Indian railway station. Her
mother was wearing a plaid coat, and a passing bird marked
the plaid with white.

The pattern of our jungle life was of course governed
by my father's work. He had to look after hundreds of
square miles of primeval forest, some heavily wooded and
some scrub jungle of wild grassland overgrown with bamboos
and thorn. He had to see that the products of the forest were
properly harvested and not spoiled or wasted, but built
up again. He had to control forest fires. He had to supervise
the work of all the forest employees in his district, and do a
good deal of office work too. If a tiger started to prey on
cattle or men instead of its natural food, he would be expected
to deal with it. Should the Indians living in the jungle get
mauled by a bear, or bitten by a snake or mad dog, they
would look to him for help. All these things he did, and a
great many more besides, such as the prevention of poaching,
the giving out of contracts for timber-cutting, or perhaps a
thing like shipping fodder into famine areas.

In the meantime my mother had to housekeep in a moving
home. There was the problem of vegetables, milk, bread,
eggs, groceries, meat. At all the regular camps there was a
forest rest-house built—a three-roomed bungalow—and some
of these had a garden, looked after by the watchman left
in charge. But some of the rest-houses had none, and at
other camps we were in tents or grass huts. Then the vegetables arrived by runner with the post. Bread also came this
way until our baker forgot us for a fortnight, and then sent
the fortnight's bread in one bundle. After that we baked our
own bread in the open in a charcoal oven.

Milk and eggs travelled around with us in the form of
cows and hens. The hens were taught to sleep each night in
a snake-charmer's basket which held all of them. Then, on

a marching morning, the basket was not opened but strapped
on a camel's back for the journey to the next camp. Once or
twice a baby camel got born in the night. Then that, too, was
tied on to its mother's back for the journey, until it was
strong enough to walk.

Sport provided us with venison, pigeon, jungle fowl, fish,
and so on. Groceries travelled in huge string-and-wood crates
which were slung each side of a camel. Even after my father
retired and we came home to live at Auberies my mother
never got used to having shops at hand. She still housekept
as if they were a hundred miles away. In her storeroom I
once counted sixteen new scrubbing brushes.

In camp we had to carry round a water filter with us
too, of course. As for laundry, it was the custom to take
your own washerman. He washed everything in the river,
beating the things clean on the rocks, and bleaching them
in the strong sunlight.

For us children, toys had to be reduced to a minimum,
but we were allowed to take some with us in a small trunk
made of spotted deerskin with the hair on. We also had to
take all our lesson books. Lessons, from our mother or
governess, had to go on, camping or no camping, and I'm
glad to say we were made to work hard.

One very necessary thing was a fully stocked medicine
chest. There were no helicopters, radios, or jeeps in those
days. The nearest doctor might be a week's journey away,
and my parents had to be prepared to deal with anything
from malaria to cholera, and sometimes with the terrible
wounds of Indians who had been attacked by some wild
animal. I remember one man being carried groaning into
camp on a litter. He had been mauled by a panther, and all
his face was covered with bloodstained rag.

But for us, my brother and me, the whole adult world
of work and worry and responsibility did not exist. I don't

mean it didn't exist for us. *It simply was not there.* Meals appeared when we were hungry. Clothes. Bed. Everything. The world was set with jewels. What shall I do today after lessons? Fish? Climb? Ride? Play by the river? Dig for the Gnome King? His kingdom lies underneath the earth, and any moment we might fall upon it. Once we unearthed a hoard of iridescent blue-and-green discs. These were not the remains of beetles, they were the coins of his realm. All the world glowed with stories and adventure. Here is the sun coming up out of golden gauze upon another blue and blazing day, and it is ours. Here is the moon rising on the black-and-silver jungle. We run out into the moonlight, to hide and catch each other and watch our shadows. I dance with mine, that funny little squatty thing down there that skips along, cut clean as ebony upon the dry ground. We lived in magic.

THREE

Our Three Seasons

This was how it went. . . .

The seasons of our year were not four, but three—cold, hot, wet. During the so-called "cold" weather, which was often very hot, we lived in the jungles of the foothills and plains, but for part of the year, the hot weather and the monsoon, when it was too hot and unhealthy to remain on the Plains, we children and my mother lived in our bungalow in the Hills, and Father joined us when he could. The Hills bungalow was set upon a forested ridge and looking out one way over rippling blue ranges down towards the distant Plains; and the other way across mountains that grew more and more savage till they lapped the Snows. Along the northern horizon from infinity to infinity went the white giants, taking the sunset and the dawn, mostly virgin peaks whose pure drifts had never yet received the footprint of Man. Between us and them went the wild hills, dark with forest, pierced by silver streams, and crimson wherever rhododendron trees were in flower. Across the gulfs of air, sounds came clear and tiny, like reverse images in telescopes. After dark, the lines of forest fires hundreds of miles away crawled like glow-worms on far hills. But sometimes all the mountains beneath us disappeared in oceans of cloud. We were an island in the moving foam that was discharging its rain below upon peak and valley inhabited by pine-marten and lynx and snow-leopard.

Life in the Hills, though, was not real jungle life, in spite of the fact that there were wild mountains and forests all around us. Here, there were other people, other bungalows, a bazaar with all its smells, a cantonment and parade-ground. Before the monsoon broke, or when there was a break in the Rains, we were taken down in party best to the parade-ground or club to play with other children, or to watch polo and gymkhanas. There were children's parties of every kind, to which each child brought his own milk, as no parent trusted anyone else's supply.

Our English governess or our Indian ayah went with us. Everyone had ayahs, those dear brown nurses whose inexhaustible patience protected the white babas all day and all night. Mine, apparently, had been perfectly prepared, when I was a baby, to set me on my mother's dressing table and let me play with all the heavy carved Indian silver and the cut glass, placidly devoting her day to seeing that nothing got broken.

One evening before our parents got home from some do at the club, my brother and I ran away from our ayah. We were very small, and we stripped off all our clothes and ran. She could not catch us, but she told our father, and next morning he sent for my brother before breakfast to spank him.

Harry returned with a tear-stained face. "Dad wants you."

"Why?"

"Go and see."

I received one of the few and well-earned spankings of my childhood. They did me nothing but good. They did not

leave me with any sense of injustice or resentment. Nor did
I ever run away naked again.

Another time I threw a stick for the dog. It hit ayah, who
set up a lamentation as if she were being murdered, and
this fetched out my father to see what the row was about.

"What is the matter with ayah?" he asked me.

"I don't know."

He then discovered what had happened. Saying nothing,
he picked me up and carried me towards the bungalow.

"Are you going to spank me?" I asked, bending down
under the edge of his topee to look at his face.

"Yes."

"I didn't mean to hit her."

"It's because you told a lie."

All the time we were in the Hills we were longing for
the day to come when we could return to the jungles and
elephants and camping. *Fishing!* That was the thing. Here
we were, wasting our days, while all the time down there
the rivers were full of mighty mahseer and flashing trout,
all waiting to gulp in our flies and spoons and then be played
with screaming reels and drawn towards the landing net
and our excited hearts.

In this hill station of Lansdowne there wasn't a river in
the place. Where the water came from for our nightly baths
I haven't the faintest idea. Once the monsoon broke, there
was rain water, and the hill sides ran with streams, but during the hot weather, water must have been carried up from
somewhere. There were no taps. Only jugs and tin tubs.

The parties and the other children in the Hills, the Indian
booths in the bazaar, and my dolls which I could not take
with me into camp, were compensation for not being in the
jungle, of course. Besides, things did sometimes happen,
even in the Hills.

It was in Lansdowne that I fell down the khud. This made

everybody run about after me and be anxious. I was the centre of attention, which was fine. There was a low stone wall built all round the compound of the bungalow. Inside this, the ground was levelled, but outside it the sheer hillside fell away sharply down and down in a precipice. The Indian staff were inclined to fling unwanted things away down this hillside where, unless they reached the road far below, they more or less vanished in the forested slopes. Hill tribes always cast all their rubbish down the khud, including sometimes the bodies of the dead.

I was walking along the top of the wall—forbidden, of course—when I fell, my blue skirt filled like a parachute, and down the khud I went. The ground was so steep that luckily when I landed, it was a glancing blow, and I went on shooting off down the hillside without breaking bones. I ended on my back, legs up and head down, and clutching the wild brambles to stop my slide. Far above me was the wall from which I'd fallen. Meanwhile my brother Harry was pasting pictures in his scrapbook on the verandah at the time. He glanced up, called out "Norah's fallen down the khud," and went on pasting pictures. Soon a row of alarmed faces appeared along the top above me, my father threw his sun-hat down for me to put on to prevent sunstroke, then they climbed down and carried me up, put me to bed and sent for the doctor. It was a great disappointment when it turned out that there was absolutely nothing wrong with me at all.

In the Hills, when the Rains began, everything frothed with ferns. Every branch of every tree bore not only its own leaf but green moss and, rooted in the moss, millions of ferns. All hung with raindrops and trembling with rain. Wild begonias grew too, and other fragile rain-flowers made of water. The sound of water never ceased. All the hillsides sang with streams, and every day rain roared over the tin roof of the bungalow so we could hardly hear each other speak.

All this wet brought mould. A box of dolls' clothes that I opened every day once grew a blanket of mould in twenty-four hours. The mould was half an inch thick, but you couldn't feel it. It was a forest of grey filaments, each one as inexistent as a ghost.

Then there were the wire-worms, several inches long, that liked to get into the house out of the wet and curl up like paperweights in corners and under things. I don't know what was done to keep such visitors out of our own clothes and to keep the clothes dry. The garments appeared in the right state when needed.

But I was not interested in clothes. In finery, yes—I loved to be gorgeous in Indian beads and silks—but not in ordinary dress. If I had been allowed to wear from head to foot every day those blown-glass beads, gold and silver and magenta, that look like Christmas-tree ornaments, they would have settled a passion. As it was, my secret wish to go to the next fancy-dress party as a fairy in tinsel was never uttered and never gratified. I went as Red Riding Hood instead. Consequently I have never outgrown the attraction of sequins.

Apart from this love of splendour, I found clothes dull. I preferred my khaki camp dresses to my party ones. It was a nuisance to change in the afternoon, and I heard with incredulity of ladies who enjoyed changing not only in the afternoons but in the evenings as well.

As I grew older, my mother insisted on gradually lengthening my skirts. I fought every inch of the way. "When I grow up, I shall cut them all short again."

"When you are eighteen," she promised me, knowing she was safe, "you may have your skirts whatever length you like."

When I was eighteen, fashion put skirts at the knees so that my threat and her promise both came true.

About this time there was a loathsome girl called Stella, I think, who always stood *still*, they told me, when her dresses were being tried on.

But however much clothes were a nuisance, we liked dressing up, of course. I rescued a pink satin evening dress that my mother was throwing away, and often put it on. It was embroidered with beads and bugles and fringes, a gorgeous thing. Holding it up, I used to peacock in it in front of an old dark mirror in a shut-up room, and I wrote a poem to it too.

Towards the end of the monsoon our excitement mounted. Soon we would leave the Hills and go down to the real jungles again and the long months of camping. In the sky over the Plains began to be seen the Cold Weather Line, purple and orange, where different layers of atmosphere met. It meant that the not-so-hot weather was beginning.

So then there was our packing to do. Not clothes. Someone else attended to those dull things. No, our job was fishing-rods and haversacks. The new flies and spoons and minnows which we had bought by post from England, choosing them out of enchanted catalogues in which they were illustrated in full colour on glossy pages, were put ready to go. Those and a selection of toys. Of course, a lot of good space was wasted on lesson books.

But most of our belongings we left behind. The dolls had to be arranged in the dolls' house for their long rest, and it was not without a pang that I put them away, choosing only my favourite to go with me. Her name was White Swan, and I have her still. Her eyes close, she has a trousseau of hand-embroidered dresses and underclothes made for me by my mother; and her bed, which folds so it can be taken into camp, was made for me by my father. One of her dresses is of pink satin, heavily embroidered with silver, and fastened with buttons made of silver cord. She, like me, could be gorgeous in pink satin.

"Ma-a-Ma-a," cried May Blue as I laid her down in her blue silk gown encrusted with golden beads.

"I will write to you," I promised.

I did, and months later when we came back from camping, there were the letters lying in front of May Blue in the locked dolls' house.

We packed and locked everything we were leaving—my party clothes, my party self. Out came the khaki shirts and shorts and dresses. Our pith helmets had bottle-green linings to their brims, to rest the eyes from glare. Everyone wore these topees in the sun then, and it was considered practically fatal to go even a few minutes without them, except in the evening in the Hills; but I believe they are now often replaced by sun-glasses.

And down we went.

The road wound down from Lansdowne to Kotdwara, looping in hairpin bends, down and down into the warm air and the jungle, into the dry, sunny days, the fishing and camping and adventure of forest life.

FOUR

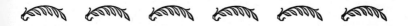

Down to the Plains

On this day we are going down to the Plains!

It's like Christmas morning, when we wake too early and in the dim light can see the knobbly stocking hanging at the end of the bed.

We're awake, we're up, we're dressed—all in one excited spasm.

"I'm not hungry. I don't want any breakfast, thank you."

My brother and I shoulder our fishing satchels. Not because we're going fishing just yet, but as a flag of joy. My clever mother made both these haversacks for us out of strong khaki drill, with a broad webbing strap that went down all round the bottom of the satchel which could thus take weight and never wear through. Everything we had in camp was khaki so that we could pass unseen in the jungle if we wished—if we remembered that now only our own actions would make us noticed. The fishing satchels were full of interesting different compartments, so we could keep everything apart and tidy, as my father approved. The tins of flies, of spoons, the lines and reels and spinners, and the gut-soaking box with its layers of flannel, all had their own

home. The satchels had fasteners which could button down
tight for those who hadn't yet got much to keep in their
haversacks, but which could be let out to accommodate
much more tackle as we earned it. Since the bags were
identical, and since there was nothing my brother and I
enjoyed more than a jolly good quarrel, the names NORAH
and HARRY were written on the outsides in ink.

So we set off.

The top part of the journey—the steep part—was performed on foot, on horseback, or in carrying chairs, either
going or coming. Lower down, where the road made it
possible, pony carts were used.

The mountain road clung to the hillside, above a misty
purple chasm with a white stream flying through it. Imper-
ceptibly, the trees changed, and the animals and birds too.
The air grew warmer. Pine trees ceased, and sal and bamboo
took their place. We saw the first brown monkeys again.

When lunch time came, there'd be cold chicken in the
tiffin basket, and hardboiled eggs and chocolate.

Half way down to the Plains, one time, a python slid
across the road into the jungle below. The men were after
it in a moment and killed it with stones.

"We'll bring it back onto the road," said my father, "and
coil it up and let the next traveller have the fun of killing
it, too."

So we arranged it on the low stone wall that ran on
the khud side of the road, and wiped the dust off him with
leaves so he shouldn't look dead, and went on.

Now here at last was Kotdwara bungalow, base camp for
all our jungle tours, the start of all adventure, with its
verandah and its few bits of rough furniture; and there
in the compound stood the two elephants waiting for us.
We were there!

Now it was a different life.

All the staff and all the needs of a large and busy camp travelled with us. The camel driver whose tender had been the most satisfactory would be there ready, with his men and his animals, to carry the luggage for the season from camp to camp. Some of them would go ahead each time with the tents and some of our men and the equipment for the new camp, while the rest stayed behind, with others of our orderlies, to clear up the old one.

Although we were sometimes in tents or grass huts, there were, as I say, forest rest-houses built at all the regular camping grounds, and these were mostly of a pattern—a verandah and three rooms, with two bathrooms behind that. The middle room was the living room, and the ones each side of it were bedrooms. They were stark plain whitewashed rooms without any fittings or amenities. They were shelter, that was all. Each bedroom had its bathroom, but when I say bathroom I mean a concrete floor and a tin tub and a hole in the wall to let the water out. Naturally, there was no water laid on, nor were there any drains. When you wanted a bath you called the waterman, who had already fetched water from the river in sewn-up goatskins or kerosene-oil tins, and heated it over a camp fire. He brought it. After washing, you emptied the bath out on the floor and the water ran away through the hole in the wall. Frogs sometimes came in through this hole because of the water, and snakes came in after the frogs.

There were no kitchens in these bungalows. The cookhouse was some way off, near the servants' quarters. Sometimes there was an outside campfire. Three tree trunks were laid like the spokes of a wheel, and a fire lit in the middle. As the trunks burned away, they were pushed inwards, and the fire never went out till we were breaking camp and someone put water on it and made quite sure it was safe to leave. The men of the camp all had their own fires to cook their individual dinners, mostly small fires between three stones, with another stone or piece of tin on top.

At every camp, shelter had to be provided for a very large staff. Fifteen or twenty servants was not unusual. This Eastern magnificence was the custom of those days, and it made things easy for what used to be called servants, each of whom did very little, nothing but his own work. For instance, one man cooked the dinner, one carried it to the bungalow, one served it, and another washed up. The pay of a forest officer was not large, and naturally, my parents had to manage on it. But a huge staff was the custom. The staff themselves expected it, and would not join a small establishment, since a cook would not wash up, and an orderly would not serve meals. It just wasn't done, that's all, and everything was performed in this style. In addition to the full staff, there were also four chuprassies (uniformed orderlies) who sat on the verandah two at a time in case anyone wanted anything. They were ready to do odd jobs such as accompanying us children and our governess to the river to carry our stuff, or helping to put up a machan in a tree if my father or mother were going to sit up for a tiger. They wore smart khaki uniforms with belts and puttees, and well-wound turbans, but usually nothing on their feet. Like all the other Indians, they could walk on stones or stamp a fire out with bare feet and feel nothing.

All the forest bungalows had only a few sticks of furniture in each. We carried round a good deal of camp furniture with us, including beds and lamps. Naturally, there was no electricity. But on the verandah of any bungalow there would usually be a typical Indian armchair. It was made of cane or wood, and the arms were extended out long in front, like skis. A hot, tired man could thus lie in it and put his feet up on the arms, and also find a special nest dug out in the arm just in the right spot to hold a whiskey-peg where it would not get knocked over.

Of course, all our camp furniture folded. The chairs would be put together with hinges made of cured sambhur leather —a thick soft bright brown leather that was easily obtainable as there were plenty of sambhur in the jungle. They were the staple food of tigers.

The windows and doors of the bungalows were provided with split-bamboo blinds to keep flies and heat out, and in the main rooms there were also punkahs hanging from the ceilings. These wide swinging fans, fringed with cloth, had a rope which went through a high-up opening over a pulley and down to the verandah. In very hot weather you employed a punkah coolie to sit outside all day, and another one at night too, perhaps, to pull the rope and keep the big creaky fan moving.

A watchman was in charge of each bungalow, and he was responsible for the house, its few contents and, if it possessed one, its vegetable garden, but this was rare.

He was supposed to keep the place in order, but sometimes there would be white-ant tunnels coming up out of the floor and branching out over the walls like ivy, as the termites built their covered-over earthen runways to try and reach the wood of the roof. Almost always the roof was inhabited by bats and squirrels. It might even house a pair of snakes.

One camp was much infested by flies. They died in millions from the poison we put out for them, and the sweeper got up half a pailful of them every day. This was because the previous year there had been some kind of pestilence in a timber-dragging camp down by the river, and the drag-buffaloes died in hundreds and were left to the jungle scavengers to clear up. We walked through this old camp, among all the bones and cattle horns. As far as you could see through the trees lay skeletons.

When we were in tent-camps there'd be hay spread on the ground, and then durries—striped cotton carpets—on top of the hay. Then the furniture was placed. Among it my father's dufta table—his office. When he was sitting at that table—"Be *quiet*. Daddy's working"—we were not allowed to speak to him, but when he came away from it, he might take us fishing.

The big living-tent was a pleasant room with side rooms opening off it. Then there were other tents for bedrooms. Hurricane lanterns hanging on forked sticks were the street lights of the camp.

If you slept in a grass hut, perhaps you could see stars twinkling through the thatch, but as it never rained at that time of year, the thinness of the grass roof didn't matter.

One night the large grass chuppa in which the men were sleeping at that camp went up in flames. All the camp woke to the roar of fire and explosions of burning bamboo, and there was the whole hut in flames, throwing up great pieces of blazing thatch. The men only just escaped with their lives, but lost everything they possessed. My parents made good these losses, so the men did not suffer in the disaster.

My camp bed had rings at the corners to take the poles of a mosquito net if necessary, though it was not often used at that time of year. When the net was up, like a misty box all around me, I used to lie and listen to the poor mosquitoes zinging about outside, trying to get in to their meal, and no doubt carrying malaria with them. But when there was no need for the net, what more natural than to push a finger into one of these rings and then not be able to get it out? Before cutting the bed off me with a hacksaw, the parents tried soap and manipulation, which fortunately finally succeeded.

One of the bungalows we occasionally used was double-storied with verandahs going all round on both floors, and an outside staircase. My parents thought they heard us playing about upstairs all afternoon one day, but it was two baby goats frolicking through the bedrooms. At one tent camp, one of our hens laid her daily egg on my bed.

Then there was another similar double-storied bungalow, again with verandahs upstairs and down, which was said to be haunted by a former forest officer, long since dead. What disturbed his rest and brought him back to this lonely block of a house, set in dead grassland beside the Ganges, I don't know. Perhaps he came again sometimes to look down the cliff across the stony shore and the broad waters, and thought of the hundred-pound mahseer which swam in that powerful current, and which he had never caught. Anyway, at this bungalow there were mysterious underground passages made of brick and very large. They were said to be drains, but they were big enough to take a stooping man, and who could have wanted such drains in that deserted place when none of the other bungalows had any at all? If they were underground passages, their purpose was lost. The bungalow was quite modern. It could not have been more than fifty or eighty years old, perhaps less, and there were no other buildings for many miles. These large brick tunnels were mostly fallen in, and they were said to harbour hundreds of snakes, so we were never allowed into them. We used to look down them sometimes, believing that at the far end lay some Rajah's treasure room where white cobras slid across blocks of jade.

FIVE

The Sacred City of Hardwar

Each camp had its own individual attractions.

From one of them we were able to journey to the sacred city of Hardwar on the Ganges, where we fed the sacred fish. There was an artificial pool on the waterfront, connected with the river. It had a little bridge going over it, and steps down all around, so that people could immerse themselves in the holy water.

A handful of atta thrown in brought all the fish to the surface so the whole pool was a jostle of glittering mahseer. They ran quite big, up to thirty pounds or more, and they were so tame they came swimming round the pilgrims who were standing in the pool.

I threw in my atta, and bought more and more from the man beside me who was selling it for the purpose. There could never be enough of looking at these great, glossy fish. But I looked about also at all the unaccustomed crowd on the waterfront. What a lot of people there were in the world.

Over there, a street barber was at work on the head bowed before him, both he and his client squatting on the pavement. And just beside them, three yards away, a little

46

brown monkey was searching a friend's head and popping his findings into his mouth.

Just then two boys came tapping along the waterfront with sticks, and as they came up to us with their hands out, begging, I saw that their eyes were all white, no iris, and looked like pigeon's eggs. Their parents had put their eyes out so they could earn a living begging.

I heard the grownups saying this, and as the boys tapped off with their baksheesh, I shut my eyes and tried to understand their life.

After that, we went down the Hardwar bazaar. My brother and I had practically never seen shops, except for an occasional visit to the Lansdowne bazaar, where the few small shops were really only booths, and this one in the sacred city was a street of Aladdin's caves. I bought an apricot china fish with his backbone painted gold.

The river at Hardwar was absolutely fascinating. A new dam had been built to provide irrigation for hundreds of miles of barren land upon which famine might any year appear. At the sluice gates of this dam, fish big and small were trying to get upriver. In the deep, fast water, strong enough to move rocks, there were big fish to be caught on spoon. In the shallow part where the water, full of sunlight, was frilling along over concrete steps, I was able to catch the minnows called chilwa with my hands. The cracks of the concrete were full of them, each one a little pencil of shadow in the distorting water. I slid my hand, brown and hot with sun, into the cool ripples, and the next moment there was the wriggle of a little fish, trapped in my palm. They were like sardines, bright silver-white underneath and jumping like squibs. We used to have them fried in panfuls, like whitebait.

The day was so hot that the sun on my skin and the river round my feet cancelled each other out. I walked in the water in the sun all day and never felt either hot or cold. But everywhere, all the time, my ears were full of the unchanging rush of millions of tons of water, and my ankles felt the ripple-movement all the time.

I stood on the lower level below the sluice gates of this dam and looked through the cracks into the great river on the other side. Of course the water was coming out through these cracks in fans of spray, but I could look through just the same into the green heart of the river. It was like being underwater. Six inches from my face flowed the great Ganges, born in an ice-cave in the high Snows near Gangotri, where the pilgrims go, and gathering all the streams of half the watersheds of the Himalayas on the way. From peak and glacier, from pure snows and from hot jungle pools where crocodiles doze on mudbanks, the water gathered into this famous and gigantic river, and now here, a few inches from my face, it flowed strong enough to kill me, and clear emerald-green.

Beside each crack clung the mudsuckers, those little fish which can climb with their suction pads and which were trying to get up into the main river beyond. If they saw me coming, they might at the last moment let go and fall with a plop, but they were reluctant to do so because it took time to climb the dam. They were easy to catch, but much too ugly to eat.

Men from Hardwar came here to these concrete steps of the sluice to spear fish. They operated in the medium-fast water, between the place where my father was spinning for mahseer, and me and my chilwa in the shallows. I should have liked to go where those men went, but they were bigger than I was, and when I approached them, the river began to pull on my legs so that another step would have had me over and away. I envied them the catches they made. A man would go off with as much as he could carry, mostly two- or three-pounders, strung on a long grass rope, to sell them in the town. The fish were free to swim here or in the pilgrim's bathing pool. In the pool they were sacred. Here they could be speared.

There was Hathikhund (Elephant Pool), so called because it was said an elephant once lost his life in the quicksands of the river there. This pool changed shape every year; one year deep, the next all silted up with treacherous sand. We had to be careful.

Indeed, there was always a possibility of quicksand, anywhere. I once sank in up to my waist when fishing along the edge of a deep pool, but luckily then found firm ground under my feet and was able to get out again. The parents told us that if ever we got into quicksand, we should try to struggle towards the nearest stones, because stones meant solid land. And, like the monkeys, we were to learn what dead wood looked like, even when it had bark on it, so as never to trust it when climbing. If we met a bear, we must run uphill, not down, because they were so much slower going up. If there was an earthquake, dive under the nearest strong bit of furniture, provided there wasn't time to get right outside, of course. In the Hills, the piano would be the strongest.

The sand of the Hathikhund held gold, and the Sona Nadi river that ran into it was thus called Gold River because of it. If you took a handful of the sand, you could occasionally see a fleck or two of gold in it, shining differently from the silvery bits of mica, but the amount of gold to be had was very small. A tribe of hereditary gold-washers lived permanently by the banks of the Sona Nadi, and scratched a precarious living from it.

We went down to watch them. The process began in the morning and lasted till night.

It was the usual bright blue-and-gold day of the Dry Weather, and the very dark brown skin of the junglis glistened with sun and water as they worked.

First they shovelled up rough river gravel, just as it came, into slotted bamboo trays over long wooden troughs, and slushed bucketfuls of water over it. The big stones were thus sieved out of the smaller ones and thrown away. Finer and finer split-bamboo sieves were used until they'd worked down to a little powder-sand in a wooden plate. Now you could really see the gold, sparkling like snow crystals, while vast quantities of discarded gravel lay all around.

Then one of the men took from his loincloth a tiny bottle of mercury, dropped one glob of it on to the wooden plate, and tilted the plate this way and that. The ball of quicksilver raced about, as they shook it, and gathered the gold flecks, amalgamating them into a tiny bead, the reward for a whole day's hard labour for several men.

They were very poor. If there had been more gold to be had, others would certainly have been there to get it. But these junglis in their two bits of cloth, one bound round the loins and one round the head, were getting it up in the ancient manner, as Bronze-Age Man no doubt first panned for gold.

But in all our camps, in all our changing homes, among all the different interests of each, the best thing was the fishing.

SIX

A Stately Pleasure-Dome

Those were no famous well-fished waters full of sophisticated fish who knew the names of the different flies. When you fished, you caught things. The rivers might occasionally be netted by poachers, but they were not fished. Most of the time, the only hunters they knew were otters and cormorants. The mahseer that lay in the pools and the trout that rolled in the rapids, reflecting sunlight off their silver flanks, were plentiful and not difficult to catch. This suited my impatience. Harry would fish all day, catching nothing, and still go on. But fortune smiles alike on the just and unjust. One day at the sluice of the Hardwar dam he fished all day with a reel which was new and very expensive, and had been given to us as a joint Christmas present. In the evening his persistence was rewarded; he caught a five-pound mahseer. I, who had frittered my day in the shallows, catching chilwa, immediately announced that it was now my turn for the reel. At my second cast I was into a mahseer. He was foul-hooked through the dorsal fin. He weighed five pounds.

A certain amount of unscrupulousness is natural to the female. Indeed, without the physical strength of man, how

51

could we keep up without it? One day I caught a half-pound
trout on spoon and killed it and used it for deadbait. Almost
at once I caught a very large one on the deadbait—one of
those big, sloppy, deep-bodied trout, running with opals. He
had swallowed the half-pounder whole. I weighed him before I took the bait out. He was a record.

One day a huge round shadow rose suddenly from the
black-emerald deeps of the pool, a livid mouth opened, and
next minute I'd hooked a turtle. It was horrible. I had to
drag him in, and when I'd got him on the sand and looked
down his mouth, the spoon was out of sight. Only the fishing
gut could be seen, going down and disappearing into un-
reachable distances. I could feel it in my own stomach. I
knew there absolutely isn't any way to kill a turtle humanely.
You can wait for the head to come out, and chop it off with
an axe, but even then the creature doesn't die at once. I cut
the gut and let the turtle go, and hoped he would survive
a spoon and hook in his belly.

Another time we called my father to look at a pair of eyes
that were staring up at us out of the sand in the shallows. He
scooped at them with the landing net. Nothing! When the
water cleared, the eyes were still there. He stepped onto a
mound of sand nearby, to go at it from a different angle, and
the whole mound heaved up. It was a monster turtle lying
buried in the sand.

This turtle was easily detained. We found we had only to
push two sticks into the sand on each side of his head, about
two inches apart. He remained there, his head poked forward between the sticks. He could see the river, and that's
where he wanted to go, so he paddled forward with all his
might, squeaking the sand. Naturally his great shell, two feet
across, would not pass between the sticks as his head did,
so there he remained. One step to right or left would have
freed him, but he did not take it. Finally we pulled out the

sticks, and he dragged himself down to the river, where he became waterborne and instantly less clumsy, and wheeled away down into the depths like a sinking plate.

The shell of these big turtles was flabby, like very thick leather, but the shells of small turtles of the same species were hard.

The fun of fishing began with buying the tackle; and since the fish knew nothing, I could choose the brightest the catalogue had to offer. Two-inch spoons, minnows painted like tigers, flies made of crimson feather and bound with silver wire—all were successful. We spent hours on our tummies gazing at the splendid pictures in the catalogues, we made our lists, we sent our orders, and at last the parcel came. Then to unpack the glorious lures and flies, and transfer them to our fishing kit. Some were too beautiful to be actually cast into water, and some became bent and chipped with all the mahseer they took and all the rocks they were hit against when badly cast.

Then there were the river picnics when, after fishing all morning in the glare, we at last reached time for food. The tiffin basket would be opened in the shade, and the water-bottle pulled up out of the river where it had been lying all morning anchored to a boulder. You massaged all the river you could out of its felt cover, but it was still wet and needed a grass nest to sit in, to keep upright; the water that came out was cold as ice and dewed the tumblers.

"Tell me the animals that went up this nullah, last night. Harry? Norah?"

"A wild elephant. Just one, not a herd."

"Yes. How big?"

"A big one. And some chital."

"Anything else?"

Ah, yes! The broad front foot and the long hind foot of

a bear. Oh, and some monkeys came to drink. In the morning probably. And that? Would that be a porcupine?

One time my father said that he would catch twelve trout before lunch time. He did too, and I went to admire them. The last one was still jumping about and all sandy, so I washed him to make him beautiful again. While I was doing so, he gave a quick wriggle and escaped. Father was kind, he said nothing, but he went home with eleven trout, not twelve, and I've never forgotten it.

To begin with—I mean when we children first started fishing—we were not allowed, because of fever and crocodiles and so on, to paddle at all, certainly not wade. So, since I must not get my feet wet, I went on hands and knees, with the feet held up backwards out of the water. The result of this was that finally we were allowed to paddle.

"But not deep," said the parents. "Not deeper than about the top of your socks."

"How shall I remember where that is?"

So my mother marked the place on our legs with a fountain pen. Each day we persuaded her to make the mark a little higher, until at last the rule was "as deep as you can without getting your clothes wet." But of course we were never allowed to bathe.

Once, however, I fell into the river, out of sight of authority. It was fun in the tepid water; I could have stayed there forever, but I caught sight of Father in the distance, casting for trout. Perhaps I had better come out. Unlike my aunts and uncles at Auberies, I had a fierce sun to help me. I took off all the wet things and spread them on rocks. All were khaki, so they didn't show up, and in five minutes they were bone dry. I crumpled them about to soften them and make them look natural and put them on again and rejoined the family.

As soon as we were allowed to wade, we could get right into the pools to fish, as Father did, and so cast into deeper water and hope for bigger fish.

Except when there was flood or melted snow coming down, the water was diamond-clear, and you could see your spoon twinkling along with perhaps a great glimmering monster of a fish coming after it. Naturally the biggest mahseer I ever saw was the one that got away. I cast my fly-spoon into the dashing water where a river entered a deep pool. Out of the black glass it came twinkling towards me, and then suddenly the darkness moved. A great shape was following the spoon—a long, powerful, dark and slender fish, a great game fish, a fighter, slippery white underneath. His mouth opened to gulp in the spoon. I saw him clearly, even the whiskers, and no doubt he saw me, but human beings meant nothing to the fish in those waters. All the same, at the very last, *last* moment he changed his mind and swung away. I am ashamed to say I burst into tears, and when asked why, could only explain "It was a fattit." I wonder if that fish is still alive, and if he remembers me.

I loved all fish, and so did one of our men who was known as Rags because of his straggly beard. Fishing is a sport that gets hold of people and never lets go, but Rags was the most passionate fisherman I have ever met. He took work only with Forest Officers, so that he could live always near a river. When anyone else caught a fish, he sat and stroked it and gazed at it as if it were his own. His rod did not take to pieces, and he marched on foot from camp to camp, carrying it like a spear.

Harry once caught a mahseer as long as himself, a twenty-seven-pounder, and he played and landed it entirely alone. He often caught ten-pounders, and he deserved to do so, whereas I did not.

The poacher's method of fishing with grass appealed to

me. You fixed elephant grass and stones across the outlet
of a pool, then you diverted the stream further up. When the
pool ran dry, there were your fish for you!

Naturally we children did not have my father's skill with
a rod, and I, at any rate, was never likely to acquire it, since
I wouldn't go on trying if nothing was being caught. But
by the time I had scared every fish in the local river, it
was time to move on to the next camp and new, undisturbed
pools, suitable for clumsy fishermen.

Of course we had to waste a lot of time every day with
lessons. Although I was longing to read and write, there
was no getting away from it: lessons were an appalling
waste of time. On a nonmarching morning, my mother or
our governess taught us every day on the verandah of
whichever bungalow it happened to be, or in one of the
tents.

In the early days, when I was setting out the alphabet
blocks in order, I could not find *Elemeno* to come after H I
J and K.

"There isn't *Elemeno*," said Harry, two-and-a-half years
younger than I was. "It's four letters. L-M-N-O."

I laughed him to scorn.

But later I read all the mildewed novels in the different
bungalows, the bound volumes of *Chums* and *Boys' Own
Paper* and *Little Folks* that people gave us, the illuminated
scripture stories written for children. I listened until I stopped
breathing to the stories told me by Gwala Ram, our groom,
and by Miss Wilkinson, our governess, who had been secretary to a Ranee. I wrote stories, I typed them, and I accepted
them for publication in a magazine I edited, called *The
Monthly Dorrit*. It consisted exclusively of the work of Norah
Burke. Also, I went in for the *Little Folks* competitions.
Norah Burke did well in *The Monthly Dorrit*, but in *Little
Folks* she won only a few "highly commendeds."

I did not mince my language in those days: " 'Bother' he cried, and with another oath he left the room."

Father always advised me on my stories, and continued to do so by post, later on, when I was at school in England and he back in India. But in those days I often lay on the floor of the tent, on the durry with the rustling hay underneath, writing my stories, and Father at his dufta table. Then the bearer would come along, in his white uniform with the green cummerbund, bringing a well-polished, well-wiped oil-lamp when it was getting too dark for us to see. After a bit, when the chimney had warmed up, we could turn the flame up to get a better light, but not before, or the glass cracked.

I knew that lessons would help me to write, but we got out of them whenever we could. Once, a totally unexpected downpour, during the Dry Weather, found a leak in the tent and filled the box of books with water, thank God, and nothing could be done till they were dried.

As soon as we could, we escaped to the river to fish and build sand castles, or to have another dig for that Gnome King.

We had to have one of the chuprassies with us when we went to the river, in case of any possible danger in the jungle. The bear, for instance, who was scrambling about on the hillside at the other side of the stream, might have been nasty if he had been on our side. As it happened, he never saw us, and ambled away.

One of the chuprassies who often accompanied us to the river was Durga Datt, a genius with sand castles. He liked a new bank of damp and solid sand in which to work, and his sculptor's fingers then produced a palace. In the wall of yellow sand he would scoop room upon room, opening one into the other, with Indian arches and windows and turrets. When it was ready in all its magic intricacy, he

searched the nullah for coloured stones with which to make
the garden. He went into the jungle to get leaves and grasses.
Flowers if he could find any, and berries, and ropes of those
little scarlet seeds, black at one end, known as lal-lal beeges
and used by jungle women for jewelry. With these he made
the palace garden. "In Xanadu did Kubla Khan a stately
pleasure-dome decree . . ."

Then perhaps we'd sit on the sand while he told us
stories. We ate the biscuits we'd brought, and sucked the
warm golden-pink juice of oranges. There was the sound of
wind in leaves, and the everlasting water-music that sang
its different notes from pool to pool, the noise of monkeys
sometimes, and the piping of birds. The top sand was hot
and loose, but if you dug into it with not-caring nails as
you listened to the story, you came to cold wet layers.

Durga Datt told us romantic Indian tales and legends, some
of them apparently exceedingly unsuitable for children. As
he continued to tell them to us after admonition, he had to
be dismissed in the end. Such, however, is the innocence and
natural resilience of a child's mind that I cannot remember a
single one of the purple stories. I remember only the sand
castles with their jewelled gardens.

After that, we'd fish some more and then walk back to
the bungalow through the jungle, carrying our fly-rods
turned backwards behind us through the trees so as not
to run the delicate tips into some branch. We did not always
take them to pieces because we'd need them again so soon. I
picked one or two of the red-and-orange bher berries as I
passed, and ate the scrap of acid-sweet flesh on the large
stone, enjoying it as much as the deer and monkeys did.

At the bungalow we'd string out our fishing lines to dry,
and separate the flannel bits in our gut-soaking boxes, drying
them too. They'd be wetted again tomorrow, and the coiled
gut set between the flannel to soak as we walked to the
river, so it would be ready the moment we got there.

SEVEN

Marching Morning

But if it was a marching morning . . .

No lessons. No fishing. We'd be up early while all the
jungle was still white with mist. We children were taught
always to shake shoes out before putting them on, because of
scorpions. I can't help it, I still do this now! My brother was
lucky with his short hair: mine was long and I could never
lie down flat in the bath with my head in the water as he
could. Now I fought the knots out of it and plaited it. We
dressed in greatcoats to begin with, though soon it would be
blazing. But we were starting early to get the cool of the day.

All the compound was in a turmoil of packing, with men
arguing, animals grunting, and the clap of wood as furniture
was folded and boxes closed. The camels, complaining loudly,
knelt down, and crates and tents and bundles were roped on
to them. Sometimes one of them, ready-loaded, on its feet,
and bored, would regurgitate its bag of water and have a
drink. This was fascinating and quite disgusting to watch.
Up came the pink-veined bladder of water till it hung out
of the side of the mouth—gobble-bubble—and then it would
be swallowed again. A new-born baby camel, made of creamy

cotton-wool, stood wobbling at his mother's side till he, too, was folded up and packed. There'd be squawks from the chickens in their baskets as they were hoisted on board. Finally the loaded camels were strung in a chain, each tied to the one in front for travelling.

Now all was ready, even to our pet tortoises and turtles in their linen bag for the journey.

The sun was getting hotter all the time. One really cold night we put out water in saucers because we'd never seen ice, but it didn't freeze.

"Write to England," said Ayah, "and tell them to put some snow in a bottle, and some ice, and send it to me so I can see what they are like."

When I first saw snow, I thought it was sugar and tried to eat it.

Now here were the elephants coming up to the bungalow to take us to the next camp. Each had a pad strapped on her back for us to sit on.

At the word of command from her mahout, who sat astride her neck, each elephant knelt down, and one of the orderlies held her tail across to make a step. Then up we scrambled, treading first on the big back foot, then the tail, and so up. We had to hold on while the animal heaved to her feet, and then we were off, the dogs running along beside us.

My brother Harry and I and, later, the baby brother Peter, travelled with our ayah and the mahout on one elephant, and our parents on another. We often wondered why we did not go with them. It was not until I had children of my own that I found out, bless them!

But there was one good game that kept us quiet. Harry and I had never been to a dentist, but we knew that dentists stopped up holes in teeth. The wooden pegs at the corners of the katola pad on which we sat on the elephant were useful things on which to sling things like water-bottle and field glasses. But what was much more exciting was that they had little cracks and holes in them. We pretended they were teeth and we were dentists, and as we travelled along we picked leaves from the trees as they swished past, and mashed them and stuffed the holes. Next day these could all be picked out and done again.

Our fingers got stained with the squashed green juice of leaves, and we soon learned not to try for bamboo blades, which cut like knives as they were dragged through our fingers.

It was a slow and rather lurching movement as the elephant walked along. An elephant cannot gallop or jump; she can hurry, but mostly she plods. As we swung along she too would pluck at the leaves that brushed past and then cram them into her mouth. Monkeys swore at the dogs, and the dogs barked back.

If we came to a river, the elephants waded through, carefully feeling for footholds among the boulders, and testing the footing before they trod. The pet turtles and tortoises clunked about excitedly together in the linen bag at the sound of the water. Indeed they always knew, long before we reached a river, that it was coming, and we decided that they must be able to smell water. They need not have worried: as soon as we got to the next camp, we'd take one of the tin tubs and send the water-man for water, and make them up a comfortable pool to live in.

Sometimes there'd be a road being made through the jungle. The gangs of road-coolies spent most of their time sitting about smoking, but if the Forest Officer's elephants suddenly appeared round the corner, every man would leap to his work as if electrified, and hack away at something.

Sparks flew from flint and sledge hammer and pickaxe. No doubt they all sat down again immediately he was out of sight.

If we crossed a plain, sometimes there'd be a tree standing up by itself, hung with strange coconuts, which were the nests of tailor birds. One time, when the nests were empty and not being used, we picked one, like fruit, while on the elephant's back. Most beautifully woven of fine grass and hair, it hung from a thin stalk on a top branch, and the opening was at the bottom. The bird enters from below, and there is a pocket on the inside for the eggs, where no snake can reach them. The nests are so beautifully woven that, like cloth, they can be kept for years.

As we travelled through the jungle, the tracks of wild animals could be seen in the dust of the path and in the sand by the rivers, which were usually dwindling and drying up at that time of year. Tracks of deer and bear and panther and hyena might be seen, of tiger and elephant and jackal, perhaps pig or porcupine or wild dog. Sometimes we saw some of these creatures themselves—a wild elephant slushing in a mud pool, a panther dozing in the heat of the day among the speckled shadows, crocodiles on the rock slabs by the river, a flight of green parrots. The animals took no notice of the tame elephants unless someone spoke or pointed and so drew attention to the presence of human beings.

Once our elephant walked into quicksands. It's dangerous to be on an elephant at such a time, for in her struggle to save herself, she may seize the human beings on her back and tread them down into the sand to get a foothold. On this occasion there was a piece of sand between two pools that looked safe enough, with quite large stones on it, but the elephant did not want to tread on it and resisted her mahout's command. He ordered her forward with a touch or two of the double-barbed ankus on her head to remind her of his weapon. She obeyed. Instantly her front legs sank in up to the shoulder, and we were thrown forward but managed not to roll off. Fortunately her back legs remained on firm ground and, calmed and encouraged by her mahout, who now realised his mistake but kept his head, the elephant then drew herself backwards out of the morass.

Now here was the new camp at the end of our journey. The elephant knelt down, and we slid off her and raced into the bungalow or tents to see what was to be seen.

First there'd be a picnic meal in the perhaps musty but getting-aired bungalow which might not have been used for a long time, and in which the disused whitewashed rooms echoed until our furniture got into them. For two or three days these bare walls would now be home. We ate hungrily of cold jungle fowl, perhaps, or green-pigeon pie or cold venison, and fruitcake, bananas, melon, oranges, and chocolate. We attended to our pet animals. Then out into the sun to see the camels unloaded, to open the chicken baskets and let them out and feed them. They cackled as they popped out, one by one, and shook their feathers straight after the journey and looked round for food. We felt in the basket for any eggs that had been laid on the journey. After that, as soon as possible, a visit to the river.

From a cliff I look down at it. There it flows, the remembered great broad stream which we have fished before but not for ages. Giant mahseer live in it. The river, too big ever to dry up, comes pouring out of the dark gorge, and spreading wide into glittering shallows. Beneath the sunny, glassy water, the sand is cut in the same ripple-pattern as the current above, and wobbles of dark gold light travel over it in lines. Over this sand, through the tremble of light and water, comes a gigantic goonch fish, sometimes known as the freshwater shark. He looks at least five feet long with a great club head and a mouth full of teeth like the bristles of a hairbrush. If he takes your spoon, he'll sink like a stone and you've got to winch him in, and maybe lose your tackle. All the same, I ache to catch him. There isn't a chance, though. He idles in peace through the brilliant shallows away off into deep water again.

In places along this river are slabs of clay. Harry and I used to dig it out and shape it into cups and bowls which we baked in the sun and stored on a ledge in a tiny cave.

Years later, when I was at school in England, my mother wrote to me "To-day we camped by the Goonch Pool, and I looked in that little cave. Your cups and bowls were still there." After I became a mother myself, I knew what she must have felt like, seeing them, and Harry and I the other side of the world.

Sometimes these bigger rivers had their banks all stranded with logs and sleepers which were being floated down to the sawmills from forests further up, and which had got left behind when the water went down after the monsoon. A sleeper was just right as a one-man raft, and we poled about on them, until men came down the river on real rafts, shepherding all the logs into the stream again.

I watched one of these timber rafts shoot the rapids. It was thirty feet long or more, made of bamboo poles lashed together and able to be rolled up like a blind. On it a little hut was built, and the men had got a fire going and their dinner cooking. The raft took the fast water like a swimming snake. It rippled its way over the rapids, without putting the fire out or upsetting the dinner.

Of course those were wild rivers, there were no boats, but we had a collapsible canvas boat which travelled round with us and was very useful. We learned to row, and to manage it, though sometimes the current was too fast for even a man to make this feather of a boat do exactly as he wished. I should have liked, for instance, to pause beside that cliff that lay in heavy shadow and look closer at the blue rock pigeon on her nest behind the curtain of maidenhair fern. But we are swept past, and all I see is the bird's startled eye cocked at us, and her grey plumage lit with a mauve-and-green sheen.

I should have liked to drift up close to that little gharial crocodile on the sandbank without frightening him, but we whisk past. He's only half grown, and he'd be harmless, anyway, however big he grew, for he's a fish-eater. The snout, which makes him look like a sword, is only about two inches wide, and set with identical long pointed teeth like a comb. It can demolish fishes but not human beings. Why the snout rises in a bump like that at the end no one knows. The eyes are raised, presumably because the reptile needs to look around before coming out of the water to bask. In a mugger, of course, the eyes and nostrils are raised so he can lie submerged while waiting for his food, much of which lives on land, unlike the food of the gharial. There were human bones in the stomach of one of the mugger crocodiles my father shot, and bracelets and anklets and beads have also been found inside them. The largest he ever shot was twelve feet long and needed sixteen men to lift it.

The crocodile is, of course, a saurian of the first magnitude, possessed of unbelievable strength. It is long-lived and slow-growing. If food is scarce, the reptile can suspend its growth and remain the same size, and do some more growing later. If one of them loses a tooth in a fight with some larger creature, he can grow another, and he has three eyelids to each eye.

The eggs, about the size of a goose-egg but longer, are laid in the sand, and the baby crocodiles will snap around at anything before they are even fully hatched. They make straight for the water and fend for themselves at once. Fortunately many get devoured, by eagles, vultures, and other things, on their way to the river, and by big fish and even other crocodiles while they're growing.

Although they live in the water, and return to it promptly at any sign of danger, they do often come out on to the land, especially to bask in the sun, and they lie without movement in or out of the water, for many hours. The tail, with all its formidable power, is a drag to them on land, but it's also a weapon, and in the water it's the swimming blade, and can propel the reptile at great speed.

As the crocodile grows, the skin hardens into an armour plate which can even keep out bullets. My parents have had bullets from powerful rifles bounce off a crocodile, and it's well known that the only place to get them is the eyes or in the soft skin behind the foreleg.

Although a crocodile is a living thing, created to be as he is, it is hard to feel any sympathy for him. The mighty jaws, the set and bony grin that goes back behind the eyes in a smile of death, the cold-blooded cruelty as he drags his prey down into the water and then stores the meat till rotten in some hole in the bank—even the greenish tone in the yellow of his underside—fill most people with revulsion.

The bones of almost every jungle animal have been found in crocodiles' stomachs.

Muggers grow fat near the burning ghats where half-burned bodies get thrown into the river. Occasionally, when we were fishing, there'd be some part of a body snagged in the current with little fish nibbling it.

Once I was going to look at some pots and pans and other things lying by some ashes on the sand, when the chuprassy stopped me.

"They belong to a dead man," he explained. "His people put them there when he was burned. He will have need of them."

Crocodiles which were out sunning themselves on rocky

ledges or sandbanks would slide back into the water if they saw us, but if we arrived on an elephant, they might not notice that there were human beings there. Then you could observe that they'd been there some time, maybe, with the mud dried white, and that it was worth a shot at the big one.

There was the sound of cartridge going into rifle. We held our breaths while my father aimed—none too easy with a tiny target and from an elephant that isn't keeping still— then there'd be a deafening report, and the crocodile leaped in a convulsion, *up* and then *smack* down into the water, all the others crash-dived too, and waves washed the rock.

We were not always able to recover the body, for a shot crocodile sinks and does not float again until the stomach becomes blown with gas. But my mother had a case made of crocodile skin, fitted with cut glass and silver and much too heavy, even empty, to be any good. The really horny skin of the back was not used, of course—sometimes it was an inch thick and unworkable—but even the underskin was too heavy.

EIGHT

Purple Blood and Norah's Glory

The river beds were often full of huge boulders as the water subsided after the monsoon. These got bleached white in the sun, and hot. Sometimes, when it was so hot that your upper lip prickled with sweat, the rock became almost unbearable to naked feet, even mine, which were getting harder, though not hard like the Indians' feet. Then it was good practice to go on the boulders barefoot and jump your way across. The hot rock kept you moving, and you had to choose in mid air where you were going to come down, missing the sharp stones, and the old snags left there by flood. These branches marked the exact height of last high water, with old grass caught in them, tinder-dry and dragged downstreamwards. They went white and looked like the bones of trees, and they became perches for kingfishers.

Flycatchers flittered along the stones, and cormorants sat in twos and threes on the big boulders where they would hang out their great green-and-black wings to dry.

There was one place between two boulders as big as tables, where the water went through in an unbroken shoot of glass; and shoals of fish, up to two or three pounds each in size used to go through it.

I lay flat on the hot rock, with a home-made spear, and waited. The heat in the stone worked up at me through my cotton clothes until I almost had to jump up again. But I knew it would go off—like the heat of a plate taken out of an oven—as my body cut off the sun's rays.

I stared down into about two feet of water, so clear it was almost not there, and so smooth that it did not show at all except where it was caught in wrinkles along the stone. But if you put a finger in it, the water feathered up your wrist, and the fish had to shoot through fast, with a dark quick wriggle or they'd never have got through at all.

Here came the first! It was through like an arrow—another and another—here they were! The yellow bottom of the shoot vanished under their slim, spotted, dark-green bodies. I plunged my spear into the shoal. Everything was shattered, foam splashed my face, and the spear came up empty.

There wasn't long to wait for the next shoal through, but I was no good at spearing. Not only did the water refract my vision, and the power of the current turn my spear, but once again I wanted the prize without the work. I went back to my rod, and put on my lucky minnow, the one with the enamel wearing off, and caught small mahseer with that instead.

Of course, not all the rivers were fast and big, and some of the little jungle streams, too small even to have a name, were beautiful beyond telling. Especially in winter morning mist, when the air was gold and silver at the same time, as the sun rose, and the trees twinkled with dew, and the footprints of a tiger might go up the watercourse like a chain before you, disappearing into the vapour.

There was one dark forest through which our jungle road wound. The trees were thick and still, and there was *silence.* No monkeys crashed and swore as we went by, no parrots screeched. Even our spaniels never barked or panted, but trotted quietly along with the elephants. Each side of us lay forest like the panoramas of coal forests in the prehistoric world. Old trees lay fallen in dark water. Creepers joined the living and the dead. There was a smell of mushrooms.

Suddenly the stream left its shadows and crossed our path, laughing out into the sunlight over coloured stones. There were cornelians and agates. There were even green ones. All brilliant with sun and water.

In another small and peaceful stream, just drying up, and the pools getting disconnected from each other, I went to pick up a curious spotted stone, when it got up and swam away. We found the pool to be full of these little turtles, and we caught some of them with the landing net, letting them all go again except two we kept for pets.

As the parents could not see how to write NORAH and HARRY indelibly on live turtleshell without hurting the turtle, we were told to choose two that were different. But all the turtles were the same size, about eight inches long, and all had dark greenish leathery shells with cream spots on them, and heads like snakeheads. Finally we chose two that we could call Three-Spots and Four-Spots because of the marking. Later, when we added two tortoises to the collection, they were called Square-Spots and Funny Face.

Being well up in desert-island stories and boys' adventure tales, we knew how to keep turtles prisoner. We turned them on their backs. Three-Spots and Four-Spots promptly shot out long snaky necks and levered themselves smartly right-way-up again. Their shells were not yet large enough to inconvenience them. This shook our faith in Robinson Crusoe.

Then there was the streamlet that twinkled its way around,

in, and through a banyan tree—the well-known tree that throws down aerial roots from its branches, and thus, as these thicken into trunks, grows a whole grove out of one tree. Under this tree you could seize a half-grown root hanging down from above, and run and jump, and be carried flying over the stream like a monkey, to the island on which the banyan grew.

There was another island on the Ganges which we visited for terns' eggs. This island was all stones, without any vegetation, nothing but a grey streak in the racing water. The crossing had to be made by elephant, since the river was too much for the boat.

Just here, the whole river bed was large boulders with the small stuff washed away, and the elephant felt her way slowly down into the flood. We were told to hold on to the katola pegs (with all their dental cavities neatly filled) and to hold tight. Every step had to be tested by the elephant and then slowly taken, and at each step the Ganges boiled up higher on her flank so she had to lean against it. The mahout cautioned and encouraged her. She did not resist him as she would have done if she had considered the danger too great; as for instance when he had wanted her to go forward on to that sand which she knew was quicksand, or if he wanted her to handle a dead panther or tiger, which she loathed. Now the pair of them worked together. Soon the water was well up over her tummy and foaming on her shoulders. It tore past, black and bubbling, just under our shoes, and no doubt the parents began to wish they hadn't brought us. But now we were through.

A cloud of river terns, in two sizes, rose with shrill protests at this invasion. The island was small, and there were hundreds of them, yet it was almost impossible to find the nests. Millions of speckled grey pebbles hid the speckled grey eggs that were of course laid loose in pockets of sand.

Still, we collected enough for a meal and brought them home and had them done like plovers' eggs. They were rather fishy, with bluish whites that remained half-transparent even when hardboiled.

Real floods came sometimes. We watched one jungle bridge disappear under flood as melting snow-water came rushing down, green and boiling, rising twelve inches in five minutes. The water raged, and rose and rose till it was pouring all over the stone-and-bamboo bridge. All sorts of flood wreckage was being rolled and heaved over and crashed along, including trees, which came down whole with their feet turned up like corpses.

Where the rock is soft, or in clay, the whirlpools of floodwater bore out deep-drilled holes. When the flood goes down, these dry out, together with anything caught in them. In one of them with a sandy floor I found a little tortoise trapped. Perhaps he could have lived there until the next flood came to release him, but more likely he would have died of thirst and starvation if I had not found him and released him into the river again. He peeled off thankfully into the pool, becoming lost not in darkness or opacity but in sheer distance of water. Out of all the uninhabited miles upon miles of wild forest, chance brought me to him, to prove that no situation is ever hopeless. Perhaps he is still alive. Perhaps he will outlive me and my children's children.

Similarly, I lost a tiny vital piece of fishing reel in the sand, and this put that reel out of action because new parts had to come from England, months and months away. Some time later, when we returned to that river, I picked the bit of reel out of the sand by chance when I wasn't even thinking about it, and so was able to use the reel again.

I lost Grey Hen, too, in the sand. She was made of lead, like lead soldiers, and I loved her. One minute she was there, and the next she was gone. I looked and looked. My governess was getting impatient.

"Come on, Norah, you've got dozens of other animals."

"Come on, Norah, we can't wait any longer."

I gave one last push at the sand, and Grey Hen popped up out of it.

A thing we all enjoyed doing was tying our own fishing flies. Of course, this can become extremely specialised. I've had a man tell me, "If you want to tie your own flies, you want to get a good red fighting cock and a blue Andalusian hen, and breed a cockerel from them and keep him for four years, and then he'll give you feathers worth tying flies with."

In those days I couldn't have waited four hours, but luckily there were materials to hand that were brilliant enough for even my gaudy soul. Blue-jay feathers were to be found in the jungle, or taken from the bird if my parents shot one. Chukor partridges and green parrots provided other colours. And if we'd had a peacock or jungle fowl to eat, every kind of fiery feather was at hand. Gold and silver thread, bronze too, and hooks, had been bought when we sent our annual order home for fishing tackle. So you took a hook, and the most dazzling feathers you could see, and bound them together with tinsel wire. Then you gave it the most gorgeous name you could invent—Purple Blood, Norah's Glory.

I even caught fish on them. There was a family prize—a bar of chocolate each day for the largest fish caught on a home-tied fly. I won it sometimes. Years and years later, long after I was grown up, an experienced fisherman said to me, "If you want to catch trout in this loch, you'll use a fly like—" he studied my fly-box—"that one," and he pointed to Norah's Glory.

The rivers were the pattern of our life. The changing

streams, the flood, the drought, the pools and rapids, the sands where we picnicked and weighed what we had caught, and built the castles, and moulded the little clay bowls.

Around us were forests where great animals lived, elephants enjoying a century of life in these wild glades, panthers and bears, sometimes dangerous but almost always preferring to get out of the way quick. Above all, tigers! The tiger, the great killer, the black-and-orange King of the Forest, ten feet long, this was his jungle.

NINE

Tiger Country

This was tiger country.

The heavy jungle, the scrub with its thick elephant grass and stripy shadows, the many pools, and the nullahs and firelines along which he could pace all night in search of his prey—all was right for him.

Plenty of sambhur lived in the dense forest, and often he could pull down a hind to give him food for several days if no one came to sit up over the kill, and if the scavengers of the jungle took no more than their natural share. He killed the stags too, coarse-haired and bearded, with the broad antlers that have to be carried laid back with the chin up when plunging through the trees. He killed other things. He liked wild pig and peacock; and he picked up buffalo around the villages when they came out to graze in charge of small boys. The stray cow or goat fell to him, or the spotted deer, though goats and chital were more the prey of leopards.

Nine or ten feet long, the most expert killer in the world, and painted like a rajah, he was one of the most magnificent creations of the Almighty.

75

At one time my father was in charge of Kumaon Forest Division, afterwards made famous by Jim Corbett in his magnificent book *Man-Eaters of Kumaon*. And the man who followed us into the Lansdowne Forest Division was Mr. F. W. Champion, whose unique photographs of tigers and other wild animals are world-famous, and were taken in these, our own forests.

Whenever we came to another camp, there might be news brought in of a local tiger-kill. Then we would go out to have a look at it, and choose the tree in which the machan would be placed.

Times change. Nowadays one prefers a camera to a rifle; the preservation of the great animals of the world is superior to their destruction; and game sanctuaries are—thank Heaven —already in being, with more planned. It was not always so. At the time when I was a child in India, the photographing of wild animals had not begun. Fast cameras and fast film were not yet invented; and the longer exposures that were then necessary made wild-animal photography out of the question.

Besides, some of these animals were dangerous and destructive to the people of the jungle villages. Would we welcome tigers and panthers and bears living wild in our own woods, close to our towns and villages, here in our own country? Suppose your dog was taken by a panther in your own garden? Suppose that if you walked down the road one evening you got mauled by a bear? The Indian villager is desperately poor. He always was so, from time immemorial long before the first British merchant ever set foot in India, and he is so still in his self-governing land. His cattle are his life, and if a tiger is eating his buffaloes, he wants the tiger killed.

It is not the sportsman who reduces the number of game. He is anxious for its preservation. It is the spread of Man, of cultivation and civilisation. Crops and big game cannot exist together. The only way is to separate the two and give land to the animals—enough land to support them.

At the time we were in India, the official attitude of the Government was that dangerous wild beasts must be shot, and rewards were permanently offered for their destruction. The jungle people counted on my father and mother to rid them of these pests, and I must add that all rewards received were given by my parents to be divided among the men of our camp.

If a tiger was causing trouble and had to be removed, and no natural kill of his could be found, it was often necessary to tie up a bait for him and induce him to kill at a suitable spot.

Every humane person dislikes the idea of tying up a live animal as bait for a tiger or panther, but the goat or buffalo is not aware of its fate, and when the killer arrives, his work is usually clean and instantaneous. This death is a great deal more humane than any other which awaits a domestic animal in India, where dreadful cruelties are perpetrated daily with complete indifference. Nature is harsh, truth must be faced, and those who live in contact with the life of the wild world and who hope that they possess both heart and brain, would wish to be neither soft nor sentimental, but nevertheless merciful in all they do.

To attract a tiger or panther, the bait—usually a young male buffalo for a tiger, and a goat for a panther—would be tied by the foot, not the neck, so as to give it a more natural appearance. Leaf fodder would be given, cut from the surrounding jungle, and the bait placed where two or more jungle paths met, or where a track crossed a nullah, but not actually on the path, which might have made the tiger suspicious. It was best if cover and water were available close at hand to keep the tiger in the vicinity of the kill after he had made it.

Well now, there lies the kill, dragged off and hidden under thorn and grass, a young buffalo with the head neatly twisted round, the neck broken, and the haunches eaten. There's a noise of flies as we reach it, a slight smell already, and fly-blows on the eyelids. Water is near, and heavy cover; the tiger is not far off.

The men set to work to fix up a seat in a tree close to the kill. A tiger can't climb trees, but he can leap up sixteen feet, and a machan must be eighteen feet from the ground to be safe. Of course, my parents often had to make do with one much lower down than that, when there was no other suitable place. The men hide the machan up with leaves, and we go home. Of course, the tiger may have been watching everything, but that's a chance that has to be taken. Possibly he moved off when he heard voices, though.

In the afternoon we see Father or Mother off with a rifle on the elephant to take up watch in the machan, but this time we aren't allowed to go too. They seldom sit up together, because one person is better able to be entirely and absolutely silent than two. I may say it did not seem in the least strange to us to have our Mother leave home to go after a tiger.

For the person in the machan, there now followed what was often a long wait in the cold malarial jungle, for it could be very cold at night. The sportsman must not move, cough, sneeze—nothing. The bite of mosquitoes, the attention of ants, the tickle in the throat—all must be borne in perfect silence without movement of any kind. And though jackals and cats and other scavengers might visit the kill, keeping a nervous eye and ear cocked for the return of the rightful and terrifying owner, often the tiger himself never came at all.

I knew about this keeping still, and I used to practise sometimes. Occasionally I managed five minutes of it.

If hours of patience and fortitude often went unrewarded, as is usual with shooting or fishing or even just waiting to look-see, there was an afternoon with a quicker reward. About three o'clock my mother set off on the elephant to sit up for a tiger, not expecting him to appear till dusk at least. But fifteen minutes later—with the elephant barely back in camp —the shot rang out. Father hurried off at once to fetch her home again and they returned with the tigress which she had shot, roped to the elephant's back.

If my parents wounded any animal, they naturally followed it up as soon as possible to put it out of pain, as well as to make sure that it did not escape and turn man-eater. Following up a wounded tiger is naturally dangerous, and we children were never allowed to go with them on these occasions. I'm afraid we were not in the least anxious for our parents—we didn't know enough—and we simply waited in camp till they came back with the tiger.

As is well known, a tiger that is wounded and unable to catch its natural prey may take to killing men, which, he finds, are easier even than domestic cattle. At first there lies between Man and Beast the invisible something which no wild creature readily crosses, but it is, once crossed, no longer there—the man-eater loses all fear of man, and comes to prefer the taste of human flesh.

Tigers are easily roused to fury, and if a tiger growls, he will hold his ground. But, apart from man-eaters, they do not as a rule molest man and, like all wild creatures, prefer to avoid a meeting. One evening, though, when it was pretty dark, a tiger began calling in the jungle near our bungalow —that soft moaning *aouh* of a tiger on the prowl. It was quite close at hand, and it came closer. The *aouh* turned to roars. Nearer and nearer he came, in spite of all the lights of camp, until everything in the bungalow, the walls, the furniture, all seemed to be vibrating with the roars, until you could feel it *in* you, like thunder. I don't remember any sensation of fear, though. We were quite accustomed to the presence of tigers in the forest. Whether my parents were uneasy I don't know. They didn't show anything. The staff were of course in the usual separate building. They probably closed the doors. But our two poor spaniels crept about under the furniture trying to hide themselves, and Harry and I went after them to comfort and reassure them. Poor old fat Squinch! There he was, trying to squeeze himself in under a tiny chair.

"Don't worry, Bunty! Don't worry, Squinch! There's nothing to be frightened of. It's only a tiger."

Perhaps they remembered that their own mother had been taken by a panther not ten yards from the house. Perhaps they could understand what the tiger was saying. Anyway, their eyes were huge and terrified, and when we stroked them, we could feel the hair on their backs standing up in the palm of our hands like the bristles of a wild pig.

After a time, the tiger went away.

In the morning, Father said "Come and look." We went outside, and the dust all round the bungalow was printed over and over with the tiger's footmarks.

Of course we saw such footmarks often, the large ones of tiger, and the smaller ones of tigress, the hind foot shaped differently from the front one. There they lay—in the dust—in the sand—the pad and four toes, with no claws visible, like a cat's. Similar smaller tracks belonged to the panther and his mate. Smaller still, to the leopard cats and the jungle cats and the civets.

TEN

A Tiger's Life and Death

The tiger is born in a litter of three or four cubs as a rule, though sometimes it is two or six. He may first see daylight in some lair in impenetrable rough grass and thorn, or it may be somewhere in the low hills, among nettles and bracken, and goldenrod and ferns, with the sweet wild air of the hills around him, and a crystal rill tinkling under maidenhair and begonias, and a golden oriole whistling in a rhododendron tree.

The parents will kill some of the litter if there are too many of them, and if food is scarce. Those that remain the tigress will defend with her life, and they stay with her until after the second year of their age. Indeed, cubs of different ages can be seen with the mother at the same time. Friends of ours once had three tiger cubs brought to them out of the jungle; but as they did not want them, the cubs were put outside the compound in a patch of thorn, and during the night the mother came and took them away.

Somewhere in his second or third year, the tiger leaves his parent. He wanders gradually further afield, and kills on his own until they no longer meet. His food up to now has been a share of what his mother killed and, on his own, small deer such as kakur, small pig, and peafowl, even a frog or two in lean times. He likes porcupine but knows he must treat such gentlemen with care if he is not to win a faceful of quills which will stick and fester. Even one in the paw may lame him and turn him man-eater. As peafowl frequent the same kind of open grassland near heavy jungle that tigers like, he can catch one now and then.

A leap at the rising peacock, a mouthful of jewels, wild screeching and flapping and wind in his face, then he's got it. He spits out the feathers that are stuck to his lips, and eats his meal, leaving behind a riot of glory to show where he did so.

It is about this time, when he's on his own and not yet come to his full strength, that he finds how easy it is to catch stray buffaloes near a village. He makes a nuisance of himself, or even becomes a confirmed cattle-killer, though he soon learns how dangerous buffaloes in a herd can be—that they can and will attack him, and are able to trample a full-grown tiger to death if they've a mind to it.

But if, instead, he keeps to the forest and his natural prey, he grows strong and dark and splendid. Power flows in the mighty muscles under the black and white and orange-red skin. See him there, upright in the sunlight, his broad handsome face alert and intelligent, all his body brilliantly electrically alive, the tail twitching, and sunlight glinting on the strong white whiskers. A few r's roll in his throat—*arrrgh.* . . .

Now his eyes are large and golden, the pupil narrowed to a hair-streak in daylight—even after death—to keep out the savage light from the ultra-delicate retina inside. But at night the pupil opens full, so the eyes look black, and every least reflected ray of illumination is collected to give him perfect sight even in total darkness.

Now the tiger, who with his enormous weight can yet tread

dead leaves in silence, is full grown and at the zenith of his power. He feels his strength, like wine in his veins. Now he paces the jungle paths and firelines with that long swinging stride that eats the distance—twenty miles at night—in perfect silence, in search of the prey which he hunts by sight, not smell. He stops and throws up his head to listen. He sinks down to wait if something is coming this way. The hair on his cheeks stands out in a handsome ruff like a lion's mane, not sleek like the face of a tigress.

Alive to the least vibration of the jungle night, he looks and listens, and though his sense of smell is weak, he sees and hears everything. He hears mice in the grass, and night-jars and owls. The dark hills run with wind and moonlight.

At the edge of the jungle appears a darkish silhouette—a sambhur hind with her long neck and large sensitive ears. She pauses. Her jaws stop. The ears twitch.

Suddenly something tells her death is at hand and she springs into flight in the single flash of a wild creature alarmed. In a split second she's racing away. A stag utters a honk of warning. The tiger is after her like a thunderbolt, and springs upon her in full gallop, his claws ripping hold of her as he seizes the neck in his teeth and twists and snaps it almost instantaneously.

They crash together.

Warm blood spurts. He forces the neck further and further round, till the dead hind is looking down her own backbone; and he holds her thus for some time after all galvanic movement ceases.

Now he drags his kill off to a suitable place, where he lies down to lick it over with his rasping pink tongue, and then to bite and shake and tear and gnaw it. The crunch of bones can be heard, and the parting of flesh. Leaves rustle as he rolls about getting his meal.

After that he hides the remains from the eye of vultures, and goes to clean his claws on the bark of a tree, standing on his hind legs, scoring the tree all down with deep claw-marks. Roaring with satisfaction, he then goes off to drink, and after that to lie up for the day.

"Hmmm——" he sighs, with his mouth shut, as his head sinks on to his paws.

As dawn comes up over the low tangled hills, and the jungle cock crows and the monkeys begin to move and talk, and the dew and mist to evaporate, the tiger, relaxed and full and content, is lying in deep shadow, near water, near his kill. His eyes are like yellow moons, the lids begin to close from above and below simultaneously to squeeze the eyes shut, he dozes, worried by flies, and hearing men near his kill, but too full to move unnecessarily.

The day advances, the heat grows until the vertical sun is scorching down on everything, and the only things at work are the bees. The tiger, panting with heat, licks and flicks one paw which has a thorn in it from his efforts to hide the kill. He chews it out.

During the day, crows, thrushes, and magpies may visit the carcass. Vultures appear also, having seen the antics of the crows, but they are so heavy, and take so long to get into the air that they daren't go down while the tiger's at hand, but sit about in trees, hoping he'll go off.

Every movement of the tiger is seen and reported by bird and deer and monkey, and false alarms are passed from herd to herd of nervous deer, that the tiger is on the move. He is not, though. He is too fed and hot to bother, but only looks up now and then with a silent snarl on his face for the monkeys.

Now evening comes. Dusk. Stars. A soft warm wind that will get colder and colder as night wears on.

If the tiger suspects anything, he will not return to his rightful meat, and in fact some tigers never come back to a kill at all; but if all seems to be in order, he arrives for his second feast.

His approach is likely to be cautious. Most tigers prefer to look and listen before going to their kills. Some have learnt to gaze up into each tree first, in search of a machan.

This time, all is well. Two jackals have fled at the tiger's approach and are calling out what they have seen. The hyena who had hoped to steal a mouthful slinks off to another stinking bit of carcass instead, and feeds on the last shreds of high and maggoty meat that still cling to the bones.

Meanwhile the tiger finishes all he means to eat of the sambhur hind, and rises, leaving the rest out carelessly in the open for the jackals and hyenas and civet cats and crows and vultures and flies of all the forest. They finish what is left, porcupines gnaw the skeleton, and the last bits of bone disappear into the earth during next monsoon.

One biggish animal will last a tiger a week, even though he may have only two or three meals from it, and even though the food itself is digested very quickly. One or two of the tigers my parents shot had only a little liquid in the stomach, although a few hours previously they must have swallowed something like forty pounds of meat.

So the tiger lives on in the jungle, killing his meat, cooling himself in pools, and coming up out slushing onto the sand to shake himself and lick the rich coat dry again. He loves water, and he's a good swimmer. Unlike the panther who, though he can swim well too if he has to, hates wet as much as a cat does, and after a night out in the monsoon creeps into his cave or hollow tree-trunk and spends hours licking the diamonds off his yellow fur.

But death comes for the tiger too. One night he fails to notice a machan or that there are human beings on the elephant that has wandered into his glade. Then he dies, and there is the measuring and skinning.

One night a dead tiger was brought back into our camp. The elephant strode into the firelight that struck upwards into the mahout's face, and shone like gold on the ankus he carried. Across the elephant's back was tied the huge orange body of the tiger, still soft. Into all the barbaric splendour of this scene, I came to watch.

Warm air drifted, with streaks of heat in it from the camp fires. There was a smell of animals, and of Indian food being cooked on those three-stone fireplaces. Mostly unleavened bread—the famous chupatties—which they baked in the open on those fires, on a piece of kerosene tin, turning them when done, then wrapping them round hot spices, or spooning up rice with bits of chupatty torn off.

Amid a good deal of excited talk, the elephant knelt, the ropes were untied, and the body slid with a thud on to the ground. The elephant reared up quickly onto her feet again, free of the hated tiger. She was taken off to be unharnessed and fed.

Meanwhile in the dark and the firelight, men bent over the striped carcass, one of them trying to pull out a whisker or two unobserved, to sell as charms. Father was there, and I still blink when I remember his anger at this mutilation of a magnificent head.

The tiger was then measured, a peg at his nose and a peg at his tail, and the tape run between the two pegs. Then he was skinned straightway while he was still warm, because the skin was easier to get off then. This was a finger-aching task. The animal was turned on his back, and a cut made all down the middle, and down the tail, and down the inside of each leg, and the royal coat opened and opened, and slowly drawn off.

Cut—cut—cut, went the little silver knives in the brown hands, severing the fat and sinews that stuck the tiger's skin to the body. There was always a special smell while this was going on, and the task lasted a long time. It seemed to go easily at first, but when it came to disengaging the toes, for instance, it was interminable. I saw that the tiger's lips were black, and his tongue pink. They kept the whole head so the skull could be dried and cleaned and put back inside the skin of the face when mounting it. They left the tongue in too, upon which the roughness was like a doormat of pink bristles. The Indian taxidermist who did our shikar trophies preferred to use the real tongues, and he was very good at producing a lifelike snarl on the mounted heads. So much so that our dogs used to give these heads a wide berth when they walked across a room. The men skinning the tiger kept also the little floating bone, which is lucky, and is not attached to any other bone in the body; then they threw the rest of the carcass outside the camp.

By morning it was covered with vultures. These huge birds dropped down with a whistle of coarse black carrion-fed wings, and squabbled and crawled all over the body, and hopped and galloped along the ground with frantic wing-beatings to get into the air again after their gorge. Then they sat about on dead branches, digesting the meal, and finally disappeared again into the blue. Usually there was a king vulture among them, with crimson on his head.

My mother photographed them, but they wouldn't let her approach until she put a cloth over her head like an Indian sari. This sort of thing was the beginning of animal photography in the jungle.

Meanwhile the men were rubbing the raw tiger skin on the inside with salt and wood ash, and then they pegged it out to dry. Later it was rolled up with the skull and tongue and dispatched to the taxidermist to be mounted. Every room of our bungalow in Lansdowne contained shikar trophies, as was fashionable at that time. We walked on chital and panther and tiger skins. There was an elephant's foot for an umbrella stand. The raised heads of these skins had to be arranged under table or piano, so people didn't trip over them; and all skins had to be wiped with citronella and other oils to keep moth out.

What were the thoughts of the small girl who stood that night in the firelight and watched that tiger skinned? Other tigers too. Nothing much, I am afraid. Such scenes were common. It was interesting to watch the skin come off, that was all. I went back to the bungalow and put my doll White Swan to bed in her folding cot.

But one evening, just at dusk, a wild cat materialised out of the ten-foot coarse grass surrounding the compound, and she peered round one of the fencing posts into the camp. In the twilight she was the colour of cream, a wild thing out of the jungle, alive. Next moment there was a bang and a flash of flame, the cat jerked over, dead, and I have never forgotten it. It was the first time I thought about life and death.

When my mother was tiny, she watched a pig bled to death, and felt no emotion whatever. All she remembers was the anger of relations who removed her from the scene.

There is a time when we are too young to feel. Then knowledge dawns, sometimes slowly, sometimes in a rip of lightning. I had seen many animals shot. I watched tigers skinned, I knew them alive and dead, and the colour and the splendour remain, but when the cream cat died I began to think for the first time.

ELEVEN

The Wild Tusker

As an elder sister, I had to sort out one or two problems for my young brothers in the jungle, and one of these was: "How can Daddy see to shoot tigers in the dark?"

A moment's thought solved that one. "Because the tiger's yellow, and the dark's black."

But of course there were things we didn't understand. One day Father set out from Kotdwara bungalow to shoot a rogue wild elephant that was terrorising the district. This rogue had taken up quarters near the local village and had killed several people. He chased everyone he saw, and he killed yet another man just before my father arrived on the scene.

We waited behind in the bungalow. Why was my mother obviously agitated and upset? What was there to worry about? I spoke to her, and she answered sharply; a thing she never did. I can remember the only two times in my life she did so, and this was one of them. I could not have been more astonished if the roof had fallen.

Suddenly a shot rang out.

Then—a second shot.

Then—silence.

What was happening? *What was happening?*

At last came news that the elephant was safely dead and all was well.

Now we were allowed to walk down and see him. This was Kotdwara, where Civilisation met the Jungle. I could hear a train. The elephant lay in thin jungle among saplings and undergrowth, his one tusk gleaming in the sunlight, and flies already round the eyes. His other tusk had been lost in some previous battle. I looked at him. That trunk had flung down human beings, and those feet had crushed them. It must be a horrible death to die, and I tried to imagine it happening to me.

We examined the bullet holes. There are only a few small places where a bullet will penetrate an elephant's skull, but my father, especially as a young man, was a cool and brilliant shot, and his first bullet had killed the rogue as they faced each other; there had been no need for a second. However, the Indians who were present begged Father to fire again to be sure the animal was dead, and that was why he did so.

The tusk of this elephant was removed, and his feet and some of his skin for trophies. The trunk was stuffed and became a perfectly hideous and useless memento, but as I say, it was the thing in those days to have such shikar trophies about the house. This was a clear fashion of the period—of Victorian and Edwardian times in England and India, and it has vanished with them.

When we were leaving India, our staff drew lots for that trunk, and Gwala Ram who won it was the envy of all. He went off with it over his shoulder, a broad grin on his face.

The cured elephant skin was eventually brought home to England. It was about an inch thick and became, in course of years, as hard as stone. A strong man—a carpenter—once asked if he could have a piece to sole his shoes. "If you can cut it, certainly you can have it," was the reply. The man took a hacksaw to the job, but after a bit he came back and said "I don't think I'll bother about soling those shoes after all." In the end there was nothing to be done with that skin but to bury it, and it lies in an English wood now, together with some antlers and skulls and other things that could be of no possible further use or ornament. Perhaps they will puzzle geologists of some distant epoch.

After I became a mother myself, my small son Tim, aged three, pointed to a photo in my room and asked "What's that, Mummy?"

"That's a photo of Granddad with the elephant that he shot."

And Tim said "I suppose the big one is the elephant."

Well then, a few years later still, when my two sons Bill and Tim were aged eight and six, they said "Tell us something funny we did when we were little, Mummy." So I told them this tale of Tim and the photo of the elephant.

There was silence. They didn't think it in the least funny.

Then Bill cried "Ha! I see that joke. The big one was Granddad all the time."

After the various pieces had been removed from that elephant for trophies, we journeyed on to the next camp, leaving instructions for burying the remains. But the ground was stony and this could not be done. It was getting towards the hot weather too. A runner came after my father from Kotdwara village to say that the body was still there and smelling bad. Now if a smell is enough to be noticed at all in India, let alone cause offence, it is quite an odour.

Father returned to Kotdwara immediately, obtained gallons of disinfectant and a gang of the low-caste jungle Indians known as chumars, the only people who will handle carrion. These men crawled actually inside the putrid carcass, in order to cut it up, and the pieces were then taken away into the jungle. Seven loaded bullock carts of rotten meat were carried off, and the job took a whole day.

The first wild elephant I saw was when Harry and I were with my mother stalking in the jungle. We were on one of our own elephants at the time, and for stalking they didn't wear the katola, but had an inconspicuous grey canvas pad instead. This had no pegs at the corners, so if you had to hang on in an emergency—if the elephant bolted—there were only the harness ropes.

We were strolling down a jungle path in silence. Even we children managed not to talk, realising that if we did so we'd never be taken stalking again. Suddenly the mahout slowed the elephant and with a slight movement of the head told us to look to the right.

There he was, the wild tusker!

He'd got his back to us as he stood at the edge of a small muddy stagnant pool, and every now and then he scooped up the slush in his trunk and flung it backward over his body. Ears and tail were going all the time because of flies. Feet too. Hot sunlight dried the mud on him at once, and all his body was criss-crossed with dusty wrinkles. He looked dirty and prehistoric.

My mother put out her hand to the orderly for the rifle he was carrying. Not because she wanted to shoot the tusker. She wanted only to be ready if he saw us and decided to charge. But the man, thinking she meant to fire, and fearing for the consequences, shook his head.

For a few moments we watched this forest scene. The silence was broken only by flies as they whizzed to and fro like sparks in the shafts of sunlight, and by the swash and spatter of water as the tusker blew like a whale. Then our elephant padded silently on, leaving the wild king to his peaceful life.

For the life of such an elephant in our jungle was very

peaceful and happy. Unless he became dangerous to man, no one molested him. Once he ceased to be a baby, even tigers moved out of his way.

Born hairy as a mammoth and with no trunk, he soon lost the hair and soon grew a trunk. He lived with the herd, adding height and strength and years, until he stood ten or eleven feet high, armed and ornamented with ivory, a giant of the wilderness.

All the jungle was his. He alone could press through the elephant grass, taller than himself, that presented an impenetrable wall to most creatures, which must travel the old worn animal runways to get through it. It opened for him, and closed again behind him, so that sometimes the only mark of his passage was a whisper in the grass, and a wave among the feathery cream grass-heads above. The deep jungle was his, adrift with green scents, so were the mud pools where he cooled his hot skin after sunshine, and the salt-licks, and the dusty nullahs where he would sometimes stand and push a little of the heavy silvery sand into the tip of his trunk with his foot and blow it up over him in a glitter of dry spray. And his trunk went all the time—this side, that side—blowing dust or water over one shoulder, then the other, along his tummy, then up over his backbone in a salute. Now a great shake and a shiver, and a cloud of bright dust flew off him.

The trunk, that wonderfully delicate and tender organ, which can pick up coins or pluck foliage, or lift tree-trunks, or seize a man and fling him down, is used for everything and it is never still. Supple, relaxed, soft, but *alive*, it plucks grass and brushes away flies with the grass, and then puts the grass into the mouth. It is raised and stretched, waving this way and that to collect news by scent from as far as three miles off. It slides like a snake over things to estimate their size and weight before lifting. It can help the mahout up to his seat on the elephant's neck. It can trumpet, and blow, and scratch. It salutes Rajahs. When an elephant charges, his valuable trunk is curled up between the tusks, under the skin, out of harm's way, the ears go back, and the animal breaks into a purposeful run.

Not a run, really, because an elephant can neither run nor jump. He has different paces, though: he can stroll or stride or hurry, and he has a slumping movement when going downhill. If it's very steep, he sits on his backside and toboggans. The tame elephants sometimes had to do this when descending a bank. Down we all went, in a slide of dust and stones.

For the lifetime of a man, and sometimes longer, the wild elephant of our jungle lived with his herd in the glades. All the food he wanted lay at hand—the fluttering bamboo leaves and young juicy bamboo shoots, tender as asparagus, leaves and grass of every kind and taste. Sometimes he would be tempted by the fruit and crops near a village, and would spend a night trampling the plantations, and crunching the crisp stalks of sugar cane to squeeze out the syrup. There were all the rivers he wanted, too, and the warm mud-pools with stagnant colours lying on the water. He could feed and idle his life away without a care.

No keddahs took place in our jungle, and no elephant was shot unless it became dangerous. Small herds wandered at will in the forest, feeding all day and night, sleeping on their feet, smashing over young trees in their loud wasteful way to get the foliage. But though they were careless and noisy, they could also be silent. Like all other animals, they preferred to get away from men, and they could vanish like a puff of smoke among the trees, if alarmed. But they never had to think where the next meal was coming from, as tigers did, nor watch every shadow—every leaf-twitch— as the deer must do to preserve life. Every other creature must swallow and look around, swallow and look around, even the tiger, and for many of them if they take two consecutive mouthfuls without looking, they are risking death. But the elephant could smash and feed and swish about in tranquil waste, without a thought for the morrow.

We always thought that one day we should find in the Hills that misty secret valley where, so the Indians told us, all elephants go to die. There are plenty of reasons why almost no sign of dead elephant is ever found in the jungle. Elephants are long-lived, not numerous; the jungle is thick; scavengers and monsoon rains soon obliterate a body. But we knew better.

"There is a Valley," said Ayah, looking with her deep-set splendid old eyes across the oceans of mountain towards the heavenly peaks.

She was right, and one day we would find it and buy Mother some new dresses, and Father every single thing in the fishing catalogue.

Although the wild elephants were always bathing, they were always dirty. The dust of dried mud, and the dust of their dust-baths all lodged in the folds and wrinkles of their loose grey skin along with twigs and bits of leaf. Some got brushed off in their passage through the jungle, but more soon settled.

Our tame elephants were bathed often.

We'd be playing by the river when a mahout would arrive with his bareback animal to wash it. Generally our sand castles meant more to us than washing an elephant, but sometimes we'd go along to help.

The mahout slid off the animal's neck.

"Down!" he commanded, and the elephant knelt in the river. "Over!" and with a sigh she rolled out flat on one side in a loud slush of enjoyment among the stones, with the bright current running a melody all around her, half her head under water, and the trunk resting looped on the upper cheek or shoulder.

"Come on, lazy!" shouted the mahout, slapping the great rump. "How can I wash a dry animal?"

She filled her trunk with a long suck underwater and hosed it out over her body two or three times, taking good care to souse the man, too, for ordering her about, but he was used to that and ready for it, being dressed in nothing but a small loincloth.

Then he took handfuls of sand and leaves, some of which gave off froth when wet, and with these he scrubbed the elephant all over, every now and then commanding the animal to help with more hosing. Halfway through, she had to get up and go down again on the other side, with a crunch of moved stones and splashing and blowing, till all was done.

Another job the elephants and their mahouts had to do at each camp was fetching in fodder, and this took quite a time because the two elephants between them needed more than a thousand pounds of green food every day. One of them, again bareback, would go off with her mahout into the jungle. The man cut mountains of bamboo and other stuff and loaded it all onto his animal, and they returned together, the elephant pacing along like a walking haystack, and smelling of leaves wilting in hot sun.

Besides all this greenfood, the elephants had twelve very large chupatties each, every evening, and they were always brought up to the bungalow to be fed.

It was really rather a majestic sight, the two noble animals coming up the verandah, and beside them the mahouts with the freshly cooked chupatties.

I sat on the edge of the verandah, my feet dangling. Under my knees, the stone was warm with sunset, and dusty too, but being clean or dirty hadn't started to matter yet. I noticed neither. Before me stood one of the elephants, her head high up above me like a crag on the sky, her tail and ears flapping all the time as usual, and her trunk too, waiting for the chupatty. I took one of the pancakes and broke it. It was warm and smelt nice, as all warm animal mashes do. I wanted to eat some myself, but I managed not to steal from an animal, and put the piece of chupatty into her trunk—between the finger and thumb of the trunk as it were. She took it gently, for all her eagerness, and shoved it into her mouth and chumped it up, and held out her trunk for more. When it came to the last piece, the mahout commanded her to throw her trunk in a salute over her head, and we reached up with our small tanned child hands to put the chupatty straight into the mouth. It was a big glistening wet jelly of a pink cave in which you could see the teeth, made flat for grinding, and saliva dripping off the point of the underlip.

Children are realists. When we modelled things in plasticine, we made what we saw. For some reason, our model of an Elephant Camp amused the grown-ups. Heaven knows why, because where there were elephants, there were always the yellow balls of their droppings. If you kicked one, you could often tell what the elephant had been eating.

Whether elephants are really frightened of mice, as is popularly believed, I don't know. They certainly don't like dogs, and they didn't like our two spaniels racing round them in usual dog-excitement when we were starting off for a new camp. When Bunty was letting off steam with an excitable small spaniel's daily joy at setting out somewhere, she tore round and round with ears trying to leave her head, and suddenly darted straight through underneath a very startled elephant. Why elephants should dislike dogs no one knows. Perhaps it makes them feel funny inside—uh! as a maggot does me.

Everyone in India loves an elephant. The people of the jungle villages, when we were passing through, always used to rush out of all the huts to look, although they surely saw wild ones often.

Once we passed a marriage procession. It must have left the family in debt for the rest of their lives, because two elephants had been hired, with all the ornament and draperies used on such occasions. The elephants were gorgeous in scarlet curtains heavily embroidered with gold. They wore gold caps and forehead bands, and gold on their tusks, and carried curtained howdahs on top. In one of these, upon a jewelled guddee, sat a small figure veiled in magenta-pink and silver—the bride. She was about three years old.

Our elephants were peaceful and obedient. They did not as a rule disobey orders, though as I say they might if asked to walk on places they considered dangerous and so on.

Still, they were not always docile. One of them once lost her temper in camp and turned upon the tree to which she was tethered, placing her rocky forehead against it and then bracing all her body to push it over. There was a loud report as the tree began to snap at the roots.

The mahout, enjoying his evening meal and gossip among the smoky little fires of the servants' quarters, shouted out a single word of command. Because he spoke without a thought in his head but for obedience—he didn't even get to his feet—she obeyed him. The tree remained leaning and broken, but the elephant was stopped in her rampage.

Elephants don't like to be asked to handle any dead things, not only tigers and panthers, though those were the worst. Indeed, ours always treated the great carnivores, dead or alive, with respect. One of our elephants had three lumps the size of walnuts on her backside where the claws of a springing tiger had dug into the skin. When my parents were beating out a small patch of grass on elephants for a wounded tiger, once, they laid all the grass flat without finding the animal, yet it could not have got out without being seen. The tiger had vanished. Finally it was noticed that the elephant would not tread on a certain place, and there the tiger was found lying dead in a dip of ground, with the grass laid flat across him.

I saw one of our mahouts ask his elephant to move a dead panther, and she refused. It was a recently dead panther, still pliant and warm. As the elephant could not be allowed to succeed in her disobedience, her rider pressed her to the task—in fact, he increased it. She had been asked to push the body, now she must pick it up. She snorted and trumpeted and backed away, shaking her head. He fought her, forcing her to it, with jabs of the ankus an inch deep into the bread-like flesh of her forehead. The holes filled with blood.

Suddenly she hurried forward, seized the panther with her trunk and threw it up high over her own back, trumpeting her disgust and triumph. It sailed through the air like a shell, and the other men had to scatter out of the way as it landed.

Every bone in the dead panther's body must have been broken in the fall, but the beautiful skin was not injured. And of all creatures in the jungle, the panther was possibly the most beautiful of all. The elephant and the tiger were the monarchs. Majesty was theirs, and romance. They appear in Indian sculpture and paintings and legends, the symbol of a continent. But they were not so dangerous as bears, nor so plentiful and beautiful as the panthers, which multiply and kill and are everywhere the vermin of the land.

TWELVE

Panthers

One evening in Lansdowne as we were coming home at dusk, something flickered at the top of the drive where it reached the small rocky compound of the bungalow.

We hurried on up, to find out what it was, but when we looked over the low stone wall down the khud, there was nothing to be seen.

We thought no more about this incident, but two nights later our spaniel Jess was taken by a panther. She wasn't supposed to go out alone after dark, but that evening the men carelessly allowed her to do so. A few yards from the house she was taken. We then found out that the panther had been in the habit of waiting on a rock just outside the compound every evening for the dog until the chance came for him to get her.

Next morning we looked for her remains, but they were never found. Father who, as I have said, was most ingenious at inventing traps for animals that were troubling us, now prepared a trap for this panther—a concealed springboard from which a wire led to a rifle in the tree just above. If the panther followed the route he had previously taken, he

would tread on this place and shoot himself. The rifle was loaded only at night, and fired downwards. One night of storm, it went off, but we never found anything, not even blood, so I daresay it was only wind that fired it.

Jess was the mother of Bunty and Squinch. In fact they, at that moment, were still blind crawling puppies, Jess having just given birth to ten of them. Ignoring the comfortable bed prepared for her welfare, she had gone out to the compound and produced her family in a flowerbed. It wasn't an ordinary flowerbed, because the whole compound was too rocky. Instead of digging down to make a bed, stone boxes were built upwards on top of the rock. One of these had just been made, and was waiting to be filled with earth from the valley. This was the spot that appealed to Jess for her accouchement. The pups were brought into the bungalow, and a few nights later she was taken, leaving us her family of ten to raise on a bottle.

Poor Jess. She had originally belonged to someone else, who gave her to us when he could not keep her any longer. She grew to love us, but the day when her old master camped near us in the jungle, she went to him immediately and sat at his feet all day.

The Burke family now had ten pups on their hands, each one of which had to be fed individually, several times a day, on a bottle. Harry and I thought this great fun. I loved holding a helpless little creature and feeding it, but of course— "I think I'm going out now, Mum. Please will you finish them?" Girls love housework just until they start to be any use at it.

Our spaniel pups had ears the exact colour of chocolate blancmange, and they smelt so nice. There's a special puppy-smell that they all have while they're little, and it stays longest with the smallest of the litter.

At eight to twelve weeks, this lot were all given away

except Bunty and Squinch, who went with us everywhere.

When we were moving in bad panther country, they wore their panther collars, but these were too uncomfortable to be worn always, and the dogs hated them. They were made of heavy leather nearly half an inch thick, broad enough to cover the whole neck, and they bristled out in all directions like a hedgehog with steel spikes. As panthers seize their prey by the neck, locking their teeth to dislocate it, such a collar protects a dog from any but the most determined onslaught. Bunty and Squinch were never attacked, but my mother shot a panther with a mouth that had been damaged by such spikes. The whole inside of the mouth was festered with little sores in a regular pattern, not irregularly as they sometimes were after damage by porcupine quills. And I saw one Bhutia dog wearing a collar that had only three spikes left.

He had come down out of the high Himalayas with the nomadic tribe of Bhutias that owned him, and they must have come through hundreds of miles of wild mountains with panthers hanging about round the camps hoping for a goat. Perhaps he had been often attacked and the collar damaged. More likely it was an old collar that had protected many other dogs before him. It wasn't much use now, of course, but he still wore it.

Of course, he could have put up a good defence of his own if attacked. All these Bhutia dogs were very large and savage, more like big wolves, with fiery eyes, a fine array of teeth, and coats as thick as bearskins. The whole pack would burst into a fury of noisy snarling and barking if anything approached the camp. They were perfectly capable of driving off a panther between them.

Each year bands of nomadic Bhutias came down out of their mountain fastnesses to the Plains to trade in salt and other merchandise, and we used to meet them sometimes on

the hill roads. The salt was slung in bags on the goats, which were used as pack animals. These gypsy people were rough and dark with Mongolian features, and very dirty. The climate of their frozen plateaux, whipped clean by icy winds, made it impossible for them ever to wash. They lived on curds and goat meat and anything else they could get.

In one caravan was a basket of newborn puppies, fat as butter, squirming and squeaking, and also smelling like nothing on earth because of the evil blanket in which they were wrapped. If their masters did not sell or trade them, the puppies would grow up around the camp with the other dogs, and learn to be ferocious, fighting among themselves for their raw meat—for life itself, driving off thieves and panthers, and usually quite unapproachable.

But one dog was different. He left his own camp and he came to us and asked to be our dog. It broke one heart at any rate that the answer could not be yes. We already had two dogs, and this one had been taught ferocity. How could he be trusted with children, and in Lansdowne with other people's children? Reason must prevail. Kolu, as we called him in the few hours he was with us, was sleek and clean and in splendid condition. There was no reason to buy him to save him from anything, and in the end he trotted off quite cheerfully with his own people, back to the wild life to which he was born.

The goats belonging to these Bhutias were hardy and spirited, and suited in every way to their bleak home. Their long thick oily hair kept out the intense cold of those fearful plateaux, their little hard hooves were sure as chamois, and they could live on bits of this and that growing in cracks of the frozen rock. Goats were used for everything, as yaks are in Tibet: to give milk and cream and curd and butter and cheese and meat, and they were used as beasts of burden. Their hides made the goatskin tents of their masters, and

their hair was woven into cloth. Even the horns were used for making household things and as phials to hold oil and spices. Their skins were used as waterbags, and as bladders on which to swim across streams.

Bhutia dogs are no doubt sometimes hungry, but they are very different from the poor lean pi-dogs who hang around every village, belonging to no one and often ravenous. Each is a walking museum of parasites and diseases. Occasionally one of these poor creatures, sick and starving, would try to join us. Mercy then had to be shown with the rifle. We all hated this, but there was no alternative. Rabies and other serious diseases were among them. The dogs could not be accepted, and if they were turned away, a miserable life and a miserable death awaited them. Fortunately many of them fall prey to panthers, and so get a happy release.

The terms "panther" and "leopard" are of course synonymous. It was at one time thought that they were different creatures, but current opinion is that they are one, with local variations; and in our part of the country they were always called panthers.

They are found everywhere, much higher up than tigers, and also nearer to mankind. They are found in the Plains and in the Hills, in the jungle, and among the fields and plantations of Man. In mountain districts they are sometimes short of food; a she-leopard with cubs is very dangerous, and all panthers are active and cunning. For these reasons, and because they like dogs to eat, and domestic animals, and because they are so prolific, they are everywhere detested. The Man-Eating Leopard of Rudraprayag, shot by Jim Corbett and made famous by him in his book of that title, operated among these hills. He was known to have killed and eaten 125 human beings, but the hill people say among themselves that it was 500. The man-eater fed on men, women, and children for eight years; and with all the name-

less travellers and pilgrims who use the hill roads, not all the deaths were recorded.

A panther hunts by night and, like the tiger, looks for a cool shady spot in which to lie up for the day. Unlike tigers, panthers don't like water, though they are able to swim well if pressed. They climb well, and sometimes carry the remains of a kill heavier than themselves up into a tree to hide it from daytime scavengers. Their method of hunting is to stalk their prey until they are close to it, and then to spring. The panther that took Jess waited for her to approach him, and made a lightning rush from a few yards' distance. As panthers can use cover only nine inches high, the chital herds of the Plains have to keep a sharp lookout.

A hill panther will sometimes bask on an outcrop of rock in the rays of the early morning sun, appreciating the heat. He too has to keep a lookout for his enemies, men.

There he lies, then, on a slab of rock in the pale yellow sunlight, a large male panther, thickset and powerful, licking his paws and cleaning them with delicacy, as a cat does. Below him are oceans of mauve valley, threaded with water music and blossom: above, a shimmer of detached and ethereal Snows. The light breeze, lifting the leaves and making the shadows run, is sweet with the call of bulbuls and a whistling thrush.

Now he stretches his claws out of the blackish pads and drags them, scratching the rock. He cleans his face. The whiskers are shorter and finer and less noticeable than those of a tiger, and the whole head has a more furry, frosty look. All time as he lies there, his ears are turning sensitively back and forward, ready for the least sound.

Something alerts him.

He listens, motionless and intent, but all is well, so he relaxes and yawns, showing teeth to command respect, and black lips, but pink inside, and a very large rough tongue.

At last the yellow eyes close, and he dozes, though never for long at a time.

The sun rises higher and higher. It's not the delicious cool haze of early morning now, but the pitiless overhead sunlight of day. Fur which had been puffed against cold, lies flat again. As always, the extraordinary colouring of the panther, the bright black rosettes on a rufous yellow ground which seems so gaudy, mixes him into whatever the background happens to be. Day or night, hill or plain, sunburnt grass or fern or lichened rock, he becomes part of it. Only movement will suddenly draw him on his background.

He is marked as in the day of Creation by Indian godly fingers held close together to print the yellow skin with ink. The spots on his head and shoulders are small-sized, becoming much larger on the haunches and backbone; and each black ear has one cream spot on it, like a tiger's. The ears are noticeably mobile, even in sleep, tilting to and fro all the time, or twitching off flies. If a leaf creaked, he'd be gone in a flash, into thin air, as a burst soap bubble is here one moment and vanished the next. But if nothing disturbs him, he'll get up presently—before he's hot enough to pant— and he'll stretch: front legs, back legs, claws out, claws in, padding his front feet on the rock, and he'll yawn and slip off with that long silent stride of his—so silent it makes you feel deaf to watch it, and he'll then spend the day in some cool cave, or among ferns and brambles.

A panther is beautiful and dainty. Brave when cornered. His body has a boneless grace that can carry him in one bound up a tree, up a rock, or down with a light thud into a nullah. He walks, he melts, he flashes, he strikes. When he lies down to feed on the goat or chital which is his normal food, he opens the skin and folds it back as he goes, and leaves it presently empty with the little rattling hooves attached, and goes away to clean and rest and hunt again.

Besides goat and chital, he eats pig and porcupine and barking deer and hog deer, sometimes a jungle fowl or kaleege pheasant, or sometimes he scavenges. He's very fond of monkey, too, and the monkeys hate him and call more loudly for him than they do for a tiger, swearing in their tree tops as he passes below.

All sorts of birds and deer also call at sight of a panther, and no tiger or panther can move by daylight without exciting comment. Monkeys post their lookouts, especially when they go to feed on the sweet shisham buds, and the deer that come to pick up any dropped buds profit also from these treetop sentinels.

At night we often heard leopards sawing in the jungle around us. The breath goes in and out, past a cog, as it were, and the result is like sawing wood. It has never been really established why and when they produce this particular sound, whether it's to frighten and confuse their prey, or to call a mate. One which I watched making this noise appeared to be just filling in time.

Like other animals, panthers appreciate paths to walk on, where it's easier to move soundlessly than on leaves, and where their tender pads find a smooth surface. For this reason, and as they are night-hunters, they often visit civilisation in search of food. This habit makes them more of a nuisance to man than ever, although a bright light helps to keep them off.

They are enormously strong and can carry a kill for miles without showing a drag-mark, though there will be blood spots, and of course the tracks show weight. Like tigers, they have keen sight and hearing, but a poor sense of smell. They, too, cover their kills to keep them from crow and vulture, and if a kill is left out in the open it means of course that the owner does not intend to return.

The mother panther has two to four cubs in a litter, as a

rule, and an occasional black cub may be among them. Black panthers are not unduly rare, and seem to go rather in districts. The mother hides her young in some tangled place where they are seldom found, and she shows great courage and ferocity defending them.

THIRTEEN

Bear

But if panthers are vermin everywhere and the scourge of many villages, the jungle man—and especially the hill man—dreads more a meeting with a bear; and more horrible accidents occur with bears than with tigers, panthers, or elephants. But bears, unlike tigers, are easily turned with a face-shot.

Two kinds of bear lived in our jungle, the Indian black bear and the sloth bear. Both were dangerous, and ready to attack unprovoked, though mostly they did so out of alarm and fear. Shortsighted and hard of hearing, they would often unwittingly stumble into man, and then they would maul him, standing up and striking at the face, knocking him over and falling upon him to inflict atrocious injuries. Men mauled by bears would sometimes be brought to camp for treatment, and one friend of ours, an Englishman, met his death this way.

He was returning by night to his camp, and was accompanied by his men, carrying lanterns. They ran into a pair of bears which attacked, and our friend died of his injuries.

Another bear came hurrying down a hillside with the

obvious intention of going for the people he could hear
talking. To his surprise, however, he found them on top of
an elephant instead of on the ground at his mercy. My
mother, who was on the elephant with the mahout and an
orderly, had time to take advantage of his surprise, and
she shot him where he stood.

The Indian sloth bear, which can reach a length of five
feet and a height of three at the shoulder, has coarse shaggy
black hair, and untidy toenails, so long they look as if they
must surely trip him up. The black bear is more neatly
made, with a shorter coat. Both have a white chevron on the
chest, and both shamble along the forest paths at night in
search of honey and ants' nests; meat, too, and they make
their own kills if they get a chance. In fact, they'll eat
almost anything they can find. Sometimes they took the
baits put out in our jungle for tiger and panther. At other
times a bear will climb trees for fruit and berries, and wild
honey. He can safely attack a bees' nest because of his thick
coat, and then he sits there with angry bees caught in his
hair and buzzing furiously, while he finishes up the whole
nest, grubs and all, as well as the rough honeycomb with
dead bees in it.

The bear cub is born by himself or as a twin, and he's
an exact tiny replica of his mother. He journeys about with
her in the forest, sometimes carried on her back, and sometimes scuttling along behind her as she ambles down the
paths and firelines by night, toes turned in and head carried
low, at a sort of hummocking trot.

Here they are at a white-ant castle, and the baby is going
to have a lesson in sucking out the termites inside. These
white-ant castles occurred frequently in the jungle, and Harry
and I used sometimes to knock off a turret to look into one.
They are built by the termites in the hours of darkness, and
they are made from the inside. Consequently the outsides

of the castles are rough, but the inside is pushed and padded smooth by the multitudes from within. Grain by grain, earth is carried by the termites along their inside tunnels, cemented by their saliva, and baked to concrete by the sun.

The mother bear now does as we did, and cuffs off one of the crags. The big ones were often too tough for us, but she manages them, though even she can't do much with the thick lower foundations of the nest. Then she stuffs her long wobbly nose into the opening and sucks and sucks so loudly that the noise can be heard quite a way off. She licks around too, and she is rewarded by a mouthful of fat pale termites that pop on her tongue as she squashes them, and taste delicious to bears.

The cub licks his share off her mouth and tongue, and then has a try himself. He's clumsy and gets only a few, but they're so good he wants more. Soon the bears have broken all the easy places, and the rest of the building resists them, so they jog away to find another.

The broken castle stands there, ruined, without sign of life for a time. But presently, deep in one of the polished corridors, something moves. The advance guard of the repair squad is here. Feelers twinkle, and then the termites arrive in twos and threes and dozens and scores to mend their home.

Deep down into the earth goes the tap root of this silent swarming social life, down to the single source of this single multitudinous life—the queen. Each particle of it is one petal of the plant, as in sunflower or daisy or sea-anemone, and is incapable of detached existence. The white-ant castle is a single growth, like a sponge.

All repairs to the broken building have to be finished during the hours of darkness, because light hurts the termites' transparent bodies, I suppose, as fire hurts us, and they always run away from it. But they are fast workers. Earth is brought up from below—from inside the building where the roots of the nest go down into the ground. The grains of soil are chewed and mixed, and the turrets built up again. When the sun rises, all will have been done, the mended part is still soft, though, still looking dark and wet, but a few hours of sunshine will harden it.

Termites build their homes sticking up out of the ground in order to be sure of a dry habitation when the rest of the earth is sodden with monsoon rain. In swampy ground, the termite castles were always placed on any slight rise of land. If you were looking for a dry patch, that is where it would be, wherever there was a white ants' nest. But also that's where there might be a snake too, looking for a dry place to live.

While the termites mend their home, the bears have trundled off into the forest. There's a sort of piglike structure about them, and an appearance of hurry as they bob along at that running slouching walk. If the cub gets tired, the mother will carry him on her back. If they are attacked from a machan, she may rear up to try and claw the man out of his tree. In fact, she rears up so often on her hind legs to reach up a tree or to look round, it makes one wonder whether there was not a bear as well as an ape in the ancestry of Man.

The mother bear, who knows exactly when each kind of tree is going to flower or fruit, is making her way to a patch of zizyphus jujuba, the bher, a small thorny tree covered with thousands of orange-red berries, and bears love them. I loved them, too. They were all skin and stone, but between the two was a scrap of sharp delicious fruit with a special taste.

The mother bear sets to work and shows her cub how to make a platform for himself in the tree. They use sticks and branches, and beat them down till they've got a place about four feet across where they can sit and eat the surrounding fruit, using their front paws to do so, or they can sleep, or contemplate, and the wind will bring them uninterrupted news of other tasty harvests suitable for bears.

After a night spent eating and wandering, the bears are feeling full and contented, so now they make for one of their daytime sleeping places. It's a shallow cave worked out of the bank of a nullah, among the roots of trees. The earth is dry and has been brushed smooth by their hair, and they curl up together there to wait for another night. Soon they are twitching with dreams, and loud snores tell everyone for some distance that bears are asleep.

It's a cool place to be in, here, against the earth, with the hot sun outside, reflecting off the white sand, but away off out there, and the bears sleep soundly.

In the evening, the cub is awake early. He rolls out of the cave and shakes himself and sniffs round in all directions to find out what's happening beyond the range of his little shortsighted piggy eyes and woolly ears. He sits up on a ridge in almost the attitude of a man, with his hands on his knees, sunning his tummy in the rays of the setting sun. And he scratches with one hand too, using the claws almost as a man or monkey or kangaroo would, not all together in one stroke, like a dog.

Suddenly his mother comes out with a rush, and dashes to and fro looking for him, angry with him for leaving her side. He gets a cuff over the ears that sends him rolling down the bank, but he takes it all philosophically and scrambles back to join her. They touch each other and snuff with pleasure because there is love between them, and will be until he can fend for himself and his mother is pregnant again. Then there'll be words, and they'll go their separate ways.

Where we were, bears sometimes ravaged the crops, and even broke into grain stores. In very high mountain villages which might be deserted during winter, the people having brought their herds down to more hospitable pastures, bears were known to break into the houses and even to live in them.

Now and then a bear cub is captured young, if a mother is shot with a cub in attendance, for instance. Such cubs are sometimes tamed and taught to dance, and men with performing bears used to tour the hill stations in India and would appear at a bungalow and offer to give a show, just as travelling actors and tumblers used to do in other countries in earlier times. The sloth bear is the *ours jongleur* of the French.

We never tried to keep a wild bear cub as a pet, though I believe they are easily tamed. But Father once kept two young panthers. They were brought to him as cubs, and were pretty little kittens to begin with, but no amount of care or kindness could change the jungle in their blood. They took to stalking and killing his chickens, so he chained them one to each end of a log. The chains were long enough to let them play together without getting entangled. But such were their natural cunning and savagery that they still caught chickens. Without even a mother to instruct them, they did not have to be taught. One of these panthers died from snakebite, and as the other was growing bigger all the time, there was nothing for it but to give him to a local Rajah for his zoo, and a zoo alas is the usual end of all attempts to keep large and fierce wild animals as pets.

For some unknown reason, the parents would not let us keep tigers, panthers, elephants, crocodiles, or bears, but Harry and I kept a number of other creatures. It is Adam's instinct to bring wild animals out of the wet woods into his cave and tame them, and produce domestic stock. The jungle cock, bronze and green, crowing in the jungle, and his bantam hen hatching her tiny brown eggs in the dried grass, were the same stock as the bazaar chickens who travelled round with us in their basket.

I longed to be like the First Men among the First Animals of the early world, before even he picked up a stone and flung it at them. I used to walk alone through the jungle, or sit alone in the branches of trees or crunched up small on a rock by the river, imagining myself a she-mowgli, with wild animals walking under my hand beside me.

Of course they never did.

But I always hoped they would. Surely if I walked as part of the jungle, and wore only khaki and sunburnt skin, and never hurt one of them, the day would come when they would accept me.

Nothing felt nicer than rough branches, holding me up high for the sun to bake my brown legs and thin arms, and the wind to get inside my loose clothes. The sound of leaves was all about me always, and the dry ground far below flowing with their shadows.

If I ever managed to keep still for even five minutes, I might see something, but alas, patience was in short supply. After a while I'd be picking bark off to look at the clean veined wood and the insects underneath; or biting the skin on the back of my hand to make tooth-marks. The lower teeth weren't absolutely even, and produced a fascinating pattern, and my skin tasted salt. All of which was most interesting, but reduced my chances of seeing wild animals.

When there were none to look at, I imagined them. An elephant coming out of those bamboos, for instance, with his ears flapping, and a torn leaf or two and some twigs on his broad back, and caked mud flaking off, but still hanging by one or two of his thick black hairs. He'd push a bamboo clump over with his forehead and knee, and bang about with a piece of it for a fly-whisk, before packing the jointed stem and sharp leaves into his mouth. It was quite a surprise to realise that, after all, he wasn't there.

Suppose I'm a panther, here on this branch now? I stretched my fingers and dug the nails, and imagined the feel of them coming up viciously out of cushioned recesses to score the bark or kill a chital and rip the pretty dappled skin away to get at the glistening flesh.

I did actually see animals too, of course, and every time I did, my heart burst out fresh into flames of passionate excitement and desire and resolution.

I wanted to be able to walk in wild places without disturbing the creatures, visible and invisible, who live there. To be part of the burnt grass and venomous thorn and the semal trees alight with giant red flowers and later strewn underneath with the silky cotton wool. To be made of earth and air and water and *unnoticed*. I wanted to get near to wild creatures without their seeing me, or being frightened if they did. To watch without hurting them. To slide myself into their bodies and look out through their green eyes and see the world as they saw it.

FOURTEEN

Where Eggs Come From

I should have been a much better stalker if I had possessed any patience at all.

In Lansdowne there was a young man who was interested in Scouts, and he offered to teach Harry and me stalking.

After demonstrations about wind-direction and silence and so on:

"I'll be here by this rock," he said, "and you two'll go off right out of sight and try and get as near as you can to me without being seen."

He sat down with his back to the boulder, and Harry and I went off into the jungle.

This was mountain land. Pines and Himalayan oak grew in alpine glory everywhere, with stretches of turf which had been grazed by cows; and a jumble of mossy boulders, and nettles and ferns, and clumps of wild raspberry spotted with yellow fruit.

We decided to move in on our man separately.

When I was out of sight of my quarry, I dropped importantly to earth, exercising fantastic precaution at the beginning of the stalk, and getting more and more careless as I approached the end.

117

At last, stung and dirty, my knees pricked into patterns by the gravel, I crawled up close, very pleased with myself.

My instructor looked up.

"Well now, I'll tell you the exact route you took," he said. "You started among those trees, and came along on your tummy behind those rocks. And by the way, if you've absolutely got to cross open land, with no possible cover, do it at a moment when your quarry isn't looking, and do it very quickly. But if there's the least cover at all, or an alternative route——"

In the meantime Harry was doing much better than I had. Two and a half years younger than I was, he got within ten or twenty yards of the man before being seen.

All the same, I was so mad-keen to get close to wild animals that I did often manage to keep still long enough to watch some.

If you climbed up high, and arranged yourself so there wasn't too much leg showing, or skirt loose to be flapped by the wind, and if you could resist rubbing those skin-prickles when they came, you might really see something.

First there'd be nothing at all, everything scared away like when you drop a stone in a pool. I was the stone. Then a wisp of hair would start tickling my face, to and fro in the breeze in unbearable irritation. I'd want to cough too. Mustn't move, though. Not even to get off that sharp bit of bark going into me, nor to tuck that horrible bit of hair behind an ear.

And presently wild life began to seep back, first the invisible, then the visible. Because there definitely are invisible things in woods, and they are the first to come back. You can feel when they have accepted you and don't mind your being there.

After that come the insects and the birds. Flies madden you by crawling on your skin, where they sit and polish up

their front legs and probes, and the daylight strikes un-
imaginable colours out of their talc wings. A bird hops
among the bushes, or tosses over the dead leaves to find
food. The little sounds begin again, of grasshoppers and
mice and such.

Now you can see what goes on in the green wild world
when human beings are not present. You are absorbed into
that secret world like water into water, and now it is going
on again because you are not there. You have become inexistent. This is what it feels like to be a ghost.

It was a great surprise to me to discover how *much* life
there is. Insects of every kind abounded everywhere. I had
only to lie in grass to see that the grass-jungle was full of
teeming life, from beetles and ants to frogs and mice and
grasshoppers. For them, this was heavy bamboo jungle, and
they swarmed in it.

In the trees, spiders hung yard-wide nets, and waited
there with huge reflecting eyes, the brown hair on their
bodies glinting bronze and purple in the sunlight that came
dappling down through leaves. Squirrels and monkeys
played in the branches. In quiet, hilly jungle there might
be a pine marten rippling through the tree tops and coloured
rather like a Siamese cat.

Birds whistled and piped, and worked away for food.
There was never anywhere without birds, as there is in
Europe where they eat them, even the song birds. There
were parrakeets and mynahs and vultures and crows and
jays and pigeons and magpies and hundreds of others. There
were always plenty of peacocks. Kites and eagles. Owls.
Nightjars. The brain-fever bird.

Next most plentiful, after insects, birds, squirrels, and
monkeys, were the deer and jackals. Every night the wild
grassland echoed with the mad howling of jackals.

There was plenty for me to watch. Of course, always,

the rustle made by the not-seen animals was like the fish that gets away, the best thing of all, and just missed.

The easiest animals for me to practise getting close to were the squirrels that lived in the roofs of the forest bungalows and that were not frightened of man. From them I learnt several very important things.

These squirrels had well-used highways between the bungalows and the trees of the compound. There was no need for them, as a rule, to stray far. Trees provided their food, and trees were everywhere at hand.

Watching for a moment when the dogs were not looking, they would streak down the verandah pillars, bounce to the ground, and then with a bounding flowing movement dart over the brown grass to the nearest tree. In the morning they went out foraging, and came home in the evening. Whenever the dogs saw them, they chased them, but never caught one. The squirrels would flit up tree or pillar and then turn and shout their triumph and derision.

I had only to notice their usual highway and then to establish myself near it and keep still. There was one special route, where a branch of a big tree dipped down like a feather towards the bungalow. The squirrels would come dancing down it with their quick frisking movements and a flash of bright black eye and floating tail. Then they jumped off the tip and dashed for home. That way, they spent less time on the ground—their danger spot—than if they came down the trunk.

This was open ground, there was no cover for me anywhere, but I found there was no need for it, so long as I kept still. The squirrels, being a great deal smaller than I was, did not notice that this lump of something-or-other was alive unless I moved. I just stood there in the direct route, not even squatting down or camouflaging myself in any way, but only clutching my skirt each side of me to stop it blowing.

Around us lay the world as it left the hand of the Creator— river and forest and hill, unhurt by Man, and peopled by majestic creatures who have accompanied Man out of the Dawn of Time.

As soon as we could, we escaped to the river.

did not seem in the least strange to us children then, to have Mother leave home in the evening to go after a tiger.

We travelled from camp to camp on elephants.

Here we are—myself, my brother Harry, our ayah and the mahout, ready for the journey to the next camp. That's one of the grass huts I was talking about, in the background.

Every few days we moved to new unfished rivers.

The tents and luggage went on a string of camels.

A jungle track.

vening in camp. One of the men is cooking in front of his grass hut. In the background one of the elephants, unharnessed, is resting and feeding.

At some camps we were in tents.

Geoff helping Harry and me to
put up our own small tent in the
jungle.

Here's how we got up on to an
elephant.

This is another way of getting up on to an elephant.

The rivers were the pattern of our lives.

y brother Harry and I used to pole about on the sleepers being
ated down river to the mills.

Jungle picnic.

Harry and I diverting the course of a stream. That's our governess on the san and Bunty and Squinch, the two spaniels.

This is Harry with our collapsible canvas camp boat.

hristmas morning, and friends to stay with us in camp. This tent belonged t
arry and me, and I've got my new doll, May Blue, standing in front of me.

Geoff with (father's) tiger!

Elephant bringing home her fodder out of the jungle.

Getting up on to the elephant.

Ayah, Brother Harry, me and the mahout. The roof means they were expecting a hot day later on, I suppose.

The big living tent with two of the bedroom tents.

Jungle river.

Our bungalow in the Hills was on the top of a forested ridge.

All along the northern horizon went the white giants.

A room in our bungalow in the Hills. The walls were covered with
ikar trophies in the fashion of the times. I typed my first stories on
at machine, and there's the trunk of the rogue elephant of Kotdwara
aning up against the wall.

In Lansdowne we did meet other children, and here I am in an embroidered dress and flowered hat, showing off to them.

The other side of this stone wall was the khud, and I'm not supposed to be standing up there like that at all. One day I fell down it.

ff to a party in Lansdowne, Mother pulling on her gloves, and Harry and m
a dandy.

Ayahs, those dear brown nurses, placidly devoted their whole days to their small white charges.

The squirrels in the tree had seen me arrive, and for a few moments all froze to the trunk, spread-eagled and up-side down. Like panthers, they then became invisible. You could expect their peppery grey jackets to disappear on a tree-trunk, but why did those black stripes down the back disappear too? Perhaps only because Krishna meant them to, same as the rosettes on the panther, for legend says his fingers made those marks.

I kept still, and in a moment the little animals one by one gave a flick and a flirt of their tails, freezing and frisking in alternate jumps until they were sure there was no danger. You could see the question mark in their minds. Is this all right? Or isn't it? Finally the scatterbrains forgot me and raced about on their business as before, eating berries, chasing each other and scolding. Sitting up briskly to shell a seed, holding it in their hands and watching out in all directions while they did so. A few quick nips, a chatter of fast little bites, and the shell flew off in pieces. You could see their long rodent teeth, capable of giving a nasty wound.

Now here was one of them on his way back to the bungalow. He came bobbing down the branch to the tip. He was within a yard of me when something suddenly gave him pause. He froze in every muscle. I could see my topee reflected in his eyes. Next moment he was back up that branch like greased lightning, chirping his alarm.

Now *why?* What caused him suddenly to become aware of me? I had not moved. The wind had not changed. It is true that I was there in full view, but I had been so all along. Why had he suddenly taken fright? Why had this wooden post that was me come suddenly into focus for him as a human being?

He taught me something which is true of almost every wild animal. I found that if I wanted them not to notice me, I must not look at them direct, but at something near to them instead. Time and again—and I can test it with birds in my own garden now—I have watched some wild animal which is unaware of my presence. Till suddenly it feels something and looks round, moves uneasily and finally darts away. We ourselves in a crowd are apt for no reason to look direct into the eyes of the one person who happens to be staring at us. Could it be that the rays of thought and watching—*the intensity of attention*—are like the sun's rays gathered by a magnifying glass into one point till they burn? Even thought is sometimes enough to make a wild animal uneasy. It's the same sort of thing, I suppose, as when there's some awkward question you don't want someone to ask, and you absolutely must not think about it—not in the front part of your brain, as it were, anyway—or that's the very question he will ask next.

I could, of course, get within inches of these Indian squirrels by putting down food on the verandah near one of the doors, and then standing just the other side of the chik and watching them through the slits of this split bamboo blind. But even here, intense scrutiny was enough to unnerve them and they'd skittle away off up into the roof again.

It must be alarming to be a small wild creature under observation. Imagine if we ourselves suddenly noticed that a hill was alive.

And so I watched the animals.

There is an extraordinary idea, fixed firmly in all the human race, that to build and cultivate is to progress. To cut the jungle and tame the land is advancement, and then to build upon the cultivation better still. Building and cultivation of course there must be; but the good earth disappears under brick, the Garden of Eden is cut back and back, and all the wild beauty of the world is tidied and destroyed. This is progress. I have even read the proud caption under a photograph: *M———, the new town! Here, before we came, there was nothing but fields.*

It might be supposed that squirrels would have been the obvious pets for us children in India. We could catch them easily enough, unharmed, in wire rat traps; and anyway, Father could have invented a trap if we hadn't already had one. They would have been easy to feed too, but we never did keep them, I don't know why. Perhaps they were too common. Or perhaps we always happened to have something else.

There was one squirrel that fell, though. It's the only time I've ever seen a climbing animal fall. He was watching me and he missed his footing. When I picked him up, he appeared to be uninjured, although he did not run away. His eye was keen, without a shadow of pain. We gave him a soft bed to curl up in, and food, and water, but in the morning he was dead. Death comes for animals, as it does for us, as a rule in the night time, and if you sit up with them, sometimes you can hold it off.

The squirrels used to run all over our parrot cage, trying to reach the nuts and grain inside, and then the parrots would nibble their toes and make the squirrels jump and scold.

These were the common little green parakeets of the jungle which are to be seen in flocks everywhere. They are beautiful creatures with a plumage of clear bright green. The rose-red beaks with which they eat and climb are squat, strong, and able to smash hard nuts or cut a finger to the bone. Some of the parrots wore a red collar, just as some pheasants wear a white one.

They nest in holes in trees, and one nest I saw was in a cinder of a tree standing up like a black skeleton in burnt jungle. It looked fine when the green birds flew in and out.

Two baby parakeets were brought to us from a wild

nest, and we kept them in a big roomy cage which was carried about with us. These parrots became perfectly tame and used to clamber all over us, but we clipped one wing of each, in case. They never really learnt to talk, though they made squawky efforts at such words as "Chuprassy!" which, as their cage stood on the verandah, they heard often. It felt nice to have one of these birds on my shoulder, his tiny glossy head rubbed on my cheek. He'd nibble my ear, fingering it with his sensitive tongue and fierce beak, and make me laugh as he tickled me. He'd overbalance and catch the ear and spread one bright wing to right himself.

They must have been a nuisance to the camp in general, one more piece of luggage. The tortoises and turtles were easier, because they just went in that linen bag on the elephant with us. Easier still were the aquariums we had, because we made a new one at each camp.

I remember going down to the river at one place and grubbing about deliciously all day among sand and running water, and coming home with tins and pails full of every kind of aquatic life.

We took the tin tub, with the name of the bungalow painted on it, out of our bathroom, and we shouted in Hindustani for the bhisti to go fetch us some water, which he did, pouring it out of his goatskin into the bath until we'd got enough. Then we fetched stones and sand and waterweed, and sticks and shells, and made a beautiful little pool. Into this we emptied the minnows and snails and worms we'd captured.

There was one poor little spider-thing, and we hesitated about putting him in because he was so nervous, hiding himself under sticks and stones, and we were afraid the others might eat him. But there wasn't time to run back to the river with him, so in he went.

Next morning, the pool lay quiet. Nothing was left alive but a gorged and bloated spider.

One other aquarium tragedy was when we used a leaky bowl for tadpoles. It was a flat enamel pan meant for setting cream, but it had been discarded as damaged. Not knowing this, we gave it a sandy bottom and the sand held the water in all day; but during the night it all leaked out. In the morning there was nothing but a little desert spotted with ink. The wretched tadpoles had practically dried away, as a jellyfish does. One of our tortoises also just dried up and died, I don't know why. We gave him everything we could think of, and he just got older and older and smaller till he died.

Aquarium creatures, which did not have to be transported from one camp to the next, but could be tipped back into the river each time, were an easy form of pet for us, though they caused a shortage of baths. Easier still, and much more useful, was a hen. Hens could live with the other hens, and earn their keep too.

I had a much-loved little grey hen—a live one, I mean, not the lead one—called Gently, who became, as might be expected, very tame and would ride on my shoulder, her hard claws taking a good grip of me through the thin cotton dress. Gently lived unharmed for a long while, escaping the hawks and the cook, too, when he came to look for a moorghi for supper. One of my other hens got eaten by mistake—a terrible day—and another was taken by a hawk before she had been mine for twelve hours.

The eggs they laid were small, because almost all chickens in India were as small as bantams. Once in Lansdowne my brother had been ill and a friend gave him four "English eggs." These were laid by hens of English stock, and to us they looked big as turkey eggs.

Harry decided they were far too magnificent to eat, so he set them instead. This was in the Hills, so we were not moving camp, and I don't think anyone knew what he had done. Grown-ups might have wondered whether the eggs had any chance of hatching.

Faith was rewarded, though, and three perfect chickens hatched.

We were delighted, although sorry about the fourth egg, which lay addled in the nest. But as I carried it away to the rubbish heap it gave a feeble cheep. Hurriedly I tapped the shell all over on the rock, and peeled it off. Inside, packed too tight to move, was a wet live chicken which I uncurled. It opened like a flower, and rocked on its legs, and blinked in the dazzling sunlight. I could see blood swell the veins. I could see the skull inside the slight membrane of skin, and the bulge of eyes—the part that was inside, and the part that was out. It was the ugliest thing I'd ever seen, beautifully ugly. But soon the sun dried it, the sticky feathers fluffed up and clothed its nakedness. I added it to the others.

The current belief then was that newly hatched chicks had to be fed on chopped hardboiled egg, and we prepared their dinners with loving care.

These were the most excellent chicks we had ever seen, bright yellow and big. We had never even imagined such big ones. The old cockerel in the hen run evidently thought so too, and believed himself responsible. When the foster mother died, and three of the chicks too, taken by a snake, he took over all duties with the remaining chick, feeding and clucking over it like a hen, scratching up titbits for it, and even trying to keep the chick warm between his horny, comfortless yellow legs.

This chick lived for a time, then it, too, died. Owing to rats and snakes and hawks and other marauders including the cook, no chicken lived very long. There were also various diseases that carried them off, and they were much bothered by parasites. One time our henhouse became infested by mites, so that one wretched hen who was sitting could bear it no longer but deserted her clutch and spent hours scuffling in a pocket of dust to try and rid herself of her tormentors.

When I touched her, the mites swarmed up my arm in millions and I had to go and be given a disinfectant bath.

In those days, without DDT, it wasn't so easy to clear a henhouse of parasites as it now is. The place had to be smoked out, or dismantled or creosoted.

It was in the henhouse that I made a big discovery. "*Mum!* I've found where eggs come from!"

The same sort of tremendous discovery happened to my own children. Having asked, and been told, where babies come from, Tim came to me later with quiet satisfaction: "*I* know where a poached egg comes from, Mum. It comes out of a boiled egg."

FIFTEEN

It's a Tragedy I'm Not a Monkey

Another hatching effort of ours in India was with the eggs laid by my pet chukor. This little red-legged partridge had been brought to us out of the jungle, and soon became tame. As with the parrots, we kept one wing clipped to stop her flying away, and she had the free run of the compound like the dogs, and travelled with us.

She was a beautiful little bird, turtle shaped and freckled, with pink about her. Man could never lay feathers down in such patterns that change like pictures in water as the wing is spread or closed—that stretch and contract, but retaining always their motif and their silken unity, sometimes with a light metallic wash over the lot. Her legs were pink as shrimps, and her eyes brilliant black with white and black and crimson near them.

Sometimes this bird vanished into the jungle from which she had come. Then the chuprassies would go out and look for her. It always amazed me that they found her in that tangle of grass and thorn and the everlasting trees, but they did, and finally we took her up to Lansdowne where she laid these eggs.

128

They were not fertile, but as far as I was concerned, and the chukor too, they were eggs, and eggs hatch. She sat for six weeks. At the end of that time, I decided to help the chickens out. The discoloration and the weightlessness of the shells ought to have warned me. I think only a dead camel ever smelled worse.

This bird finally went off into the jungle and was not recaptured. I hope she was rewarded for her patience, and that she found a mate and laid other eggs that did hatch.

Hawks often made attacks on this and other chukors which we kept from time to time. The partridge would leave the security and shade of the verandah and wander out into the sun, idly searching the grass for food. Zigzagging over the land like a butterfly went the tiny ominous shadow of a hawk high above. Suddenly the shadow would grow darker, or there'd be a whistle of wind in wings, and then the partridge came streaking for home with the hawk in close pursuit. Sometimes we had to rush out and save her, and the hawk braked with barred feathers spread and showing cream among the brown. Then *zoom*—he banked and was off again, climbing into the sun.

Besides squirrels, there were bats living in the roofs of the forest rest-houses, and every evening they emerged from the eaves with a drop and then an opening of silent umbrella wings as they flittered off into the twilight for insects, looping on the rose-coloured and turquoise sky.

We caught some of them with a butterfly net, waiting at the edge of the bungalow for the moment when they dropped out, each with almost an identical swoop from the same spot. We had to be careful not to injure them, they were so light and delicate—winged mice. The bones must be like thistle-thorns.

I held one of them up by the points of its wings, on which the tiny hooks grow, and it was almost too light to feel.

How big the wings were, but thin like jap silk, and the body covered with exquisite brown fur as fine as mouse fur. And in this speck of life beat a heart. If you held it up to the light, you could see the blood system in its wings like the veins of a leaf, pure scarlet. You could smell its musty smell, and feel the tug as it struggled to escape. Huge ears, pink as sweet-pea petals, rose above its tiny head, and the little thing gnashed its teeth at us.

I put it on the ground and it could not fly, because its wings were too big. Like a swallow, it had to have air under it before it could be airborne. It dragged itself with a webbed ungainly crawl to the nearest tree and climbed the trunk, then suddenly launched off into the air and away. All without a single sound of either voice or wing, though sometimes you could hear the needle-note of bats everywhere in the evening air.

We never kept a monkey for a pet: we played with the wild ones. Of course, they would not let us touch them, nor even approach too close, but they joined in the fun.

They watched us making the sand castles, and when we left the river, they came to inspect what we had been doing. Sometimes they sat in a row watching us, and sometimes they copied what we did. It was difficult to avoid the feeling that they were only another kind of us, and so perhaps they were. I've done things to annoy them, maddening their curiosity, and I've had moments of fear when a big grey langur sat staring at me and then edged up closer. I was only a bit bigger than he was, and I hadn't got his teeth.

Langurs are the common long grey apes of India. They have black faces with white ruffs. When I watched them swing on those lanky arms and let go and whoosh through the air to the next tree and catch a branch and never fall, even when they had a baby clinging to the breast, I longed with passion to be able to do the same. Why didn't my skinny brown legs and my sunburnt hands behave like that? Why wasn't I dressed in fur instead of khaki skirt? Why couldn't I sail through the air too?

"Mum, it's a *tragedy* I'm not a monkey."

Imagine looping from branch to branch like a travelling pendulum, crashing and flying through the tree tops, and never coming down to earth unless you wanted to, throwing yourself from tree to tree—away on those trapeze swings with eighty feet of air beneath you, and landing with perfect assurance on the whip-thin branch you'd chosen, dipping on it with your weight, but away again before it could break. Free air flowing cool all round you, without clothes. Your fingers long and double-jointed and black inside, with fur on the back.

And then sitting up there among the fresh buds and the flowers, feeding on petals, on berries and fruit, and throwing them down half eaten because there were plenty all around. Bounding off to somebody's garden to feast on mangoes that were all stone, and the peppery nasturtium seeds. Or peeling the loose brown shell from litchi fruit to get at the white flesh inside that looks like an onion but tastes sweet.

Looking down and calling out rude things to a panther if you saw him below. Following him in the tree-tops and shouting to everyone to look out. Never having to dress and undress or wash or go to bed or get up or do lessons. Just to live in the air in the green leaves. Sometimes so high up there were enough leaves beneath you to shut out all the ground, so you could be there above everything in the blue sunlight with the wind moving the foliage all round as far as eye could reach. Secure in your skill of climbing. Sleeping there too, in the arms of the wind.

We used to bend and crack our fingers to make them like

the monkeys' hands; when we weren't fishing, we spent all our free time climbing; but we never learnt to climb as the monkeys did.

Nevertheless, we scuttled up high—high. . . .

"Look at me, Mum. Look!" And we swung on our hands, legs free.

She turned away.

I was repaid for this later, when my sons did it to me.

Langurs were common, and at one place the bungalow itself was one of their aerial stepping-stones on their way to the river. They woke me early every morning at precisely the same time as they bounded *thump!* on to the flat roof above me, and galloped across off into trees on the other side. You could count the size of the troop by the number of thumps they made. They went down for their morning drink and then came back over the bungalow again.

Hanuman, the Hindu monkey god, is a langur, and he appears in carvings and paintings and in some of the temples. So does Ganesh, the Elephant God, and all the other gods of the complex Hindu hierarchy which, if it has fear and ghastly cruelty and filth, has also comfort, for there are lots of little local gods to attend to you and who are perhaps not too busy to listen to personal troubles.

I found a god in the jungle one day, carved in stone. Ganesh, with the elephant's head symbolising wisdom. He was only a baby Ganesh, and he lay in the rough grass under a tree, without a throne or temple. There was no village for miles. I wondered how he got there, and I left him where he lay.

Hindus do not care to take life, and all monkeys are sacred. My father once had to help in the transport of a trainload of monkeys from the city into the jungle. They had become too numerous for the town, where they could steal what they liked and must not be killed. So they were caught and let loose in the woods. Here, most of them must have fallen prey to panthers, or died of starvation, as they were town-dwellers and not able to fend for themselves in the wild.

Such was the way of life. I remember a dying pony that had been left by the roadside, since the owner did not wish to take life. The man could be as cruel as he liked, but he must not kill. Vultures were all round the pony, waiting for their meal. One or two, overcome by impatience, waddled closer and snatched a mouthful of the living flesh. It was left to the wicked imperialistic Englishman to end the pony's suffering with a bullet.

SIXTEEN

Our Best Pet

In the towns it is the small brown bandar monkey that is seen everywhere; the langur is more a forest dweller. But even in the jungle, bandars were more numerous. These little pinkish-brown monkeys, always looking rather mangy and flea-ridden, were everywhere. They too could climb and swing about, of course, but they had not quite the lithe long-limbed grace of the langurs. The mothers had to carry the babies till they were quite big, and once or twice I saw a poor mother weighted with twins, one at the back, one underneath. She still jumped and climbed, but you could see her weight as she did so, and her range was shortened.

At one river I saw a row of bandars come to drink. Some bent their faces to the water, and some raised it in cupped hands. I was reminded of the picture of the tribes led to drink, in my Bible.

I noticed that whenever we saw monkeys in the jungle, they left whatever tree they were in and got into another one, even if they had to come down and cross open land to do so, and even if the second tree were smaller than the first. In the presence of possible danger, any kind of action felt better than none.

I never handled a wild monkey, not even a baby, nor did we ever keep a deer for a pet.

Once a chital fawn was brought into camp from the jungle, either stolen from his mother or abandoned. There were friends camping with us at the time, and they took the fawn away with them to be a pet. This tiny brown dappled jungle baby of the sweet smell and velvet feel and wet nose lived in their town house, chewing up slippers like a puppy. I think in the end they gave it away.

I had wanted to keep it myself, but apparently we already had enough creatures on hand.

Some time later I had jaundice, and had to be carried in a litter when they moved camp. During convalescence it was decreed that the patient needed a good long walk. The patient was in a difficult mood, and complained and whined so, that everyone set off without her, and she was left behind to sulk alone.

Believe it or not, they came upon a wild chital fawn which showed not the slightest fear of human beings, but allowed everyone to stroke it before it finally wandered off into the jungle to find its mother. This was the only time a real wild animal, free and uninjured, allowed any of us to touch it, and I was not there. It was a sharp punishment and I learned my lesson.

Animals usually disappeared at sight, of course—earlier, if possible—and naturally they showed savagery if caught. The wild-dog pup that was brought to us was tiny, the size of a peke, but he'd have killed everyone if he could, and snarled and snapped at everything.

We chained him to a verandah pillar, with the intention of trying to tame him. The only thing he would eat was raw meat, just as it was, with the fur still on. I watched him tear up a crow. He fought his way into it, with black feathers tossed out in all directions.

One day he broke his chain and raced off into the jungle with the chuprassies in pursuit. I saw them silhouetted on the ridge behind the bungalow, the pup stretched in a gallop, and the men falling further and further behind. They never caught him, and I am afraid the chances are that he died miserably of starvation, being cut off from his pack, or else, as he grew, from the collar, though one can only hope not.

Wild dogs, of course, are hated everywhere. They hunt in packs like wolves and pull down their quarry after relentless pursuit. They can clear a piece of jungle of all game in record time. The highest government reward was for wild dogs.

I once saw a poor terrified sambhur stag crashing through the jungle with his chin up so the horns didn't catch. There were wild dogs on his trail. I don't know what happened. I suppose he was killed. And if not—if I had been able to save him, I suppose they'd have eaten some other animal instead. That, or the dogs themselves would have starved to death. Life is harsh. It is impossible to be kind. The instinct to kill is in Man too, side by side with the equally strong instinct to save life.

We once smoked out some earths in open grass-jungle which were supposed to contain dogs, but there was only a hyena in one and a porcupine in the other.

Both are nocturnal and spend the day in their burrows. At night they come out and trot about looking for food. They steal from panther and tiger kills; and they often came to the kills where my parents were waiting for bigger game. If we found an old natural kill in the jungle, the bones would often show marks of porcupine teeth.

But on the whole we didn't see much of either hyena or porcupine.

The hyenas were silent slinking carrion-eaters of the night.

They didn't mind how high their meals were. Occasionally one got shot and made into a rug. Their fur was coarse, though, and for a carriage rug jackal was better.

We collected jackal skins for such a rug, and it makes a fine car rug now. About twenty skins were needed, and they had to match. As jackals vary a good deal in colour, matching was none too easy, and we wanted the best dark winter coats. However, one often came on jackals in the grass in the daytime, when we were moving camp, for instance, and so the twenty matching dark skins were collected.

Jackals seemed to spend the daylight hours in ones and twos. Then at dusk it was as if a leader called them together with his first long howls that soon collected them up into a yelling chorus.

They are of course susceptible to rabies, and I knew this. Sometimes, if I thought about it, a quite unreasoning terror took hold of me, and the only way to get rid of it was to climb a tree. As I got to the height where no mad dog or jackal could possibly have reached me, that curious special mad-dog feeling used to drain out of my legs, and after a bit I could come down and be quite all right again.

Do ponies count as pets or transport? We had two. One was my father's, but he did for us as well. He was called Ponko, a small dark mountain pony, bright as satin and strong enough to carry a house. The other was a beautiful pink strawberry roan. We went riding, accompanied by Gwala Ram and a chuprassy, and we had biscuits buttoned down in our khaki pockets, to eat at the furthest point of the ride, while we sat and chatted to Gwala Ram and heard what he had to tell us. Then we trotted home again.

Most small girls love riding. They pour their hearts out on a pony if they can get one. So there must be something wrong with me because I never liked riding. I had riding lessons in India and at school but as soon as I was old enough to have the courage I at last admitted I didn't like it.

But of all the pets we ever kept, the best came to us in Lansdowne. A nurse was staying in the house at the time, and one morning she came along to Harry and me and said "Your mother would like to see you."

Mother was in bed, and in the crook of her arm lay a baby.

I've never had a happier shock in my life. My own babies did not arrive quite so easily or unexpectedly. There I was, a little girl of ten, passionately loving every small and helpless creature I could get hold of, and intensely interested in the reproduction of the species, to judge by the stories I was writing at that time. Every animal in every yarn had large litters of delightful young. The heroines had baby after baby at remarkable intervals. In one story a shepherd lost his flock in a flood, but saved one lamb only. It grew up and "Luckily it was a female, so he soon had a large flock again."

Here I was, then, suspecting nothing, but longing for a baby brother or sister. "If that's what you want," our governess had told me previously, "you'll have to speak to your mother about it!"

And now here was a baby brother.

We adored him at sight.

Cots in those days had head draperies to keep the draught off small bald heads, and there our baby lay in the pink light of the cot, looking like a wizened angel. He smelt so sweet, like the puppies, I took some of the baby powder to powder my dolls. He could wrinkle his forehead right over to the back of his head, and he still can, having the most mobile scalp I've ever seen. He can move his ears too, each one separately as a dog can; and sometimes in a railway carriage he'll do it to see what happens to the man sitting opposite.

What to call the baby? My parents had no idea. At last they took a Service list and looked down it and found a name they liked—Peter. So the man he was named for is not even aware of the honour. For a second name, Peter got Walter, the name of my grandfather, the one who used to snap his gold watch shut in church, to end the sermon. Names go in cycles, and it is curious that this name Peter, chosen from a list, apparently appealed to the parents of a great many other boys born at that time too. My kid brother has even been on a party with four young friends of his, all called Peter.

If it was a job to look after a baby in camp, to wash the nappies and obtain the necessities, I never knew it. None of the work or disturbance fell to Harry or me; we never had to get up in the night when he squawked, or wash things or be responsible. As far as we were concerned, he was nothing but pleasure.

He travelled with us on the elephants, in that laundry basket. The nappies were washed in the rivers, smacked and smacked on the rocks in the ancient way, with thousands of gallons of fresh soft water flowing past all the time to get everything clean as clean. Then the linen was put in the sun where it dried immediately and dazzling white in the disinfectant rays. It was better than any washing machine. When a cushion had to be cleaned, it was simply put under a waterfall, and pure water flowed through it for twenty-four hours. In fact, at one country hospital where supplies were short, the doctor ordered that washed bandages should be thrown up on the roof for the fierce sunlight to sterilise.

A baby in camp. I did not look ahead, as my mother did, and wonder what would happen if the baby were ill, with

the nearest doctor a week's journey away. Suppose he had
colic, croup, fever, dysentery, diphtheria? As I say, there
were no trucks, helicopters or radio. Suppose a scorpion
got into the cot? Or a snake? She and Father had to be
ready to deal, personally and alone, with everything. Nothing
must frighten him. They might even have to cut or cauterise
their own child.

But for Harry and me, all we knew was that we had a new
plaything. Better than the turtles and aquariums. Better than
the parrots or squirrels or monkeys. Everything he did was
wonderful. When he waved his hands and we found a fly
squashed in his fist, nothing could stay our admiration.

After a time, he became able to stand, and then he stood
alone! We used to get him balanced, and then we'd start to
count, gabbling on as fast as we could to see how far we
could get before he toppled over.

Presently the ninepin could walk. Now it was my job to
distract his attention while Harry built a tower with all
our bricks. Then the baby, armed with a mallet, was aimed
at the tower and released. He toddled fiercely forward and
hammered it flat.

Minding a baby brother was perhaps a more womanly
occupation than any I had attempted yet. I did not cook,
I did not sew, and those were the days of embroidery and
piano for girls. My mother often sat in our wild camps by
the light of oil lamps, doing her exquisite needlework. Not
me. But I was a girl-child, just as vulnerable as any other.
How did I make out in this man's world of rifles and tigers
and elephants, where the smell of gunpowder was more
familiar than the scent of flowers?

SEVENTEEN

My Mother's Duties

It was a man's world, but women had the good fortune to share it. Contrary to the usual film story, where the wife is always unhappy in the wilderness, thus providing conflict, real-life jungle wives love the life. When my mother got married, my father worried about taking her into camp with him. Camp life was so different from everything she had known up to then. "But what will there be for you to do?" he wondered. She loved every minute of it.

There was plenty to do. She organised the meals and comfort and orderliness of our jungle home. It was absolutely never makeshift or chaotic. She shot tigers, and raised a family, and did beautiful needlework. Some of the house linen in my bottom drawer when I got married was magnificently embroidered by her in camp in the jungle.

She could make lace, or haversacks, or cloth heads for my dolls when the china ones got broken. She could ice a wedding cake, make every kind of confection—anything. When pen-painting was the rage, she mastered the art at once and painted beautiful designs with a pen on satin cushion-covers. It was a rage that did not last because the paint faded and broke off. Mother went back to her embroidery.

But I was no needlewoman or chef. I liked fishing and climbing, and watching animals. In these pursuits, being a girl was a handicap, even though I had a mother who was prepared to wait up alone in the jungle at night for panthers and bears.

Well, my hair and skirts, for example.

That was in the days before shorts for girls, or short hair either, so I wore a skirt and long hair. Both were a hated nuisance.

I was a thin child, skinny, even. I went thin when I had whooping cough at six months old, and I stayed that way. Later, when I came back to England and school, they told me I was sallow and that all my strength had gone into my hair. Hairdressers in England always exclaimed over it. It was long thick hair, fair to begin with, and dark brown by the time I was grown up. It was perfectly straight, and I got it out of my way into two plaits, either of which by the age of fifteen was thicker than any other school friend's one plait. But it never did me the slightest good. As a child I found it a nuisance, specially when they wanted to wash it, and the minute I grew up I cut it off. Now recently I've had the trouble of growing it again in preparation for an equable old age.

But in India, there it was, always in the way. When it was in plaits, they slipped about and fell into things; and if I went to a party in Lansdowne I had to wear it loose, which was worse. If I crawled through undergrowth, my knees tripped on it. I wanted to be like a boy, with no skirt or plaits, and sometimes I knotted the two plaits together behind me to be rid of them.

The daily brushing, too! The tangles. And then when they washed it—the fuss! The rubbing and rinsing. Jugs and jugs of water, always too hot or too cold. The last one ice-cold, supposed to be good for the hair, made me shiver right down to the toes. Now came the white towels, and the brushing with my mother's heavy silver brushes, freshly washed. Another lot of wet tangles to be got out, and the pain of someone else doing it for you. It brought tears to my eyes. Then out to run in the hot sun, but with a topee on. Topees had webbing inside, so the air could circulate between scalp and pith, but the head part of my hair always took a long time to dry, however fierce the sunlight was. I couldn't climb, either, till the wretched stuff was plaited again. Absalom. But Harry could just swim in his bath and be lathered and towelled in a moment.

Still, at those Lansdowne parties, people always said "How thick her hair is, and long! What do you do for it to make it like that, Mrs. Burke?" so the listening child began to be vain about it, to compensate for hating the beastly stuff.

Every day we had to lie down for an hour after lunch in a darkened room. My hair was sometimes loosened, to rest it, and if it were a hot day I would spread it up on the pillow to cool my neck. I lay and sang one of my own doggerels, made up mostly of the "British Grenadiers," I think. I never got tired of it. Others did. After a bit they'd give me a book to look at, instead.

One afternoon as I lay resting in a darkened tent, the singing came to an abrupt end. I had noticed a snake lying on a chair the other side of the room. I must have charmed it out with my singing, and now here it was in answer to my call. This was precisely what I was always longing to do with animals, but now that it had happened, I lay paralysed. So did the snake. I discovered just what birds must feel like, hypnotised by a serpent. I did not move till someone came to call me, and threw back the flap of the tent, the daylight came in, and the snake wasn't a snake at all but a dressing-gown cord.

Another time, in Lansdowne, we were in bed, and I arranged my plaits out on the pillow so as not to lie on the lumpy things. I had plaits at night too, to prevent tangles. Just as I was thinking "But no, perhaps better not, someone'll get a fright thinking the plait is a snake," an earthquake struck, the whole house shook like a train, the parents rushed in, snatched us from our beds and ran from the house. Snakes and plaits were forgotten.

It was only a small earthquake and no harm done. My mother, however, had been in the big Darmsala earthquake and there was always a chance that there might be another one like it, when all the houses fell down.

My governess was absolutely maddening one day. She rushed us out for an earthquake and stood in the compound clutching our heads into her skirt. I struggled to get free, but by the time I succeeded, the earthquake was over and I had seen hardly anything of it.

Almost everything to do with hair was a nuisance. Skirts, though, had one great advantage, for which the boys respected me: you can carry things in a skirt. When it was necessary to transport earth to make a mud fort for the lead soldiers, for instance, or sand, or stones, I held my skirt like a bag and filled it and ran along to the place where the stuff was wanted. They couldn't do that with shorts. It's true their shirts and shorts had dozens of useful pockets, whereas my dresses frequently had none, but they couldn't carry mud in them, and often they really needed my help.

Only when fishing was I allowed to tuck my skirt up. Otherwise it had to *be* a skirt. I wasn't the only one to suffer from this, of course. It was worse for adults. Ladies in those days still wore their skirts long. My mother's shortest jungle skirt was at least calf-length, and she could not possibly have worn such a thing in the hill station, where even ankles hardly showed. Neither could my father have worn his shorts in Lansdowne. As for riding, all ladies rode sidesaddle, in voluminous habits.

The dreadful doom of long skirts hung over me, the prison closing in. My object was to keep skirts as high and socks as low as possible: my mother's was gradually to close the gap. But my generation was fortunate. Before us, centuries of small girls had been trapped in the dreadful prison of clothes. They fought too, no doubt, but it was a losing battle. For us, daylight dawned. Chains were falling off women all over the world.

My generation were the first women to earn their own living. The freedom and independence which now we take for granted were won only in this very century. I was probably one of the last to watch my skirts go down at each birthday.

After the first world war, when we were back in England, the process was still continuing with me. By that time my parents had returned to India, leaving us at school, and the next step in my subjugation was stays. I was thirteen, and they wanted me to wear whalebone supports. I remember now that nightmare garment with its bones and metal clips, and the two cups which I couldn't begin to fill. Crack! went the whalebone when I bent down, and it dug into my thirteen-year-old flesh.

I cut the tucks and pulled the bones out. Even then, I hated the thing.

Then one day an angel came to the house dressed as an old lady, and she said to the old ladies in charge of me, "Why make the child wear stays? It is unnecessary. Look at me. I am healthy, I am straight, and I wear nothing but soft underclothes. I will show you." I never had to wear stays again.

My mother would not have made me wear them, and in India all she wanted was the gradual and usual lengthening of the skirt, and raising of the stockings. The day I first wore stockings to the knee, I kissed my socks goodbye. I thought I would never wear bare legs again. What if the sun had browned my English skin? What if it was making little hairs glint on the brown? I did not care. I hated clothes altogether, and now I was being made to wear more and more of them.

Not gaudy ones either. Not red and yellow such as the Indians wore, with necklaces of, say, silver bugles strung on cyclamen cotton, and turned-up slippers stitched with gold. That would have been different. If they had given me the bunch-dyed skirts that are tied tight in rings and dipped in vermilion and saffron—if they had given me the anklets and nose-rings, or painted caste marks on my forehead with white and ochre, how different the story would have been.

Then I'd have worn all the skirts they wanted. Then perhaps I'd have changed twice a day without grumbles. Then I'd have rustled with thousands of those glorious blown-glass beads, so light you hardly knew you'd got them on but had to remember not to lean on things or they'd pop. They never cut you, though, any more than a Christmas bauble does when it breaks.

I did have lots of these beads, and wore them sometimes. Almost the only sewing I ever did was to string them by the hour into necklaces and bracelets. They were dirt-cheap, and I used my pocket money on them, and on glass bracelets. We collected also those red seeds called lal-lal-beeges out of the jungle. They were hard as beads, and bright scarlet, with a black tip one end, and they lay about in thousands wherever they grew. Each had to be pierced before it could be used in a necklace.

The coral necklace which I possessed, and the christening-present brooches of gold and seed-pearls were for parties only. But I had a blue enamel watch with microscopic flowers painted on the face. This was so beautiful that it had a steel case with a wire grid in front, to protect it from harm, so that all the blue and the flowers hardly ever showed. I did not keep this watch long. It disappeared, and presumably it was stolen.

Two dresses once came for my mother. They were evening dresses, for Lansdowne dinner parties. One was grey. One was flame.

"Which do you like best?" the grownups asked me.

My eyes caressed the flame dress.

"Oh well," they said, "it's only natural a child should choose the bright one."

It wasn't natural in the least! I had chosen the best because of my good taste and knowledge. It was nothing to do with being a child. I boiled.

I'm afraid I often boiled; though seldom to any effect. "I hate you all. I'm going to run away into the jungle with a puppy."

How humiliating it was, when feeling so angry and disdainful, to burst suddenly into tears.

I suppose most small girls learn early to do the shopping. I don't think I went in a real shop at all until I was about twelve years old. There were the Indian booths in the Lansdowne bazaar, and the same kind at Hardwar—mostly a room full of gorgeousness, with an open front and a special Indian smell. Here sat the goldsmiths, and if you went to one for a filigree bracelet, he would take a brick of gold like a half-pound pat of butter, and dig into it with a butter-knife and pull and work it out thin as thread, and spin it into spider-web. But we practically never went to the bazaar, and the only shopping I ever really did was by post or from the travelling Kashmiri wallahs who visited the bungalows in Lansdowne and spread out their silk and carpets and jewelry for sale.

One of them, riding ahead of his retinue like a caliph, would approach the bungalow, followed by servants carrying the merchandise.

They had cashmere shawls and carpets and exquisite saris to show us, and opal and turquoise. Rolls and rolls of silk so delicately coloured they could not stand daylight. Plenty of the blown-glass beads. I should have liked to buy everything, but naturally we had a set amount of pocket money and had to manage on that, saving or spending it as we wished. The silk was expensive. I bought one square yard of shell pink, and one of apple green. They were so lovely that even I felt the desire to sew them, and I hemmed the edges as neatly as I could and used them for sheets on my doll's bed.

The love of Eastern gorgeousness and the hatred of clothes went hand in hand in me. I liked either khaki or vermilion. I did not want to enter the adult world of long skirts and everlasting washing and changing and brushing of hair, and yet I longed to be grown-up enough for a love affair. Sometimes I pinned my plaits up and tried to see myself as a lady with a man coming to kiss me.

Those novels left behind in the bungalows contained many romances. I read them all. Since I knew so few unmarried gentlemen, I was obliged to fall in love with fictional heroes out of boys' adventure stories.

I naturally supposed that all this interest in love was my own secret, so picture my blushes when I heard my mother saying "Books? Norah likes a passionate love story."

I was writing them, too. And to illustrate them, I cut pictures out of magazines and catalogues. I pasted the picture onto a sheet of paper and then typed round it. For one story, an interminable novel that never did get finished, the only picture of a man that I could find handsome enough, was an advertisement for pyjamas, so I had to include a bedroom scene in the story.

EIGHTEEN

Clothes and Dolls

One might have supposed that this keen interest in love would have brought a reasonable interest in one's appearance. With me, it did not. Apart from the adoration of oriental gorgeousness, which was a hunger and which could be assuaged by the sight of a sunset or a rhododendron or semal tree in full flame, but more easily by covering my own body with colour, I did not care what I looked like.

The large and clumsy khaki topees which we wore in camp did not distress me. Nor, on the other hand, did I appreciate my huge Lansdowne party hats covered with piles of white lace. Not a single one of my party dresses remains with me now, though I am sure they were lovely, and must have been decorated with real lace, and hours of Mother's embroidery.

I do remember that I never wore gloves. We just didn't have any. When I returned to England I could not get used to them. Wool gloves set every nerve on edge, and they still do. My hands at school were always bursting with purple chilblains. Sausages took the place of my thin brown Indian fingers until I was grown up, when I suddenly became immune to chilblains, and had no more.

In India the thought of decorating my face never occurred to me. Make-up had still not appeared even for grownups. A little vinolia talc powder in the bathroom was probably the first, and a powder-block and buffer to get a polish on your nails. After a bit, the nail powder, you remember, began to be lightly tinted with pink. The same thing happened with lip-salve, didn't it? The first sticks of these were white grease to prevent chapped lips, and gradually they began to be tinted pink, then darker and darker till they were red. I can remember one of my governesses biting her lips and pinching her cheeks to get colour in them before setting out for a party.

As for me, I brushed and washed, I plaited my hair, I cut and scrubbed my nails and that was all. The first make-up I ever put on my face was at school when I was about fifteen. One of the girls had been sent a simply unbelievable birthday cake with whole crimson roses on it, and when we ate the much-too-sweet petals we found the colour came off. So then we licked them and used them for lipstick, and we put bath powder on our faces. It was then highly gratifying to look in the glass.

Sewing and cooking are normal occupations for girls. I did neither. Under Mother's supervision, I made one cake, a madeira mixture with fruit in it. The moment it was in the oven I had a lick-out of the mixing bowl, because uncooked cake tasted so much nicer than the finished ones. Then I was off out into the compound again. "Call me when it's done, Mum. Don't anyone take it out except me, or it isn't my cake." Well, I have to cook nowadays, the same as most people, but I still hate it.

As for sewing, I sewed for the dolls and I made myself those bead necklaces, and that was about all. But occasionally I got seized by a need to make something beautiful.

"Mum, I want to embroider roses."

She found a square of white satin for me—a piece of wedding dress, was it?—and a transfer, and fillets of coloured silk. We ironed off the blue transfer, and I embroidered my basket of roses, with one of course fallen out beside the basket, and in the end I made the thing into a blotter. This terrible blotter represented many hours' work and much determination, but it did not harm anyone so much as a jumper I once knitted in artificial silk. It was white, with two yellow bands at the bottom. It turned out broader than it was long. It was a present for my mother. She bravely wore it at least once.

Except when there's no escape, I neither sew nor knit even now.

But all the reading I did, and squinting in the sun, and I'm afraid temper too, made the parents warn me, "You scowl too much. You have quite a wrinkle between your eyes."

I rushed to the mirror. A wrinkle? It was true. Every day I massaged away at this sign of age. I was about eight or nine years old.

As there was no radio in those days, all girls learned to play the piano, so that they could be of some use at parties. I also. Thank Heaven a piano could not go with us into camp, though. I was no good at it, and was presently allowed to give it up. I remember one musical child, however, who was really brilliant. For him his parents had a small portable piano which could be taken into camp and he gave us a recital on it one day in his tent. I have often wondered what happened to him afterwards, with such talent.

He was an only child, without even a brother or sister to play with in the jungle, and he had been told that we two children were coming into camp with him for a few days. All his hopes were built on this, but when he first caught sight of us on our elephant and saw the identical round topees, tears filled his eyes.

"They're both girls," he said.

However, the tears dried when he found that one was a boy, and very much a boy, and that the other, I hope, did not disgrace herself when it came to climbing and fishing and mud pies.

Because of my brother, nearly all the games I played as a child were boys' games, such as soldiers and stalking, and a game of our own called Squatimy. This had to be played in the moonlight in the jungle, and got its name from the short squat shadows that the full moon threw on the dusty ground.

In Lansdowne the nearest people to us were a family of three boys. We divided into two sides and built those mud forts and filled them with our lead soldiers, and shelled each other's forts with stones. When all the soldiers were flat and therefore dead, the battle was over. We also melted the soldiers, dropping them in at the top of a charcoal brazier and getting them out at the bottom in what looked like silver coins.

It was most exciting, but I was a girl, and I hated killing the soldiers, or even just spoiling their newness. I *hated* it whenever one of those poor mangy homeless pi-dogs who had never had enough to eat in his life had to be shot because there was nothing else to be done with him. I hated it when the boys had a beetle-swimming race, because I was sure the beetles were drowning, not swimming. The boys would never have been cruel to anything, any more than I would, but they did not agree that beetles could not swim.

I was soft. I was silly and feeble. I loved people and things. It hurt horribly when they had to go. I could not lose even one of my thirty-two dolls without crying. When the two pieces of a cracked china head grated together like broken bones, I shuddered right through.

One of these dolls, a lesser one—not one of the queens

like White Swan and May Blue and Melinette, but nevertheless one of my family—was christened by Ayah. She gave
her the name of Gordon Gurriah—Gordon Doll—because the
doll's beautiful face reminded Ayah of a Mrs. Gordon we
knew.

One of our tents had windows with some sort of window
ledge. I dressed Gordon Gurriah and made her lovely, and
set her upon this ledge to look out at the jungle. She fell and
was killed, her head in a thousand pieces.

This was when Mother first came to the rescue about
dolls. A dead doll can be brought to life again. If only our
other losses could be healed in like manner.

Mother took Gordon Gurriah's hair, and she took linen and
her sewing basket and paint box, and she made a new head
for the doll. It was a different face, of course, and the doll's
name now had no meaning, but my dead doll was restored
to me.

Many of my dolls—White Swan, May Blue, Melinette,
Jappy, Mr. Brown, and others, are alive now. Mr. Brown is
a Teddy bear, rather a hard one, and has survived the love
of several small boys.

I first got married when I was ten years old. I chose
almost the only boy I knew, and he hadn't a chance.

My mind had been on marriage for some time. Those old
novels left behind in the forest bungalows by other Forest
Officers and their wives had fired me. In one exciting tale the
heroine's long hair always tumbled down at what I called
the cru-ical moment. At any crucial or critical time, down
it fell to make her more appealing.

In addition to this, the chuprassies often whiled away
their time telling us those old tales and legends, and there
was that governess who had been secretary to a Ranee. This
Indian queen was writing a book of fairy stories, and so we
were told some of them. One was about a girl whose mother

married her to a serpent, but the serpent turned into a prince who covered her with jewels. Another governess used to read me her love letters, as well as some of the romances she bought. In one of these stories, the poor working girl walked with her lover to meet his people. As, footsore and weary, they approached a castle, he pulled out a huge ruby ring, put it on her finger and confessed "I am the Earl."

Besides, as I say, I had begun writing stories myself and typing them on my father's machine.

But now, great Heavens above, here I was, ten years old already, and not a man in sight.

For great lengths of time, Harry and I never saw any children but ourselves. There were hardly any in our lives that we knew well, and we called each other Boy and Girl instead of by our names, because we were Adam and Eve in our world. But there was this other boy, Geoff, who did sometimes appear in camp because he was the son of the Conservator of Forests for the district. He was a most attractive lad with a delightful smile; but more than that, he could make extremely powerful magic.

"I have an Air House," I announced. "It is invisible. You can't see it, but I can. I go there sometimes. Two people live in it besides me. Big Fairy and Little Fairy."

"I" said Geoff "have a magic box." He brought a matchbox out of his pocket. "Inside this box is my magic."

"Show me."

He rattled the box. "Listen!" he whispered. "Can't you hear the magic?"

Well that settled it, but presently we wanted to see some of this magic at work.

"All right," Geoff offered. "This afternoon my father is going fishing. I will make a magic that he will not catch any fish."

His father returned empty-handed.

You can see why I chose Geoff. But how to get the matter arranged?

He was coming into camp with us very soon. I consulted my family.

"Well, if you want Geoff to marry you and he hasn't asked you, you'll have to ask him, won't you?"

"But I thought it was the man who asked the woman."

"Oh well, there have been many instances the other way round. You try."

I waited in a quiet fever of excitement. Would time never pass?

At last we saw the Conservator's elephants coming into camp. The cru-ical moment was upon me.

I do not remember putting on any special clothes for this great occasion in my life. I did not even re-plait my hair or look in a mirror. I was wearing my usual khaki cotton dress for the jungle, and the khaki sun-hat, and brown socks fallen down round my thin ankles.

I went to find Geoff and make my proposal.

NINETEEN

Christmas in the Jungle

I did not beat about the bush.

"Geoff, I have been thinking," I said. "Would you like to marry me?"

He considered the matter.

"Oh, all right."

"But I mean really, when we're both grown-up. Will you?"

"What I've said I'll do," said Geoff bravely, "I do."

But of course, when the time came we married other people.

Perhaps I knew this all along, because in India, on that day in the jungle, I hastened to make sure of him.

"Very well then. We will be married this afternoon."

It was the usual brilliant hot day. The ceremony—and I think we even used a prayer book—took place in our own small tent which was set up in the shade of a grove of dark green mango trees, and was an exact replica of a real big tropic one, even lined with red. Like them, it was made in two pieces, the inner room and the outer roof, for coolness, and so it didn't matter if you touched against the ceiling by mistake in rain. The tent had two poles, and windows, and proper loop-fastenings and everything.

157

We collected leaves and creepers from the jungle, and whatever flowers we could find, and decorated the place. During the winter, which was when we were in camp, there weren't many flowers to be had, the jungle mostly khaki-green and the grass dry as straw. We were often told "In England the grass is *green*." There were always trees with leaves on, though.

When the tent was suitably decorated as a church, we were married, with brother Harry as the padre. I can't remember if we sang hymns or not. I think we ended with "God Save the King."

The tent now became the hall for the marriage feast. This consisted of biscuits, chocolate, and oranges. We sat cross-legged on the cotton drugget on the floor, and the breeze blowing through the tent and mango grove cooled our bare sun-hot legs and bodies prickling with sweat.

The Indian oranges were small, and loose in their skins like tangerines, and had that taste of fruit just off the tree. Ayah used to sing us a child-song about oranges. Like all Indian lullabies, it was a chanting nasal drone accompanied by monotonous movements guaranteed to send anyone to sleep. It was all about a bungalow leaking in the monsoon, and a child stealing oranges—*ek narengi chor-dia*—and getting beaten for it and sobbing herself to sleep. In later years, when I sang these old Indian child-songs to my own babies, they always started to nod.

As soon as I was safely married to Geoff, I drew a breath of relief.

Harry must have felt a bit out of it, because he now decided that he must marry too. Fortunately some friends whom we knew as Aunt Ethel and Uncle Frank were coming to stay with us soon for some tiger-shooting, and bringing with them their two daughters, Margaret and Molly. Harry chose Margaret for his bride, because she was his age, and

Molly rather young to think of marrying yet. Margaret naturally had Molly for a bridesmaid, so I suppose I must have married them.

Anyway, the bridesmaid threw up the flap of the tent at the end of the ceremony and commanded "Bridegroom, fetch the water for the baby's christening."

Margaret and Molly and their parents used to come to us for Christmas Camp sometimes.

Christmas in the jungle! The mist of early morning giving way to sun and heat. The tiger shoots. The roast peacock to eat instead of turkey.

Excitement woke us early on the Day itself, and in the dim light we found that Santa Claus had visited us just the same as he did other children, though once he gave all girl-things to my brother and all boy-things to me. I suppose because, as we were in camp, our beds never stood in the same place twice and he muddled us.

Harry and I gave each other our presents as soon as we woke up. His to me were usually things for authorship, such as blotters and diaries, because I was always writing, and I think I gave him mostly fishing things; all of course bought by post. At breakfast we gave presents to our parents, and had gifts from them. These were absolutely wonderful things, like the folding dolls' bed or that special fishing reel that we shared.

Since there was no church, we could not attend it. In camp, we said our prayers, and read the Bible or our book of children's Bible stories, but I don't think I went to church on Christmas Day till I was twelve years old. In England, church bells are one of the sounds of Christmas Day. No bells rang in the jungle.

After breakfast there was an ancient and romantic ceremony. The Indians of the camp came to the verandah with the largest coin they possessed—a rupee, if possible.

This they offered in the palm of the hand to the sahib, who touched it, but did not take it, and they salaamed and went away again. Their action meant "All that I have is yours, Protector of the Poor," and his, "I understand and thank you. Go in peace."

This was a gesture significant of something much deeper than even its known symbolic meaning. It is customary nowadays to assume that Britain bled India for what she could get out of her, and the word "imperialism" is one of blame and disgust. It used not to mean suppression and greed; what it used to mean was the protection of a hitherto ignorant and superstitious people, backward and weak, practising the many cruel rites of savage times; and the incorporation of such a people into the Commonwealth and jurisdiction of the strong. Civilisation and education followed, until the country was able to govern itself.

But when you have a land where widows were expected to burn themselves to death on the husband's funeral pyre—where goats were skinned alive to get the fourpence extra for the larger skin—where these and thousands of other atrocities were daily practised without any glimmering that they were wrong—education, advancement and enlightenment take time.

From the day when the Crown took over India from the East India Company to the time when the great subcontinent achieved self-rule was about ninety years. During that century, the Englishmen who went to India did not grow rich on what they could squeeze out of ignorant savages. On the contrary, they gave their life's toil, their sweat and blood, their health, even their lives, too, to India. They built hospitals, schools, railways, irrigation schemes to prevent famine, and every other kind of necessary thing. They prevented the most ghastly but quite common cruelties to women, children, and animals. They conserved the forests and other natural riches of the land, so they should not be wasted away. They fought poverty such as has never been seen in Europe or America. They fought ignorance and super- stition and indifference, and squalor and filth and disease. They said goodbye to their children for years and years, in the most sad and bitter partings, losing years that could never be replaced. They lived on ordinary pay, and in the end they retired on small pensions. It seems a pity that their memory should now be blacked by the lies left behind by those agitators who, towards the end of British rule, could see rich prizes for themselves by fishing in troubled waters. *De mortuis nil nisi bonum.*

The Indian servants who brought their rupees to my father on Christmas morning in the jungle, to have them touched and returned, were not bowing to a tyrant. They knew that here indeed, in absolute reality, was a protector of the poor —that all security and justice came from him and others like him. No Indian went for justice to one of his own country- men unless he could afford to buy it.

On Christmas morning, some of them sometimes brought necklaces of marigolds, the flower which is used for every kind of special occasion. A marigold necklace is a sign of honour, and is placed about the neck of any special person. But also it may be given in mere flattery or as a conventional gesture. My father's face (hating flowers as he did, even in vases) when he was obliged to put on one of these sycophan- tic flower necklaces was a picture.

Occasionally at Christmas there would be offerings from Indians of dhalies of fruit, vegetables, and flowers. These baskets might contain oranges, bananas, mangoes, pome- granates, litchis, all ripe with their sunny sweet juices and delicate different flavours. There would be vegetables such as bringhal and bindi, tasting altogether different from all other vegetables ever grown. The baskets might be gorgeously decorated with marigolds. Unfortunately many such gifts had to be regretfully declined, as they were all too often intended as bribery to the man who could give out Government contracts in his forest block. On appointment to one new district, Father received at his first Christmas embarrassing gifts from various local contractors, including a magnificent doll for me. This, a custom of the country, where it is perfectly normal to buy favours, had to be stopped. It is not for us, especially now, to criticise the habits of another country. Bribery has always been looked upon in the East as natural, and the sahibs were mad to try and stop it. They did, however, try.

In camp, by the time the rupees and marigolds were dealt with, the day would be getting into its stride. The cold of morning was gone. We threw off our greatcoats and ran about in cotton again. Ran, to make wind to cool our legs. And dashed back into the bungalow, for a drink of orange juice or filtered water. There were no ice-boxes. We had to be content with drinking water that had been boiled or filtered or both, and that was keeping cool in those aluminium water bottles with khaki felt covers that had been dipped in water to get evaporation and hung in a draught, instead of put into the river as we did for picnics.

Excited by Mrs. Beeton's coloured plates showing tables laid for banquets, I decorated the table for lunch, taking a clean white linen tablecloth and leaves and creepers. My father bore it as best he could. Most of the year he had his plain utility furniture and straightforward man's life of marching and rifles and cartridges and jungle work. This was Christmas. He allowed me to decorate the table.

Meanwhile the peacock was being roasted, and the plum pudding steamed. There was bustle in the distant kitchen, the other side of the compound, far from the house. Coils of sky-blue smoke rolled in greater abundance from the fires, smelling of the different woods that were being burned, and making our eyes sting if we ran through it.

My mother always had the coins for the pudding wrapped each in greaseproof paper and cooked in the pudding like that, because even silver money—even washed—was always looked on in India as suspect. Heaven alone knew through what dirt it might have passed before it came to be cooked.

But before that, the coins would have first been tested for silver. There was a good deal of counterfeit money going about, and it was the custom when paying a man to drop each coin on the stone of the verandah to let it ring true before he accepted it. Father used to cut any dud coin thus discovered, with a chisel, so it could be thrown out and not used again. Harry and I knew there were sixteen annas in a rupee, and had often wondered how sixteen coins as large as an anna fitted inside the not-so-very-big rupee. We did not expect anything of counterfeit money, of course, but asked Father please to cut open one good rupee and show us the sixteen annas inside.

TWENTY

Wild Peacock and Auberies Ham

We filled up Christmas morning until lunch time playing
with our new toys, climbing, shouting and running about,
with no lessons to do.

I visited the place where the peacock had been plucked,
to collect some of the feathers. They were too beautiful to
waste, and yet what could you do with them? No one could
ever arrange them again so that daylight could reflect off a
thousand feathers in a single green flush, the design on the
plumage squeezing small or stretching large with the bird's
movement. No one could get back the snaky sapphire neck
and the dark speckle of the wings, or the cascade of shot-
silk eyes sliding down the back into the splendour of the
tail. From the crest of blue-green tippets on fine stalks that
crown the tiny brainless head to the end of the plumage—to
the final triangles of feather, atremble on wire supports, that
finish the tail, the peacock is impossible to believe.

I stroked my cheek with the right side of one green
feather, where the gold was, to absorb it, and get all the
colour into me by touch. The end of the quill was still pink.

I gathered up the best feathers, lots of them, more and more, and took them to add to the dozens I'd already got, wrapped in pages of the *Pioneer*.

We saw peacocks often in the grass-jungle, standing still as posts before they finally decided to fly for their lives, and rose screeching with great beating wings, and the grass blown about, and a shiver of glory as they got into the air. Or dust-bathing. They'd lie there, sifting the dust all into them, then stand up, one good shake, and there all the feathers were again, perfect, lit with heavenly fires.

Our dogs, being sporting spaniels, were not supposed to chase things, but sometimes they couldn't resist doing so. For instance, the squirrels and the shadows of blue butter-flies that skimmed over the ground. One of the spaniels, bursting through discipline, once leaped and caught a flying peacock's tail, and got dragged along till at last the scream-ing bird broke free and sailed away, leaving one or two long blue feathers shining in the dog's mouth.

If I regretted it when a peacock was shot, though, I ate my full share of it when it came to table!

And now it was time for lunch, with all the good things of Christmas—peacock and stuffing and plum pudding and crystallised fruit, crackers with table fireworks inside them.

Every Christmas we had an Auberies ham, sent out from England. This splendid pig had been raised on the Home Farm in sties deep with yellow straw, and fed, among other things, on fallen apples from the great vegetable garden where rich fruit lay under the espaliers, making wasps drunk, and waiting for children to spike them on sticks and feed them to grunting piglets over the bars of the sty.

The hams were cured to the special Auberies recipe, and one was sent to us every Christmas in the jungle, where it was boiled in a kerosene-oil tin—the only container large enough—and now here it was at table, complete with breadcrumbs and paper frill, to remind everyone of home and family and far-away Christmas at Auberies.

I won the wish after pulling the peacock's wishbone with my brother, and the parents wanted to know what I had wished.

"It doesn't come true if you tell people," I reminded them.

"But mothers are the exception to that rule. A wish is more likely to come true if you tell your mother."

Now dolls were all right, but—

I whispered in her ear, "I've asked for a real live baby in a pram."

"They don't usually send babies to people until they're grown-up, because babies need a lot of looking after. I should wish for something else," she advised me.

"Ayah could look after it for me," I planned, with more wisdom than I knew.

Well, my wish did come true in the end, but not for many years.

The pudding was all that it should be, smoking with blue brandy flames, and everyone got something out of it.

Then the crystallised confections. These were made in India, so we met all our known favourites like mangoes and papita, as well as apricots and greengages and peaches from the flowered orchards and snow-meadows of Kashmir. And whole little oranges, skin and all. These made up for the wonderful-looking confections that we were not allowed to eat but which we had seen in the Hardwar and Lansdowne bazaars and on the trays of travelling sweetmeat sellers. Honey blown into figures of eight, crisp-sweet on the outside and running with liquid honey in the middle. Things like that. All the colours and shapes you could imagine, all open to the stinking dust of the bazaar, and free for flies to sit upon.

Now the table fireworks! We liked the smouldering brown-paper ferns that looked so much like those forest fires on distant hills in Lansdowne; and the snakes made of glistening bronze-black ash which foamed like lava out of the so-called snake-eggs when you set one alight. We kept the sparklers for after dark when we could dance in the open with one in each hand, in showers of harmless fire, and breathe in great mouthfuls of the wonderful sparkler-smell.

It was at Christmas that I was given a box of certain famous chocolates, a wonderful white box with a scarlet satin ribbon. One of these chocolates was even more magnificent than the rest. It was shaped like a crown, and inside it I knew there were strawberries and cream. Before offering round the chocolates to the family and to the friends who were camping with us for Christmas, I took the precaution of removing this chocolate to a safe place first.

I can only hope I was ashamed of myself when one of the guests, a young man, subsequently shot a tiger and, since it would not then have been the done-thing to make a present of jewelry to my mother, had the tiger's lucky bone—that small unattached floating bone—set in gold as a brooch, and gave it to me. But I fear not.

For the grown-ups I suppose the shooting was the thing, the big days with elephants and beaters, and the sitting up over kills at night. We were not allowed to go with them, so all we usually saw of it was the preparation and then the return home. If a tiger had been shot, or a panther, bear, chital, or anything else, we saw the bag brought back on an elephant and unloaded and skinned. We heard people talking the day over, the parents in English, and the chuprassies among themselves in Hindustani.

I went and stroked the dead tiger, and put my finger on the points of his wiry white whiskers to feel how sharp they were, and lifted his black lip to look at the teeth and the rasp-like tongue. The canines were longer than my finger, and the tongue rough enough to wear my skin off just by licking. Its whole surface was like a forest of needles, with a narrow border that was smooth.

It is said that a tiger can pass through any opening which is wide enough for his face and whiskers. I looked to see how wide that would be; and in spite of the broad golden head, and the spread of stiff white whisker, the place would be narrow indeed for such a king. But, yes, he could certainly pass through it. The chest was deep but not broad; the flanks and shoulders narrow, and lithe as lightning.

I could smell cold blood, and there was a bullet hole, with blood in it, from which the men would presently dig out the bullet.

What a *weight* a dead thing is. When the men wanted to heave the tiger from one side to the other, in skinning, they used all their strength. To carry the unclothed meat away out of the camp afterwards needed at least four of them.

While they were skinning it, I examined a dead sambhur. I looked at his rough brown hair, and the nose, wet and brown, and his large ears—large eyes too, but dirty with earth where he had fallen. There was dirt on his tongue too, and the leaves he had been eating still in his mouth.

Presently all edible meat was divided among the camp, the non-edible stuff thrown away to be squabbled over by vultures next morning, and the skins pegged out to dry.

Although naturally children could not be taken tiger-shooting, we did sometimes accompany our parents on the lesser Christmas shoots to get game for the pot and so on. Then there was the quiet ambling through the jungle on an elephant, the deafening roar of a rifle going off right by you, the recoil, the smell of gunpowder smoke. Then there were the jungle tiffins, with big picnic baskets being unloaded from one of the elephants, and unpacked, and things set out upon a white tablecloth under trees by the khit and bearer in their white uniforms. There'd be cold chicken and peacock to eat, and Auberies ham, and you were allowed to use fingers to hold drumstick or wing bones. You could bite off the last stubborn slips of dark meat that tasted so greasy-good; and lick your fingers too, if no one was looking. Green-pigeon pie, with the gravy set into jelly. Hardboiled eggs. Mangoes. Melons. We opened the big ripe melons, and a slush of loose seed bulged out and was spooned away. Now for a huge slice of the orange-pink fruit with heaps of sugar. When we ate round the big mango stones, we were juice from ear to ear.

Never believe, when you are icing a cake for children that perhaps you are wasting your time. The work of hours may be destroyed in ten minutes, but there is sure to be some little girl at the party who remembers that cake for the rest of her life. Me, I remember the one that was covered with sugar mice, and another which, when we cut it, wasn't a cake at all but an iced paper drum full of toys. I remember the table decoration that was a lake made out of a mirror surrounded by moss, and it had boats on it, too.

One of Mother's most exciting Christmas cakes, made in the jungle, was done this way: she took a branch shaped like a Christmas tree and dipped it entirely in icing sugar and stuck it into the cake, then hung little presents on the frozen sugar tree.

Once Christmas was over, the next one seemed so very far away that surely a whole century lay between us and it. Even the months until Harry's birthday, in May—or until mine, in August—seemed as long as years.

Of course, not every Christmas of our Indian childhood was exactly the same. Once we journeyed through the forest on an elephant to another camp where there were other children and a Christmas tree out in the open under the stars. Right on the top glittered a fairy doll—the present no one ever gets, like the coloured glass balls, the best thing of all. But when the time came she was taken down and given to me. I carried her home on the elephant through the starlit jungle, and we saw a panther on the way back. He was sitting in the middle of the track, but he got up when he saw the elephant and lolloped away in front of us, his tail held straight up in the air like a cat's.

Next day I sewed loops of gold and silver beads to my fairy's tinsel dress, and gave her a crown and jewels as well.

I called her Melinette, because it was the most splendid name I could think of. Years later, after I was grown up, another little girl said to me, "She's the most beautiful doll I've ever seen, Auntie Norah," so I gave Melinette to her.

One Christmas we visited friends who lived in the capital of an Indian state.

We went *in a train!*

It was an unforgettable experience. This time we did not have to get out again before it went. We got in, we sat in, we stayed in! The train grunted. Our hearts jumped. It began to move and gather speed until it fairly rollicked along, singing "Gotta-go-fast, gotta-go-fast . . ." The upholstery of those marvellous seats was held in by buttons, one of which was the magic one that made the train start. This magic button was a different one at every station. At each stop we tried and tried, and at last we hit on the right one and the train started.

The stations were a seething mass of humanity, people of every kind travelling, sweepers, coolies, merchants, a mohammedan with two wives in purdah, one veiled in pure white from head to foot, and the other in pale pink. The sellers of tea and cigarettes pushed their way through the crowds, shouting their wares in high-pitched nasal tones.

"Char! Char! Gurrum char!"

"Cigarettes! Dirsalai! Matches!"

Monkeys—too sacred to be denied—snatched at what they wanted, and raced and chased everywhere.

I bought some coloured-glass bangles off a man who had hundreds of them on sticks for sale. The glass had patterns inside it as marbles do, and flecks of gold-dust.

In the city where we stayed was a zoo, and in this zoo a hyena that ate monkey nuts. Our jungle hyenas were nocturnal scavengers of putrid meat, and we were much amused by the nut-eater. But perhaps he was no more strange than one of our spaniels who used to go blackberrying by himself. Or rather raspberrying, for he ate wild raspberries off the bushes.

During this Christmas the grown-ups attended various dinner parties at the local palace. Round the Rajah's dinner table travelled an electric train, carrying an assortment of wine. You helped yourself, and when you lifted a bottle the train stopped till the bottle was replaced. But these parties were chiefly famous for wonderful cracker bonbons. I was given one. It was an artificial rose, each pink petal edged with silver, and I was told they cost ten rupees each. All these showy cracker bonbons contained paper hats, and it was the Rajah's pleasure to slip among his guests and set a paper hat or two on fire from behind when the wearer wasn't looking.

It was during that Christmas visit to civilisation that I made my first phone call, went to my first cinema, and had my first ride in a car.

TWENTY-ONE

Life in the Hill Station

Even in Lansdowne we had never before seen a telephone, and I picked it up gingerly.

Uncle Jack was in his office which was, I knew, about half a mile away and so almost out of earshot.

"HULLO, UNCLE JACK!" I bellowed.

"Hullo, Norah."

"HOW ARE YOU?"

He had left us in excellent health about half an hour ago. "Quite well thank you. Don't shout, my dear girl! I can hear you. How are the dolls?"

"Quite well, thank you." I could think of nothing more to say. "Well goodbye, Uncle Jack."

"Goodbye. See you this evening."

The first motor ride lasted longer. The car was one of the earliest-shaped models, rather like a bath chair. I sat in front, looking straight down past my toes and the funny sloping bonnet of the car to the ground that came racing along towards us and disappeared underneath.

We went *fast*—I don't know what the pace was, I suppose about 18 or 20 m.p.h.—it was wonderful. The wind tore past our faces, filling my sleeves, nearly blowing our topees off, and I had to hold my skirt down. Not that I cared, but still. Flies dashed into us, I kept my eyes half shut to hold them out. Each side streamed a kaleidoscope of pony carts and staring people and bicycles and dusty trees.

When we got back, pink and breathless, a man appeared —a groom, I suppose—to take the machine back to the stables and dust it, and polish all the brass, and make sure the lamps were full for the evening drive.

I never went in another car in India. Not again till we got home to England in 1919. By that time, the very early body designs had already changed. I'm glad I went in a bathchair-shaped car; and not because it was a curio, either, but because it was a smart new conveyance.

What wonderful cars they were, too, nothing cheap any-where. If you look at one now, you notice the good leather and the solid brass. In the first hoods there were little side-windows, and these were rimmed with brass as well. The lamps were like carriage lamps, and must have taken hours to fill and trim and polish and probably even then smelled of paraffin. Plenty of clean rag and well-used rag and tins of polish were needed in the first garages; but when the car was done, it blinded you, with a sun shining in every piece of brass.

It must have been around that time, back in England, that a relative of mine bought the first car in Exeter. It arrived by train, and no one in Exeter could drive. He unpacked it at the station, read the book of instructions, and drove it home.

Our first visit to a cinema was no less exciting than the first car ride. We were taken into a dark hall, and there on the wall was a huge photograph in which the people were moving. We stood stupefied.

Grownups pushed us along to our seats and we sat down in a trance, our eyes glued to the screen. Next moment the folks

were making us stand up again so they could put down
the seats under us, for we had sat on the bar instead. We
rose and we sat down again as bidden, and our eyes never
left the picture.

Those were silent films of course, with an orchestra to provide music and sound-effects, or more often just one man
with a piano. He had to be agile, suiting the tune to the story,
sad or gay, producing a thump when the soap sent the fat
man flying, or brilliant scales when people ran up and down
stairs. Parents often used to read the dialogue out to their
children, so that there was always a murmur of reading going
on, too. It was of course these early pictures which earned for
films the name of flicks, because they flickered so.

The film we watched was called *Civilisation*, and all I
remember of it was that the Kaiser leant against a wall, and
his ghost came out of his body and was led about the battle-
fields of the world by an angel to be shown the damage
he had wrought. Then he went back into his body and
was sorry.

I came away burning with ideas for stories to save the
world and show mankind the error of its ways.

Another thing we saw was the Rajah's private mint, which
provided the special state currency. We watched rupees
being stamped out of sheets of silver or copper that rang
like a gong when moved; and we were told that the punched
sheets were then melted down and rolled out and punched
again so nothing was wasted. But I worked out that however
long you went on doing this, there'd still be metal over.
You could never use the last drop up.

This worried me. Another thing I used to lie awake and
worry about was the National Debt. Debt was a terrible
thing, and how on earth was this gigantic one—for which
I, as a Briton, was partly responsible—ever going to be repaid?

But, to listen to grownups, it was clear that the main person responsible for everything that went wrong was someone called Government.

I could see the answer to that one. It was obvious surely, and I offered them my idea. "Why don't they put Government in prison?"

During that wonderful train journey, by the way, Harry and I got left behind on a platform, when we were changing trains. On arrival we had stepped out to look about us, while Father, Mother, and our governess put together the luggage ready for the porters, when suddenly the train pulled out again, taking them all away from us. We were small, quite unused to crowds, and very frightened. I seized Harry's hand to keep him.

"We must stay here till they come back and find us, Boy. We mustn't move from this spot, however long they are."

"All right, Girl."

Father leaped out of the moving train, though, and came back to us, and in the end the train itself came back too, and everything was all right.

On another station we were told there was time for a meal at the refreshment room, so my mother, my governess, and Harry and I went to get it. I ordered a poached egg. It came and it was a perfect egg, sitting on a beautiful piece of toast on which the butter could still be seen as it melted. And the plate so hot I couldn't touch it, even to put it straight.

I was hungry and I hurried to cut the first mouthful. The yolk ran out on to the butter and some on to the plate, where it would congeal and be so good to eat cold at the very last, if no one caught me and stopped me knifing it up on to my fork. "Don't scrape your plate, Norah." But then again if I left anything, it was "Lots of little boys or girls would be thankful for what you are wasting."

Well, I cut my egg but I did not have even one mouthful of it, for Father arrived at a run to say the train was leaving that *minute*. So we jumped and ran, and I suppose someone threw some rupees at the waiter. We scrambled into the train just in time, and had to make do with biscuit and tepid water instead.

I have never trusted trains from that day. The family say that I arrive at a station in time to catch not merely the train I want but the one before it.

Apart from those rare visits to the world, the hill settlement of Lansdowne was our nearest approach to civilisation; and even Lansdowne lacked many things which now we take for granted. Neither telephone nor cars nor movies appeared while we were there, nor electricity, nor ices. I used to lie in bed looking at the hurricane lantern in our bathroom, left there for a night-light, and rats used to dart across the doorway between me and the light. I don't know what the arrangements were for water and drainage. We bathed in a tin tub, the same as in the jungle, and tipped the water out on the floor just the same. Nor do I know what the fuel arrangements were. It was never cold enough to need a fire, and I don't think I ever saw inside the kitchen. It was, of course, a far and different world. Most passengers in a liner never see the engine room.

Lansdowne was a small hill station 6,000 feet up in the Himalayas. Although called a station, this did not mean there was a railway. No train came nearer than Kotdwara, twenty-five miles or so away down the mountains. There was a European population of a few score people, with a small bazaar of Indians, and two battalions of Gurkhas were quartered in the place when we were there.

The bungalows of the Europeans were scattered about on the wooded mountainsides, and there was a club with tennis courts and other amenities, as well as a parade ground which was useful for things like gymkhanas and hockey matches, besides drilling. Most of the Indians lived in or near the bazaar, which was more or less a one-street village. And the Gurkhas lived in their cantonments. The bazaar, of course, was on a steep slope and had deep steps all up it that made my legs ache. No vehicle could use this sort of street stair-case, only people walking. We were not allowed to go there very often.

That was the India of the Sahibs—the India that Kipling wrote about—a good place for both high and low.

The men had their work to do, of course, and so had their wives, though different work from that which we all do now. The ladies attended to their children's education and upbringing, they gave time to charity, they ran their houses, supervised the large staff, attended to such arts as piano, embroidery, painting, and they organised the enter-tainments, of which there were plenty. Because there were no such things as movies, TV, or radio, people had to make their own music and shows.

The life of an Indian hill station, with two battalions in the place, was very gay, no matter how small and scattered the station might be. Many of the ladies, such as my mother, had come in from the jungle after seeing nobody for six months. So there were parties of every kind for everyone: bridge, concerts, theatricals, gymkhanas, dinner parties, picnics, tennis at the club, children's fancy-dress parties and birthday parties—everything.

Besides the Kashmiri merchants who visited the bungalows to sell their wares, we were visited also by jugglers, con-jurors, snake charmers, and nautch girls; and these travelling show-people would sometimes be engaged to entertain at a party, thus living out the most ancient form of show-business in the world.

I remember one conjuror who made rupees drop from

the roof of the bungalow, and his concern when Father teased him for a minute or two by pointing out that as they came from the Sahib's roof they must belong to the Sahib.

A favourite trick of the conjurors was to plant a mango stone in a pot, cover it with a cloth, sit at a distance and play a flute. While they played, the stone germinated, threw up a shoot, some leaves, and finally a ripe mango. At any stage of the show, they would lift the cloth and let us see the developing plant.

Another man had a little water fountain which he set at a distance and it obeyed him, playing or ceasing as he commanded. Father bought the secret of this fountain: it was black cotton attached to the man's bare toes.

We never knew when such entertainments were coming our way. One of the chuprassies from the verandah would come in and salaam and tell Father, "There is a snake-charmer outside the verandah, Sahib."

Out we went to see what he had to offer. We sat on the verandah, and he gave his show in the compound just outside. He needed only his flute and his basket of snakes, and a boy to carry the basket and generally attend to him. Sometimes a charmer will get his cobra to kill a chicken before the show begins, to prove that the snake has not had its poison fangs extracted, but this of course helps to milk the poison glands before he begins. Many of the snakes have been rendered harmless, though. However, snake-charming is always thrilling and picturesque. The cobra lifting to strike, shining like pink metal in the sunshine, the famous hood opening to show the spectacle marking, the darting of the snake as its forked tongue flickers in and out—it's a wonderful show, no matter how often it's given.

But perhaps it would be dancing girls instead of snakes. I remember one pair, in their rippling gold and scarlet skirts with the little weights in the hem, and their rose saris and silver nose-studs. They stood in the dust and sunshine, doing a snake dance, without a single bone in their bodies.

Some wonderful jugglers and tumblers appeared at a children's party in Lansdowne. One of the men strapped cow horns to his feet, point down, and walked on a tightrope on the points of the horns.

Naturally I enjoyed the children's parties, though never so much as the fishing and camping and elephants of our other life.

I announced blandly "I am going to take my new doll to the party and make Margaret jealous!"

"Oh no!" Mother promptly squashed the idea. "That wouldn't be very kind, would it?"

I relinquished my plan with reluctance, I remember, and can only hope that nicer instincts grew in me later on, when I learned how to behave with other people, instead of looking out only through my own jungli eyes.

In Lansdowne of course we did meet other children.

There was one little boy, Eric, whom the Indian climate did not suit, as it did me. Maybe I was thin and sallow, but I throve like a marigold. Eric, however, often looked small and ill. At the parade ground one day he mentioned that he had never had a jelly, so Mother promised to send him one down as a present.

"And look," she said, "I'll tie a knot in my handkerchief, so I don't forget. When I blow my nose, I'll see it and remember."

He gazed at her with his huge dark eyes.

When he went home, he said nothing about this. Not even his parents knew of the promised jelly, but that night he appeared at their bedside at midnight.

"Please," he whispered, "what will happen if Mrs. Burke forgets to blow her nose?"

Every afternoon in Lansdowne all the children collected

at the parade ground for games, while the nurses and governesses had a gossip, and the ayahs too among themselves. Almost every family had an English governess as well as an Indian ayah.

We children had an absolutely pointless game called Green Grarvels which we played every day, dancing hand-in-hand in a circle round one child, and adding another to the centre from the ring until the ring was no longer big enough to circle the centre people. While this went on, we sang:

> "Green grarvels, cherry marbles,
>   The grass is so green,
>   The fairest of maidens
>   That ever was seen.
>   I dressed her in silk
>   And I fed her on milk
> And I wrote her name down with a gold pen of ink."

Now and then the governesses vaguely called out to us to behave, or an ayah came across and remonstrated with her charge. Otherwise we played by ourselves, although so heavily escorted.

How beautiful the ayahs were, with their dark brown skin and pure white clothes, and sometimes a jewelled nose-ring. They wore miles of skirt and sari, and glass and silver bangles in dozens, so you could always hear them approaching. Our own ayah was old and dark, and dressed in countless yards of snow. Someone ought to have painted her.

TWENTY-TWO

Affairs of the Heart

One of the governesses we had—I must call her Miss Golden and not her real name, because afterwards she disgraced herself—was much beloved by me because she was so beautiful and sometimes wore such lovely clothes. Not in camp, it had to be khaki there, but in Lansdowne.

Goldie was a bright-gold blonde, the pin-up girl of all the barracks. She used to sigh "I've always longed for brown hair, and yet here I am, golden. It's a shame. My hair grows dark, too, as you can see at the parting. It's dark at the roots and then it turns yellow."

One day she sent me to fetch a measuring glass that was standing on the washstand in the bathroom which she shared with Harry and me. There was a little something which I took to be water in the glass, so I emptied it and it fizzed.

"It had water in it," I told her. "I tipped it out, and it bubbled."

She was furious with me.

Well, it served her right for sending me on errands, I thought darkly, remembering the time she dispatched me all the way home from another bungalow where we were playing with other children, to fetch some blouse she was making, to show the other governess.

I meditated evil to that blouse on the journey back, but hadn't quite the courage to put it into action.

Rage boiled up in me so easily and so often, and usually with the people I loved best. I remember thinking "This time I *will* stay angry—I *won't* go and say sorry," but the fiery resolution generally died an ignominious death, because it felt so horrible to be not-loved.

But Goldie was beautiful. She was fair as a lily, and she shone. Now and then she would buy twelve yards or so of some exquisite white material such as net or lace, and she'd employ a durzee who came with his hand machine and needles and scissors, and squatted on the verandah and sewed away under her direction, making a dress. He was a Mohammedan, and several times a day he spread his prayer-rug, turned towards Mecca and went through the prayer-ritual—standing, kneeling, prostrating. Then he rolled up the rug and went on with his work.

When the dress was finished Goldie put it on. She cut short a wisp of her bright hair and damped it into a kiss-curl and stuck it to her cheek, and put on a white hat. She owned some scent, with violets painted on the outside of the bottle-green glass: she put some behind her ears and in the palms of her hands.

Then we walked down to the parade ground.

Oh, the beautiful white folds of her dress and the cream shadows! The loud whisper of it as she walked! The cloud of scent that accompanied her.

When we got to the parade ground, if there were no sergeants about, we'd walk on towards the cantonments to "see Mrs. Fayer."

Mrs. Fayer was a sergeant's wife, and she and Goldie

discussed clothes and love affairs over cups of tea, while we played with Mrs. Fayer's little boy, Johnnie.

Goldie's love affairs did not go smoothly, and there was much to-and-fro-ing of letters. She wrote reams on blocks of thin lined paper, and also on some special pink paper that had a bevelled gilt edge, and smelled like pink soap, and she always read me what she had written. If the replies were satisfactory, I heard those too. She read me also the letters from her married women friends offering advice on the treatment of males. But she was dazzled by romances like that one of the Earl and the ruby ring, and by stories of sheikhs, so she passed up present offers of marriage for future chances of a brilliant match.

One night I woke up in the middle of the night. The door of our room was slowly opening, and in the dim light from the turned-down hurricane lantern standing in the bathroom, I saw a great bear-like thing come stealing into the room. For a moment I was stiff with fright, then I recognised one of our Indian servants with his rezai over his head. All Indians slept in this kind of cotton wadded quilt. However cold it was, and if they had only one rezai, it did not cover the body but the head. We often wondered how they breathed in it. The man tiptoed in and lay down at the foot of Goldie's bed.

I fell asleep again at this point.

In the morning I said to her "Why did the bearer come into our room last night?"

"He was feeling ill," she replied promptly. "He came to me for some medicine."

I did not think of the incident again once until I was grown up, when I at last heard the true reason for Goldie's abrupt dismissal.

I loved her so, and I cried so much when she went.

One morning, for no reason at all, there were no lessons, and Goldie told us she was being sent away for ever. She packed all her things, the exquisite white tulle dresses, and the bottle-green flagon with the violets painted on it, and the bottle of fizzy stuff that she kept hidden in one drawer, the stockings that were real rose-silk as far as right halfway up the leg. She strapped her trunk ready for it to be sent on after her, and she was lent Father's pony Ponko to ride down to Kotdwara with the saice Gwala Ram in attendance to carry her suitcase and bring the pony back.

I could hardly see her through my swollen eyes, but she looked beautiful in her dark habit on the spirited mountain pony, with her golden hair done up tight under the neat topee.

She rode away down towards Kotdwara, the saice walking behind her.

I never saw her again. I have often wondered what became of her. Is she keeping a boarding house in Ilfracombe? Or did she marry a Rajah?

For a time we had lessons with Molly and Margaret from their Governess, Miss Frankinson. One day I had done well, and cried out "Oh, Mummy *will* be proud of me."

Miss Frankinson checked me. "No, Norah," she explained gravely, "you must not say that. Your mother is a good woman. Good women are never proud."

With Goldie gone, we did not see so much of Mrs. Fayer as we used to do, but we still sometimes played with her son Johnnie.

Johnnie was only three, so he was really much too young for us, but he was in with all the Gurkha soldiers, so we admired him. When they were off-duty, the men used to let him drill them, as his father did, for play, but they would not take orders from Harry or me. This hurt us rather, though on reflection we had to admit they were right. After all, our own saice and chuprassies would have refused orders from the other boy.

In the India of those days there was this loyalty—yes, even in spite of all the bribery and corruption, lying and thieving that went on as well. But of course theft, lies, and bribery were not sins, except to the Sahibs: they were the time-honoured and normal customs of everyday life. No other way was known.

But there was this loyalty too, between Master and Man, both ways. When that small boy drilled those soldiers, and they would obey him but not us, it was a symbol much more significant than we knew at the time. Now, recently, in the ghastly massacres of partition, when Hindu and Moslem at last got at each other's throats after a century of British control, families we knew had the privilege of saving their servants in the general butchery, and so perhaps partly repaying the long debt.

After we had left India, Gwala Ram in one of his letters to my parents wrote "Cold as it must be in England, I would prefer death a hundred times to see the kind faces once more; is it His will that I should perish without once more seeing you all? Thousands and thousands of salaams to Miss Norah and Baba Peter and Harry Sahib. If ever Miss Sahib comes to India, I shall join her immediately and serve her faithfully to the last. Harry Sahib will, I hope, come to India sometime. It will not be difficult for him to do so when he is in the Air Force." Such were the people whom we, as a nation, abandoned to their fate when we walked out of India on a sudden weak impulse called statesmanship, instead of handing over power slowly in a secure and orderly way.

But at the age of three, one does not always keep one's mind on the job. Johnnie Fayer took four Gurkhas and he ordered "Attention! Quick—march!" in their own tongue. Then he forgot about them. They set off down the road, and though it was not towards a precipice ("For Heaven's sake say something, sir, even if it's only goodbye") they marched on, and away out of sight. For all I know, they're marching still.

Everyone has heard of Gurkhas, the fighters from Nepal, about whom their British officers used to tell us such affectionate and unbelievable tales of toughness and loyalty. In Hitler's war, they were about to be taught to jump from planes, and asked for their first jump to be at a hundred feet, not more.

"But then the parachutes won't open," the C.O. explained.

"Oh I see, sir. We had not realised that we were to have parachutes."

The Gurkhas in Lansdowne were, like all their race, stocky broad dark smiling men. They told us wonderful tales of battle, murder and sudden death in the hills, and illustrated them with flashing strokes of their kukries.

The famous kukri! The broad deadly double-pointed sword-knife of the Gurkhas! It can slay the enemy, cut silk, or heliograph a message across the hills. A Gurkha with a kukri in his teeth can stalk a sentry and slice his head off without a sound. The English ladies belonging to Gurkha regiments had this famous knife copied in gold for brooches.

With two such splendid battalions to ornament the place, Lansdowne was colourful, although so small and primitive.

TWENTY-THREE

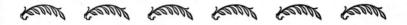

The Social Conventions of Kipling's India

The social conventions of Kipling's India were strict. Especially the laws governing calls and calling cards, which were different from those operating in England at the same time. Every bungalow had a calling-card box at the gate into which one dropped one's cards instead of actually making the call. I remember walking down our drive through the great trees and the millions of ferns and wild begonias in all their rain-diamonds, and seeing my mother look into her calling-card box fixed to a tree at the gate, to see who had called on her. Sometimes these card-boxes would be left at the club, an even more convenient place for collecting cards.

Thus a great deal of the preliminary social feinting was got through in a businesslike way. The tedious afternoon calls of England, strictly between 3:00 and 3:30, with a stay of only ten minutes for a first call if the lady were in, and a thankful leaving of cards on a silver salver instead if the butler said she was out, were thus all done away with.

When a lady sent out invitations, one of her chuprassies brought round the lot. He could not read, so he sent the whole batch in to each bungalow, and the lady chose her own and gave him back the rest. He then went on to the next house.

And when, in answer to these invitations, one visited other houses, how different the rooms were from those we live in now.

The drawing room, for instance. Ours, in Lansdowne, was full of Indian furniture and ornaments as well as all those skins of animals, each with its mounted head. The piano of course was the main thing in the room, and upon it stood photos in carved silver frames.

One of the photos in the drawing room was of my father. After we had had a battle one day, I expressed my feelings— but frugally—by taking a half-anna stamp and sticking it over his face in the photo. My satisfaction was shortlived. I was sent to take it off again.

Most Indian drawing rooms had one or two of those tables with legs of antelope horn, and a movable top of black teak, inlaid with ivory, and a thickly carved teak screen, all made in India. There was always plenty of brass to be cleaned, including probably a brass standard lamp that stood usually behind the sofa where it would not be knocked over. If you ran a finger down it, you could tell with your eyes shut if it had been polished that very day, because of the satin sheen.

A variety of lampshades was in use for the different lamps. You didn't always have to have the same one. The yellow silk one, covered with gathered cream net—well, maybe you'd seen enough of it, so you had a change, and used the red roses with the fringe of glass beads.

Everywhere there were dozens of ornaments to be dusted. There were lots of tables, and all the tables were covered with them. Japanese ivory statuettes, things in jade and turquoise and soapstone. Perhaps an ivory fan. I had to be careful not to turn quickly in this room, especially in one of my starched muslin party dresses, or there'd be a crash.

Of course, as well as all the ornaments, there were always the pot-plants brought in by the mali who was in charge of the garden. There were a great many flower vases to be done as well. The memsahib's vases were all cut-glass or silver. A plain vase was not admired.

Even the shapes of the vases were of the period—the silver rose-bowl in particular, and the cut-glass bowls with their heavy glass flower-holders which always acquired a green stain that couldn't be got at to be removed, and in which the holes were never big enough for the thicker-stalked blooms. Then there was always the set of four trumpet-shaped vases of slender silver for the dinner table, each of which held three carnations and a little maidenhair or asparagus fern. They decorated the table, but allowed space in the middle for the lamp or candelabra, and did not hide the conversationalists from each other.

All dining tables were laid with a white damask linen cloth. There were no polished tables or mats. One spot on the linen, and away it went to the dhobi. How he did his washing in Lansdowne where there were no rivers or lakes, I haven't the faintest idea. In the dining room the table servants were in charge, in their white uniforms and turbans, and their bare feet. It was their job to lay the table, to receive the dishes from lesser minions who brought them from the kitchen, and to serve the meal. It was their task to see that the many courses with all the etceteras followed smoothly from soup to dessert; and to see that the bowler-glasses, as they called the dessert bowls, contained water and perhaps a jasmine flower, and sat clean and bright upon the embroidered doilies on the dessert-plates, with the dessert knives and forks in place, the mother-of-pearl handles just so, ready to pick up, and the silver part polished by the man who did the polishing.

At the head of the table would sit, naturally, the master of the house, and opposite him his wife. The disposition of the guests often caused her anxious arranging beforehand. No doubt it had been easy to decide which lady was to sit on her husband's right hand, by order of age and seniority, by the husband's position in the station, and how well they knew the lady. But the rest? Could one ask Colonel Forbes to take Mrs. Mellor in to dinner? It was known that her conversation, such as it was, bored him. The Miss Langs? Captain Dashwood? One could not ask Mrs. B——— and Mrs. Y——— to the same dinner party, since it was impossible to establish which should sit on the host's right hand.

All this having been sorted out beforehand, the guests having gathered in the drawing room—but without, of course, cocktails to help them—and dinner having been announced, each gentleman gave his arm to the lady he was to take in to dinner, they formed up in the right order, and the little procession went in.

And so to dinner; the men in their immaculate black-and-white, with their fine moustaches, and handsome sunburnt hands on which the lamp made the hair shine tangled gold; and the ladies in their beautiful evening gowns showing the pearly shoulders and the jewels, their hair dressed on their graceful heads in gleaming coils. No lady ever wore imitation jewelry. It could be cheap, but it must be real. If she could afford nothing better, she might wear seed pearls or coral. She could wear a cameo or a gold heart on a chain, containing a secret photo or lock of hair. She could wear cornelian, even, or an aquamarine or topaz pendant on a ribbon, but *nothing imitation*. Perhaps it is a pity we ever changed. Nor did any lady use scent. A little cologne water for headaches or travelling, perhaps, but that was all. Scent and make-up were for wicked women only.

A dinner party was a work of art, and everyone from the least member of the staff to the most important guest had his part in the gracious picture. The clink of silver and china, the sparkle of jewels and conversation, the turtle soup, asparagus, quail—everything, from the warmth thrown by lamp or candles, from each drop of hot clear wax, to tulle and garnets and after-dinner cigars, was Art and Beauty.

The hostess devoted herself to charm. If there were a pause between courses and she feared some disaster in the kitchen, she must not show her anxiety. No wheels must be heard turning. As far as her guests could see, the dinner arrangements were nothing to do with her. She was as untouched as a goddess by work or worry. She was enjoying herself with as much carefree pleasure as they themselves. But for the menus in the silver menu-holders, she knew no more than they did what was coming next. Her task was to keep the conversation dancing, to give opportunities for each guest to shine, to be witty and informed and gay, but more than anything to cause each lady to feel beautiful and admired, and each man a golden male who could do no wrong.

At the right moment, the hostess caught the eye of the lady sitting on her husband's right hand, and all the ladies then rose and moved to the drawing room, where they could relax and gossip, and smooth their hair. The gentlemen meanwhile drank and told stories, and presently joined the ladies.

There would then be some piano-playing and singing, or bridge, until it was time to send for the jampanees to bring the dandies to the verandah for their memsahibs and carry them home.

There was time and opportunity for flirtation. More so, of course, in the large fashionable hill stations such as Simla. But even in Lansdowne, which was only a small scattered place, there were all these parties, as well as the club, and you could always go riding together.

Naturally it was of the keenest interest to everyone to watch the different attachments, and all my stories became love stories. I could not think what to put in the love scenes, but did my best. Usually they walked in the twilight, his arm about her waist, and then there was a fallen mossy log on which they sat down.

Home Chat was sent to my mother from England every week. She collected the cooking recipes, pasting them into a big book as all good wives did, so as to guide the cook and to look in it for ideas when neither could think of a pudding. I read the serials, especially one called *The Man with the Square Chin*. Mother invariably knew in any story who was going to marry whom, and it was only a matter of time before she was proved right. But to me it was always touch-and-go. At last, wedding bells rang, and nothing but happiness lay before the lovers.

I believed that if a man kissed you, what he meant was "Will you marry me?" and that is what I thought until I was at least sixteen years old.

Girls did not then live as they do now, earning their own livings at an early age, their eyes open, their lipsticks handy. I did not go to a dance or use even powder until I was seventeen. That was still the era in England for the daughters of good families to remain in the schoolroom until seventeen or so, when they came out. They wore a white dress for the first ball, they were presented and they then led a social life until marriage.

Lansdowne was a beautiful and romantic place. Apart from the natural grandeur of the hills, it had rides through pine woods, and an old ruined garden that was haunted and fallen into weeds. This was a place of wire-worms and millipedes, of greengages lying in the long grass and split with too much rain, and a centipede curled in the heart of an apricot.

I remember seeing a couple walking in a twilit garden in the hills. They must be grandparents by now, but to me she is still there with her fair hair taken back loosely without a wave into a bun, and the man walking beside her. Not enough light to see their faces.

All flirtation, of course, was reserved for the numerous young unmarried girls who had come out from England to stay with relatives in India for the express purpose of finding a husband. They lived a sort of pink-garden-party-hat life, attended by dashing officers. A wife on the other hand had to be careful not to flirt even with the eyes, or she stood in grave danger of losing her reputation.

Divorce was almost unheard-of. It was as remote as murder is for most people. The thing happened, but not to anyone you knew. A divorcée was not received. There was one such woman who was not seen anywhere. Another lady we knew, with a kind and generous heart, once spoke to the outcast; and immediately scandal flew round the station that Mrs. Kind-Heart was obliged to do so because Mrs. Outcast knew something detrimental about Kind-Heart ("My dear, she has a Past") and was insisting upon being known.

How firmly entrenched were all the laws of conduct and social behaviour. You must not only obey them, but draw your skirts away from those who didn't, or you would be splashed with mud too. Was that code better or worse than our own? Who are we to say? The line between Right and Wrong was firmly drawn, black and white. Were they right, or are we with all our greys? A marriage made could not be unmade. Was that a good thing or not? Was it right or wrong to give so much time to the play of social contacts? To have a thing called Charity? Were those dinner parties an art—a living picture of gracious things—or were they greed and selfishness? Were those people wicked? Priggish? Without social conscience? Was the safe conduct of another nation from ignorant squalor to self-government and a seat in the Councils of the World a bleeding of the weak, or was it a duty undertaken in knowledge of greatness?

Nothing is certain but change, and the 1914 war made the first crack in the impregnable fortress of all that life and behaviour. Some time in August, 1914, Harry and I were walking down to the club in Lansdowne with our mother, and she was stopped by a friend on the way. They spoke together, then Mother said to us "Stay here for a little while, children. I have to go back to the bungalow and tell Daddy something."

"What's happened?"

"England has declared war on Germany."

She went back to the bungalow, along the path that looped its way up and up above us, with tree-roots for steps. She was wearing a blue dress.

I did not know at the time that that was the end of an era. The rule of two centuries of British merchants and then of soldiers in India was drawing to a close. Thirty years of stress were still to come, but it was the beginning of the end.

As far as I personally was concerned, the 1914 war kept me in India more than four years longer than I otherwise should have stayed. Children could not remain in that climate much after seven or eight; they had to come home to England, or they acquired permanent sallow complexions and a chi-chi accent, besides losing health to malaria, and never getting a proper education. I was just about due to come home when war broke, and so I stayed.

TWENTY-FOUR

Snakes, Butterflies and Spiders

Our months in Lansdowne had compensations for not being so much fun as the ones in camp. One of the most
thrilling of these was hunting tree-crickets with the three
boys who lived in the bungalow on the next peak. They
were Scotsmen, bra', bricht, and extremely adept at the
sport. One of them flexed his bare arm to show a small girl
his muscles. She has adored Scotsmen ever since.

A gulf divided their house from ours, but we could all
stand at the edge of our two compounds, and shout to
each other across the tree tops in the ravine, and say what
lessons we'd got to do, and make arrangements to meet afterwards.

Once, when I was blowing soap-bubbles, I put my bowl
of suds on the compound wall here, and set the bubbles
adrift on the wind. One blew right over to the other compound, and by the time it got there, it was such an old bubble
that all the changing colours on it were dark. I could see it
hanging there, crimson, before it burst, and one drop of
soapsud fell to earth.

Hunting tree-crickets was entirely a Scottish idea, and it
was very exciting.

These crickets were two or three inches long, shaped like huge grasshoppers. They had glass wings and three rubies in the head. I truly believed them to be real rubies and that if I collected enough of them I'd have a fortune. Then all the family could buy all the rods and fishing flies they wanted, and when the Kashmiri wallahs unrolled the delicate mauve-pink jap silk for me, out of the sunlight, I'd say "Twelve yards please."

We called the crickets cha-chas because of the noise they made. Every evening at dusk, for precisely fifteen minutes, they made this deafening noise. All the air shrilled with it. Father had one singing outside the room he used for a dufta, and could get no work done till he had found and killed it.

Found! Aye, there was the rub. For they were extremely difficult to see. The hill trees were overgrown with moss and lichen and ferns, and these insects, though not exactly transparent, appeared to be so, and blended into their background in a general indistinguishable muddle. Each would sit in its chosen spot on branch or trunk, and shrill its song with all its vibrating body. Your best chance to locate one was to get it sideways against daylight. Then it could be seen like a leaf-skeleton on the fading sky.

Now came the job of climbing and stalking it. The insects believed themselves to be invisible, so they did not move till the last moment, but then they'd be gone in one snap of leg and wing, whirring off to some other inaccessible branch, and you had to begin again.

Up I climbed, brushing through ferns that showered me, kneeling on squelching moss in an odour of squashed toad-stool, until there was the creature again, fastened to a branch and chirring away for all he was worth. I got my hand ready in a long cup-shape and stretched out, nearer and nearer. Now a quick dab and he was mine.

So then down again, soaking wet, with scraped knees,

and my hands smelling of everything as child-hands do when it's ages since they were last washed; and all the primitive bloodthirsty passions of pursuit and capture inflamed, no matter how humane I thought I was.

The Scots one day appeared with a jam jar containing twigs and moss, and covered with gauze. Inside the glass, in the lilliputian forest, there darted and jumped a tiny jet-black mouse. He was the smallest, most beautiful mouse I have ever seen, electric with life and quite shining black. It was like a scene in a glass paperweight. This mouse afterwards escaped, thank goodness. We never learnt his scientific name.

One morning two mice were caught in the same wire trap. Harry came running with the news. "And Mother Mouse has had some babies." He ran off. He ran back. "Father Mouse has had some too."

There was not much shooting to be had in Lansdowne. Certainly no tigers. Although bears and panthers lived in the hills, we were not bothered by them on the whole, with the exception of the panther that took Jess; and there were no other large wild animals in Lansdowne. Not even jackals, hyenas, wild dogs or other similar jungle animals from the Plains. In the high mountains, sportsmen found things like goral and tahr. There were birds of course, but not parrot, peacock, or jungle fowl. Eagles had their eyries among the rocks, and there might be a lammergeier vulture invisible in the blue.

As there were no rivers except the annual torrents of the monsoon that came bouncing down with wild white manes, there were no fish, crocodiles, turtles or tortoises. Fish to eat in Lansdowne was so unusual that I remember the only time we had it. A man brought round a basket of them to sell, and he'd got several kinds we'd never seen before.

There were snakes. The men killed one in the compound

one day, prodding it out of the stone wall with sticks and then flattening it. I was not allowed out while this was going on, but watched from the verandah, and then went across when the excitement was over, to see the beaten, dirty body before it was flung out far down the khud.

One day, earlier, as Father and I were walking up the path towards the bungalow, he was teaching me to count.

"You know as far as ten, Norah. Then it goes in tens up to a hundred. First there's ten, then there's twenty, thirty—now, listen, because if you understand the method, you'll soon learn. Oh well, if you're going to be silly, I shan't show you."

But I had seen something in the path.

The gravel was rubbed away, and something white was showing up from underneath. A snake had chosen this spot to lay her eggs. I suppose because it got the sun. But she must have had a job digging out the hard path, and then people's feet going over the place had exposed it.

I got a stick to fork the eggs out. Father opened his pen-knife. He was never at a loss for any weapon or tool. His numerous pockets—and he always knew exactly which one, too—contained everything that could possibly be needed during the day, from string to notebook. I have even heard people discussing a new rifle and saying that presently, when they could get hold of a target, they'd try it out. "Here you are," said Father, producing one from his pocket.

We dug out the snake eggs. They had shells made of dirty white cloth, and were not yet on the point of hatching, when you can see the shape of the snake inside. We *counted* the eggs—*I* counted them, even up beyond ten, and then we destroyed them and threw them down the khud.

Did the snake watch us? Was she in the stone wall close by, looking on with her hard glazed eyes that have no lid? Some snakes remain in the vicinity of the nest until the eggs are hatched, and some even show solicitude towards their young.

The chief inhabitants of these loosely built stone walls in the hills were lizards. They came out to sun themselves, but they were sharp-eyed and you could never get really close to them. They'd watch you coming as they sat there, spread-eagled, head up, and throat pulsing. Before you were close, they'd flick back into their crack of rock. Then if you peered into the slit, all there'd be would be a little dry rustle, and pinpoints of light on the eyes. If their escape was a close shave, there might be a lizard tail left behind jerking on the stone to distract your attention while the owner disappeared, and presently grew another one.

Lansdowne was also the haunt of the most magnificent moths and butterflies.

Collecting lepidoptera is a fever endemic among the Burkes, bursting out without warning. Quite tiny members of the family will suddenly announce out of the blue that they are making a butterfly net and, please, have you got any green mosquito-netting, Mum? Or "Daddy, what is sugaring for moths?"

We were no exception.

There, across the compound, goes a Mourning Cock, the big velvet black beauty with drops of molten orange on his wings. He is travelling in the usual aimless butterfly drift like a blown leaf, and because of his great size and of the absolutely unreflecting black of his attire, he is more noticeable in all the sun-dazzle than the brightest-coloured ones ever are. What more natural than to go after him? And what more difficult than to catch him, too! The moment he sees you, he's out over the khud, with thousands of feet of air below him, and the points of pine trees.

Then there were the window butterflies, which were turquoise-blue and black, with places in the wing that were transparent like fly-wing and you could see through. Every now and then, as they flew, a pair would meet and whirl upwards in a spiral *valse bleu* at great speed to separate again at the top.

There were leaf-insects that looked like dead leaves, and the caterpillar like a broken stalk.

Naturally, the rarest moths and butterflies were little dull dirt-coloured things that fluttered their feeble lives away in the dust and shadows of heavy vegetation. I was not interested. For me, the fast red-and-orange ones that zagged about everywhere.

For me, the great clicking stag beetles that moved with the slowness of Jurassic reptiles on land, and on the wing banged about like dragons. They were four to six inches long, dressed in suits of mail. Suppose I was small enough to be afraid of them? But I could not imagine how appalling it must be to be eaten by those passionless mandibles.

Moths of every kind, large and small, bumped and whirled round the lamps every evening. When one of them sat on the shade, the light shone through him from underneath, and you could see his furry legs, and his cream or black or pale green eyes. There was one made entirely of powdered white lace. And one of them that lit on a pane of glass and was unable to get in at the lamp, had a proper face, just the same as anyone else has a face; and the undersides of his wings were like parchment, scribbled on with brown ink.

The most magnificent moth of all was one which we called the Moon Moth, pale pearl-green with two long tails, and peacock eyes on its wings. It was huge. Full-length, it could be six or eight inches long. And such was the fragile bloom of those exquisite wings—a bloom made up of millions of almost unseeable feathers—that only a newborn insect could be undamaged. Sometimes not even then. For only a few hours after the perfect insect crawled feebly from its cocoon to cling, wet and crumpled, to some twig in the dark while its wings straightened and dried—for only the first few hours of ethereal flight could such beauty remain whole. No human hand could touch it without hurt.

The Indian night in Lansdowne contained these dream moths, and also fireflies. Not many fireflies, but sometimes you would see suddenly that one of the sparks in the darkness was not a lantern jogging along some distant mountain track but an insect close by you, instead. Just as once I thought I saw nothing less than a gorilla in a distant tree, and it was a housefly on a pane of glass close to my eye.

The Death's Head moth was also to be seen in our forests, one of the few moths with a voice. Even the caterpillar can produce sound.

The biggest caterpillar I ever saw was six inches long, and looked like a head chopped off a snake. It was thick, and green, and on its back were painted two eyes like snake-eyes, but the caterpillar's real eyes were tiny and much further forward. This creature had the fat, wandering, changed-colour look of a caterpillar that is about to pupate, and we left him to his own devices. He wanted to get into the right place, whatever it might be—earth, or chewed wood, or grey silk hammock—and go to sleep there and turn into an angel, as perhaps we do also.

We had no setting boards for our collection of moths and butterflies, so we kept them folded in triangles of newspaper, not knowing how interesting those columns of the *Pioneer* would be to read, thirty years later.

In Lansdowne there appeared one day a cloud no bigger than a man's hand; it grew and darkened the daylight, and it was a cloud of locusts. They streamed across in billions. They were on their way elsewhere, but a few fell on us, and in a matter of minutes the trees they covered were stripped of all their leaves. The insects fell everywhere in our compound, and one of our men, the mussulchi, the dish-washer, picked one up and held it between finger and thumb. It struggled with its long glass wings and grasshopper legs and its three-inch body, and waved its feelers and clicked its dry jaws.

"They are said to be good to eat," commented the mussulchi, and he put the live insect into his mouth and bit it in half.

In the Hills, as we had no larger creatures to interest us, Harry and I paid a lot of attention to insects. We watched ants, we caught butterflies, we fed spiders.

There was one fat spider, shaped like a bumblebee, striped orange, yellow, and black, and dressed in silken hair. He had spun his web in a creeper by the wall, but we were sure that he could not, alone, catch enough to nourish that plump body, so we killed flies and put the dead insects into his web. He would rush out at once, knit madly, and envelop them in white cobweb. One day he did not do so, nor the next. By the third day we saw that his body had shrunk and lost weight and colour, and his web had the unmended untended look of a house where the owner has died. Frag-ments of leaf lay in it, untidy. Perhaps he died of over-eating.

Another spider I tried to feed gave me an unpleasant bite, and we found he'd got a beak like a parrot. We left him to sink or swim unaided after that.

Yet another one went skimming over the floor of a bed-room in the dolls' house. As the insect was carrying a white bag underneath it, I tried to capture it to see what the white bag was. The bag burst, and out swarmed hundreds of tiny spiders that ran off in all directions.

Other insects which we fed were the ants and the pit

insects. It was extremely interesting to place a dead fly on one of the tiny smooth runways frequented by ants. The first ant that came to it stopped dead, stunned by excitement. Then it sized up the prize and scuttled off to fetch help. The ants then worked and pushed this enormous piece of meat towards the nest, where it had to be inserted into quite a small hole in the ground. Soon the dead fly was disappearing down into the nest till it was out of sight; and even if you looked close, right down the tunnel smoothed by insect bodies, you could not see even a glimmer of fly-wing or black shell down there, any more.

The pit insects were, I suppose, some kind of spider. They had to have loose sand for their traps. In this they dug a small inverted cone, and hid themselves in the sand at the bottom of the pit. Any ant or beetle that stumbled into the trap was unable to keep foothold on the loose sides and rolled to the bottom where he was captured and devoured. I'm afraid we sometimes tickled the sides of the pit with a hair to see what would happen. The sand at the bottom of the pit wrinkled, up heaved the spider, only to find there was nothing there. However, we did sometimes drop a real dead ant or beetle into one of these traps and watched the excited owner draw down the meal into his home of dry quicksand. Soon all had disappeared, and the little dimple of a trap waited for its next victim.

Of course, feeding insects was boring compared to fishing and camp life; and when the monsoon broke in Lansdowne, even the spiders and ants seemed to disappear. Day after day the rain roared over the tin roof, drowning everything, the earth steamed, the hillsides ran. Cloud foamed in all the valleys below us, like a white sea, and above the foam soared the Himalayas of Garhwal—Nanda Devi, Kamet, Trisul—twenty-four and twenty-five thousand feet high, the greatest mountains in the world.

Majestic scenery was lost on us children, though, alas. We were too used to it to notice, and it was not really till we had left it behind in our lives that we could look with eyes that understood. I remember the grownups exclaiming over a tree in the Hills. I don't know what kind of tree it was—almond or peach, perhaps—but it was in blossom, a shower of pink lace. It grew on the lip of a dark blue gorge.

"Just *look* at that tree!" they exclaimed. "If this was England, it would be put in a garden."

I took a careful look to try and understand what they meant.

There is no doubt that rain added to the beauty of the great hills, with all its music and rainbows and all the magic of growth. But we found it boring.

I suppose it was boredom, really, that made Harry shoot me in my bath.

TWENTY-FIVE

Jungle Medicine

It may have been boredom, or perhaps it was sudden irresistible temptation. Anyway, he drew a bead on my back with his popgun, pulled the trigger and scored a bull's eye.

I set up a roar—far, far out of proportion to any hurt I could possibly have sustained. The cork that stung my wet back left nothing to show for it, not even a bruise, but I screamed like a banshee.

So did Harry. Partly because he thought he had killed me, but more because he thought his popgun would be taken away.

The whole household raced to our bathroom and tried, in the uproar, to find out what was the matter.

"I didn't know it was loaded," Harry sobbed.

This was a heaven-sent opportunity for the parents to press home what they had already told us so often: never point a firearm, loaded or unloaded—never point even a stick at anyone—*never*—NEVER—not even in fun. Always unload a weapon the moment you're not going to need it any more. All the other rules too. We never forgot them.

The parents sometimes slept with a loaded revolver under

the pillow, if there were dacoits in the district for instance, but that was different.

To clinch their teaching, they reminded us of one of the forest guards who, carrying a loaded gun carelessly in thick jungle, shot off one of his own feet. Like everyone else, he walked barefoot even in uniform, and the charge of shot destroyed the front part of his foot. The loss did not seem to inconvenience him, though. He walked on what remained.

This man was not one of my parents' patients in the jungle —the accident had happened some years before—but they did often have to deal alone with similar wounds. Their medical books and chest of medicines were one of the main and natural pieces of our camp equipment; the smell of medicines and gun smoke, the taste of quinine, were a sort of signature tune of that life.

Jungle Indians would arrive at the verandah at any time for treatment for anything from toothache to mauling by a bear. They had perfect faith that Father and Mother could cure them of everything, and their great pleasure was to receive a bottle of medicine of some kind, no matter what. Perhaps we are all alike in this. Anyway, I've seen a man who had been given a large dose of castor oil swallow it at a draught and come back grinning for more. They liked everything.

They could not understand about doses, though, nor that a bottle must be made to last, say, a week. Their argument was that if one dose did good, it would be best to swallow the whole bottle at once and so be cured immediately. As we were always moving, we often did have to leave them with bottles and hope for the best.

One tragic case was a man who had been severely damaged about the head by a panther. His wounds were cleaned and dressed, and he was told he must be taken to hospital. All arrangements were made. We did not return to the district for six weeks. When we did, we found he had refused to go to hospital, had left the first bandages untouched, and gangrene had developed. This man subsequently died.

The junglis of course had not the faintest idea of hygiene or daily treatment. Nor could they believe that a medicine which had relieved one condition would not necessarily cure another. Indigestion pills might thus be expected to put right a poisoned toe. Any kind of oil or ointment would be applied to any wound. Ayah, for instance, had been given eye-drops. Later, she was found to be using typewriter oil instead. But far worse things than that are put on to open wounds.

However, if the jungle Indians applied the potions of civilisation in peculiar ways and had no idea of hygiene, they did often have their own forest remedies, some of which were surprisingly efficacious. Country people do often have good remedies which at first sight seem strange. Even in some English country districts, cobwebs and puff balls are still used to stop bleeding. In India, Ayah could stroke out sun-headaches with her old brown magic fingers alone.

Toothache was always a problem. Contrary to popular belief, Indians do not necessarily have excellent teeth. An argument on this subject was going on, one time in England, and my parents had with them an ayah who had travelled to England with one employer and would return with another —a brave woman to cross the Black Water—the Kala Pani, the sea, to visit what were then still unknown worlds to many Indians. This woman was sent for, to settle the argument.

"Now you, Ayah," they said, "have got beautiful teeth, haven't you?"

She was delighted. "Yes, haven't I! I got them in Birmingham."

There was no dentist for us children, either in the jungle or Lansdowne. I never saw one till I was twelve years old, and often suffered from toothache. This was made up to me, afterwards, because I'm lucky enough to have good teeth now, but as a child it was a different story. Often the exhausting ache began, and got worse and worse, refusing to yield to hot bottles, and to wisps of cotton wool soaked in strong-tasting iodine or whisky or camphorated chloroform and stuffed into the cavity. I sat with tears trickling until it stopped.

Finally one tooth got to the stage where it had got to be removed, and the doctor at the Lansdowne military hospital said he'd have a go. This hospital was for the gurkhas and did splendid work, but it had not the equipment we now expect. Poor man, it can't have been very pleasant for him to extract a tooth without anaesthetic or proper instruments from a small girl-child. And my poor mother had to walk down with me to the hospital and see it done.

Meanwhile the patient, quite unaware what lay ahead of her, and free of toothache for the moment, danced blithely along to the appointment. Father had promised me a rupee when I came back. A whole rupee! It would buy me a yard of that silk, or dozens of glass bangles, or a boxful of gold beads, or a fishing minnow. As I thought of all the different things it would buy, it became as if one rupee would buy the lot.

The road lay along the khud-side, and in the stone of the walls grew docks and other delightful weeds. We always stripped the red dock seeds off as we went along. The tall plants were just the right shape for a hand going past, and it was a nice feeling—nice sound, too—to get the seeds ripped off into your palm. Then we sowed them all along the wall to be sure of a good crop next year. Then there was another plant of which the leaves were lined underneath with silver-grey. You could peel off this silver skin in one piece in the most entrancing manner.

I was busy all the way down to the hospital. But now we were there. Some of the convalescent patients—gurkha soldiers—lay resting in those long easy wicker-chairs on the verandah. Silence fell as we approached.

The doctor came out to us on the verandah and gave me a reassuring smile.

"Now you sit here, Norah. Open your mouth."

Next moment piercing agony shot through me. I'm afraid I yelled, but it was over in a few moments—a baby tooth but a back one, and it gave a bit of trouble. I sat sobbing in the chair, while all the soldiers gazed at me.

But now the pleasant part of having a tooth out lay ahead. We walked home and I got my rupee, and the Scots were there to tea. I was able to show them the money and also the black wound in my mouth. They were gloriously impressed. I felt like having another tooth out next day.

It was a feeling that disappeared fast enough when the time actually came to have another one removed. This journey to the hospital was not the carefree skip-and-hop of last time. As we approached the dreadful building, I dawdled and hung back, not yet having learnt that the only way to tackle an unpleasant thing is to go at it quick and straight and get it over.

"Do come along," my poor mother pleaded.

Well we got there, and it was the same thing over again. Another baby tooth and therefore easy to get out, of course, but it didn't seem so at the time. Again a molar, but this time the tooth had one of its fangs turned up like a fishing hook. I don't suppose this made the slightest difference to the extraction, but I was able to boast about it for years afterwards. A hooked fang! It sounded terrible.

My toothache went away after those two extractions, and I felt a lot better. No more sitting crouched over a book, holding a hotty to my face, my mouth running with the violent taste of iodine, and tears blistering the pages that I read.

Now, however, I did understand the junglis who feared hospital and would never go there until they were dying. Now I knew what it was like to be frightened of what they would do to you. Suppose I actually *was* a jungli? I looked down at my hands and imagined beautiful ivory-brown Indian hands lying there, instead of my own scratched ones. If I were a jungli the nails would be cream brown, for instance, and perhaps I might have one or two bangles of blue glass with the sun in them. Suddenly I knew *really* what it felt like to be a forest woman, fond of beads, and scared of hospital.

Most Indians would not go there until it was too late to do anything for them; and so in the jungle villages it came to be believed that hospital did not cure a man, it killed him. All the villagers, and our own staff too, would beg and plead with my parents to treat them in camp and not send them to hospital. Often they refused point-blank to go. The parents thus often had to treat cases much too serious for amateur doctoring. I expect that nowadays, with trucks for transport on jungle roads, and better facilities at the hospitals, and enlightenment among the people of remote areas, these conditions no longer apply.

Fortunately my parents never had to do anything really serious to any of their own children, though they were prepared for anything and would have faced whatever was necessary. But none of us, thank heaven, had appendicitis, diphtheria, cholera, or anything like that, nor were we ever bitten by a snake or a mad dog.

Treatment for hydrophobia at that time could be given at only one hospital in India. Anyone bitten by a rabid dog or jackal had to travel there as fast as possible. A Forest Ranger once turned up in camp saying he had been bitten on the wrist by a mad jackal. The place was cauterised and he was sent off to this hospital for treatment. I'm glad to say he recovered.

Snakebite was a constant danger, and we replenished our stock of anti-venines each year. There had to be different ones for the different venoms, and they had to be fresh. It was essential to see what snake had bitten you, the most likely ones being cobra and krait.

There is a good deal of variety in the colouring of cobras. Some were a metallic dust-colour, grey with a note of pink, and some darker and more patterned. But, unless you were bitten in the dark, you would always recognize a cobra by the characteristic hood which is spread before the creature strikes.

The krait however—the little dust snake—was far less noticeable, and more easy to tread on, and absolutely deadly.

The bite of cobra or krait could be fatal within a very short time. Murder by snakebite is fairly common, and the murderer seldom brought to book, since snakes can be captured without undue difficulty, and left in a suitable spot.

Hamadryads or king cobras are rather rare. They lived in our jungle and grew to twelve or even sixteen feet long, varying somewhat in colour, just as ordinary cobras do. There were also nonpoisonous serpents such as grass-snakes and pythons. Father sometimes shot a python, and the men now and then killed a cobra with sticks.

Once they dug out a well-used hole at the root of a tree, expecting a snake, but there was only an old goa lizard at home. They killed him instead, I'm sorry to say. He lay there, unattractive, a big scaly bag covered with blue ticks that almost matched the scales; but he had done no harm, merely appealed to the prehistoric part of human nature that makes us kill. He was about four and a half feet long,

with a lizardlike head and big claws to climb with and a
tail like a dinosaur's.

There was always great satisfaction at the death of a
snake, rather naturally. Death itself was dead. But even when
the creature was dead, no one would touch it, and it would
be taken up with sticks to be thrown away.

Then the body hung limp and dusty, all the strength and
liquid beauty gone out of it. Never again would this serpent
glide along, leaving marks in the dust behind it, while each
curve of its body copied the one in front in follow-my-leader
fashion, so that if the snake took a loop back towards its
own tail, the front and the back of the body would be
travelling in different directions at the same time. Never
again would the small deadly head and restless black tongue
stretch out far into space from the branches among which
the rear of the body was intricately knotted—stretching
rigidly out—out—to reach another branch. Nor rear up *high*
and stiff as the snake explored a wall or other obstacle for
an opening. Nor utter the warning hiss, nor strike like lightning and squirt death down the poison-teeth into the blood-
stream of its victims, animal or human.

Time meant nothing to snakes. They could feed once a
week or once a month, it didn't matter. They would lie
unmoving for days, twined in branches, slopped in a hole, or
under a stone in a pool, breathing so slowly they almost didn't
breathe at all, and all their colours brilliant with running
water, or gleaming with dry reflections in the sun. If they
were not disturbed, their movement from one place to another was smooth and slow, the head forging forward in one
steady push, the body reaching and drawing up behind it,
as the snake walked on its ribs.

Gwala Ram once claimed that he had been bitten by a
cobra in Lansdowne, and that he had saved his life by run-

ning round the station all night. He had no other treatment, so the chances are that it was not a cobra that bit him.

People sometimes kept a mongoose for a pet to discourage snakes, as one may keep a cat to discourage mice.

Of course Harry and I were taught, within reason, to be on the look-out for snakes and scorpions. Apart from shaking out shoes and boxes before using them, we must never put a hand into any hole in tree or wall, and so on. Once we were digging in a bank, when there was a fall of earth, and a coil of reptile was disclosed. Harry was still very young at the time, and went to pick it up. The chuprassy struck his hand out of the way, and then Father picked up a spade and drove it down with all his force on the reptile. Out fell a poor old toad, chopped in half. But it was safer to kill quickly and ask questions afterwards.

I've seen a chuprassy strike a child's hand away from a scorpion, too. A big one can give a very painful sting indeed, and a child might even die of it. We saw scorpions trotting about sometimes, and killed them when we could.

Malaria and accidents with jungle animals were probably the most common things my parents had to treat, though they were asked for all sorts of things, including "spectacles for a man aged about fifty."

TWENTY-SIX

I Suffered but Not in Silence

Actually, I thought it rather fun to be ill sometimes. Not too ill, and not for too long, but I always hoped for a bit of a temperature—a small go of fever. Not too much horrible shivering, of course, and so on and so forth, but enough to be important. Then you were put to bed and had special things cooked for you—chicken broth with rice in it, and meat jellies made of nilghai hoof, red jellies too, with fruit in, and honey to sip for a cough. The men smoked out wild bees to get this honey, collecting it in buckets, and then straining away all the rough comb and dead bees through a cloth. Honey was supposed to be the best thing for coughs and sore throats. We certainly agreed it did more good than any of the nasty-tasting things ever did. Quinine, for instance.

But in bed, besides all the little good things they brought you to eat, there were all the interesting things to do. Jigsaws, and cutting out and threading beads and so on. That time I had jaundice in camp was fun, once I stopped feeling bad. It was exciting to travel in a litter instead of going on an elephant. To lie and listen to the squeaking ropes and the men's gossip as they carried me along.

One evening I watched a mosquito on my arm, and hoped it would give me just a tiny go of malaria. It had a long slender pepper-and-salt body and exquisite wings. I could not feel the six legs on my skin nor the sucker probing down into my blood. Then I killed him, and all that fragile singing body was squashed beyond repair. The place on my arm began to irritate.

Harry had whooping cough in Lansdowne for six weeks. Whooping cough was worse for children then than it is now. There was little that could be done to help patients, and when he started to cough it was beyond any dosing with honey. He would stand and hold on to something while his face went blue because he could not get his breath, poor child, and you thought his insides must all come out.

I escaped, of course, owing to having already had whooping cough as a baby.

Harry was always so good and patient when he was ill, and so brave, it broke your heart to see him. And he was the unlucky one in all these things too. For instance, one of the governesses—this was in Lansdowne—read in a magazine from England some theory about the value of raw meat as a food. She fed raw-meat sandwiches to the four children in the house. Naturally in a country like India raw meat was dangerous, but we all escaped trouble except Harry. For years afterwards he was the victim of a tapeworm which refused to yield to any kind of treatment. Everything was tried. Many of these so-called cures involved prolonged starvation, and he would go patiently to bed hungry, without complaint, although he was quite a little boy. Next morning Mother would be up at five or six preparing whatever was necessary for the morning dose. Freshly ground melon seeds was one thing they tried, and it took two hours to grind enough for one dose.

Always, some weeks later, it would be found that he was

not cured, and another effort must be made. For a time, all this set him back in health and growth, and it was not until we went home to England that he was cured. He then forged ahead, making up for all lost time.

Harry died in 1942 by one of Hitler's bombs from a lone raider on the R.A.F. hospital at Torquay.

In India he was always good and patient, and put up with everything that had to be done to him without a murmur.

In marked contrast to me. I'm afraid I always complained. Someone said to me recently, "While your husband does that, Norah, I suppose you'll suffer in silence?"

"Norah will suffer," my husband put in, "but not in silence."

It was the same in India.

I carry a piece of India in my arm to this day. Running down a steep drive in Lansdowne, I tripped and fell and shot down the gravel. There was what I considered a really horrible place in my arm which of course had to be washed and squeezed to get the gravel out. Iodined too. Iodine, carbolic, and permanganate were about the only disinfectants in those days. I'm sure I made the most of all this.

Anyway, when the place healed, there was a little stone left inside. It's there now.

But luckily none of us broke bones or suffered any really dangerous illness.

One of the chuprassies became seriously ill and delirious in camp, though. He lay in his hut in the servants' quarters and refused to eat what the others brought him.

"They are poisoning me," he whispered to my parents through his dry delirious lips, rolling white eyeballs in the darkness. So they themselves looked after him and fed him.

Father had to leave camp that day. While he was away, the sick man rose, dressed in his uniform and presented himself for duty at the verandah. He was in high fever, and nothing my mother could say to him would make him go back to bed, so she sent a message post haste to Father to come back and reason with the madman. Meanwhile she told us to keep away from the man. I peeped at him from a distance, and first I thought it was a new chuprassy standing there. He was unrecognisable, he looked so ghastly. All the other men nervously kept their distance too.

After a while, Father returned on his pony. On his way he had come upon a man unlawfully cutting Government timber, and confiscated his axe. So in reply to Mother's call for help with the chuprassy, Father galloped into camp brandishing a hatchet.

This chuprassy recovered soon after this. His life had been saved by my parents, but as his religion forbade him to eat food touched by Europeans, he at once went away to purify himself after their ministrations.

When he came back, he told me all about his illness. He was then entirely recovered and quite normal again, but he still told me quite firmly that the others had been poisoning him while he was ill.

Many of the jungle Indians could have had much done for them, if only they had consented to the necessary treatment. For instance, in Lansdowne there was a hill woman with two thumbs, the extra one sprouting out sideways like a branch. This ugly deformity presumably could have been easily put right, but it was considered lucky, and her husband was looked upon as most fortunate in having such a woman for his wife.

The parents had to doctor animals as well as human beings.

Poor old fat Squinch, the spaniel, tore a triangle of skin down from his chest, on barbed wire, and had to be sewn up. Father did the job, and the place healed well.

After Harry and I were back at school in England, Squinch became very fat in his old age. He'd always been a heavy dog, and he became even fatter. Then one day he jumped down rather a steep place and broke both front legs. His injuries were too severe to be repaired, so Father had to render him the last service of Master to Dog, by putting him out of his pain with a rifle. The life of a dog is so short, and it is not very pleasant when this time comes. It seems to come so often, too, and then a member of the family is gone from the house.

Our dogs in India were sometimes bothered by leeches. These loathsome black worms would take up residence in the spaniel's nose, and could be got out only by drink-starving the wretched dog for a day. He had to be tied up, away from water, and when he was really thirsty, the leech would be, too. Father then held a sopping sponge under the dog's nose, and a pair of forceps in his other hand. Soon the leech would stretch out of a nostril to have a drink, and it could then be seized and drawn out. After that, a long cool drink for the dog.

Our cows and goats sometimes got maggots in their feet and noses. This trouble was caught from the ground, and the animals got it when grazing on infected land where other cattle had been. The men used to winkle out the maggots with paraffin rag, and the condition could be cured.

In the villages, though, the chances were that nothing would be done. One saw animals with half a foot eaten away, and they could not be killed because they were sacred. The tiger or panther that prowls near cultivation looking for stray cattle is thus a mercy-killer, and the only hope that such diseased animals have for release from suffering.

TWENTY-SEVEN

Fire

Often the grassland near habitation is burned on purpose as a precaution against forest fire, and this no doubt helps also to kill infection in sour grazing land. It produces beautiful fresh clean green grass afterwards, too, for the animals to eat.

But fire—real fire—was one of the worst dangers for the forests themselves, for the great trees and all the wild creatures who lived among them.

A fire, of course, would turn out animals whose presence was not suspected, just as a beat for game did.

Naturally the Forest Officer and his staff preached and practised the strictest care with all possible causes of fire. Our camp fires were always pulled apart and stamped out and well-doused before we left them. If we lit one for a picnic, it must be on clear ground, away from all sticks and grass and undergrowth—preferably on sand—and we had to cover it with sand or water or both before we left it, even if it looked dead.

Generally, forest fires could be seen at once—the column of smoke by day, and pillar of fire by night, as in the Bible—

and of course the Rangers and Forest Guards were always on the watch. They'd send a runner at once to Father with the news, but generally he was already on his way. Whenever there was a fire, all the men of the camp turned out to deal with it. If it had got a good hold, there might be anxiety and danger. Sometimes it was hours before they got home, black and exhausted.

All the jungle had firelines cut through it, from which a fire in any section could be fought. These lines were kept clean of growth; they ran like broad roads through the forest, and were much used as such by the wild animals, especially the carnivores as they paced the night in search of meat. The usual method of attacking a fire was, of course, to light a counterfire from one of the lines across the path the blaze was taking so that when the two met, both would go out, as there was nothing left to burn.

Left to itself, the counterfire might try to travel the wrong way, creeping back across the short grass of the fireline. So men were needed all along the lines to beat out these efforts and so force their counterfire to travel towards the main conflagration. Many hands were needed to fight a fire; one day one of the chuprassies, a new one, declined to help, saying that he had been engaged as a chuprassy, not as a Forest Guard. He remained in camp while everyone else was out fighting the blaze.

When Father returned, this man came to him in some astonishment.

"You have dismissed me, Sahib?"

I gazed at them both in acute unhappiness. I liked this man. I loved Father. Surely they did not have to quarrel? Mind you, I was perfectly prepared to quarrel with everyone myself. I could push off restraining hands, and roll up my sleeves with the best of them. But as a spectator, I could only blush hot with discomfort.

The chuprassy left, and another took his place—someone who would not refuse to help when the forest was alight.

One year we were there at the right time when one of the bungalows was to have the grass and scrub all round it burned as a precaution against fire. The bungalow stood in flat grassland, with two or three tracks going out from it like spokes. In between grew heavy elephant grass. The men took one section at a time. They armed themselves with rough brooms or branches cut from the forest, and posted themselves all round the area which was to be fired. When they were ready, one of them took a swash of grass, twisted it and bent it over to make a club-shaped torch. He lit it and, holding it to the growing grass, he raced down the line.

And then!

In a moment flame was everywhere. It forked like lightning from his torch into all the grass with such speed that in a few seconds there was all the wind and noise and heat of a forest fire, complete. Great flames tossed, wind tore pieces off them, thick smoke poured up to eclipse the sun. Bash! Bash! went the men with their brooms and branches, shouting if the fire seemed to be getting the better of them, and dancing about as they did so, to stamp out flames with their bare feet as well.

We helped them, beating away with our branches of green leaves, until the leaves dried up and kept catching on fire themselves. Then we had to get new ones.

Now all the grass was in a molten roar, making its own wind that sucked at my skirt and topee. The heat was too much for our faces—we had to turn away—and the smoke made cloud-shadows on the compound, a thing we rarely saw.

When one triangle of grass was done, the men did the next. In one there was a clump of trees which had been spared in the fires of other years but now had to go. When the flames reached it, they tore through the undergrowth, the trees at first resisting them because they were green. But soon the leaves began to curl and catch, and the trunk to char. Presently flames were flying from the whole of every tree. On the topmost branches they looked like flags.

Piece by piece, all the grassland was burned, until the bare whitewashed bungalow in its compound of worn grass-stubble stood alone on the smoking plain.

Next day I walked through the cinders. Warmth came up at me through the soles of my shoes. If I kicked at the ash that lay sometimes still in the shape of different knots of grass as they had been, I uncovered the embers throbbing inside. I walked through the black trees. Two days ago when I came here, these had been alive, there had been green leaves and shadows. Now everything was dead and the tree trunks, still standing, were charcoal and too hot to touch.

We moved camp, and when we came back to this bungalow, a little later, mushrooms were growing as usual on the burnt land. Some of them were gritty with ash in their pink gills, but there were so many we could select those that were clean. There were thousands more than we could ever eat. Mother instructed the cook in the making of mushroom soup. They used cream and mushrooms—so many mushrooms that the soup was black, and all the fine elusive never-to-be-recaptured flavour was caught in the black milk. One can imagine a Frenchman, remembering a soup like that, devoting his life to the rediscovery, by trial and error, of the recipe. He would never find it.

After the mushrooms, in due course, came the grass, springing up from deep uninjured roots in blades that were tender and actually green in all the faded jungle. Deer loved this grass. They would come out of the forest to graze on it, morning and evening. And, of course, they were followed by the beasts of prey.

In those days deer were plentiful. Chital, the beautiful brown-and-white dappled deer of the Indian jungle, were the ones that were to be seen most often, and the ones on which many of the jungle panthers lived. There were also hog deer, barking deer, and others.

Occasionally chital stags would be seen together in numbers. One early morning in the mists of a dried riverbed, Father saw a herd of more than a hundred chital stags—a moving forest of antlers. Such numbers are probably never seen now. Even when we were there, the grandfathers would mutter that already the numbers were decimated.

For unknown centuries, Man has preyed upon his fellow inhabitants of the Earth. He, too, was created to be a beast of prey; and in the last hundred years or so, he has had more deadly weapons with which to kill. Now is his last chance to preserve some of the wonders of the Garden of Eden before they are lost for ever.

When we were in India, we shot animals, too, though in the case of deer it was usually for food. We ate chital, and their skins were made into rugs, and into trunks and boxes. The live deer is a beautiful golden-fawn colour, with a darker line down the back and a double line of spots down the back-bone, as well as spots on the rest of the body, but the skins faded to a pale biscuit shade, and the hair soon wore off.

Chital stags often have irregular or deformed horns, the result sometimes of an injury when in velvet, or by infection and other causes. My father made a collection of these irregular horns, and finally gave it to the Natural History Museum in London.

In the jungle, chital have every reason to be nervous, and their large ears flick to and fro all the time, twitching off flies and listening for danger. If they are suspicious, they freeze and stare, and stamp a warning. Then suddenly the herd breaks into headlong flight and disappears.

As I have said, chital can sometimes be located because they so often feed underneath a troupe of monkeys on what the monkeys fling down, and the monkeys do the sentinel work for all. But though deer are always in danger from men as well as from their natural enemies, it is obvious they are not constantly thinking of death. Out of sight, out of mind, and most of the time they seem to be happy and at peace. If a panther kills one of them, they will even stand near, calling out about it. Then they will continue their life as if nothing had happened.

They know perfectly well when a passing tiger or panther is merely moving from one place to another and not hunting. They will call at sight of him, but they know if they are in danger or not. The moment he is out of sight, they cease to worry; and that of course is when their danger is likely to begin.

After chital, sambhur were the most common deer of our jungles. They are forest-dwellers and nocturnal, and practically never seen on the open plains. The stags have beards, or rather manes, and have hairy brown coats which we used to make into leather, as the hair itself is too coarse to be used for rugs.

Then there were the nervous little kakurs or barking deer, whose agitated cry might mean that one of them had sighted a tiger or panther or python. But they were unreliable, because also they call from sheer nerves, at nothing at all. They are only about the size of a greyhound, smooth reddish-brown, and they creep about the forest paths with their tails down.

Python often feed on kakur; when they have crushed the life from their victim they open their mouths and, beginning at the head, draw in the whole crushed carcass, horns and all. An elastic ligament allows the serpent's jaws to open wide enough, his recurved teeth act as hooks, and he draws himself over his meal like a stocking over a foot. The horns of the dead deer can then often be clearly seen under the python's skin. To absorb such a meal takes time, and the python will lie in some secluded spot for days while digestion takes place.

A rare denizen of the jungle, and something like the kakur, is the little four-horned antelope. About the same size and colour, but an antelope, not a deer, this little creature has four horns instead of two. But he is rarely seen. We had one mounted head of this antelope, but I never saw one alive.

Nilghai would browse on the new grass growing on burned land. Although their name means blue cow, they are antelopes, and ugly ones, but they were useful as food in our large and hungry camp. Of course, the Hindus among the staff would not eat them because they were called cows, and cows are sacred. One Indian prince, wishing to shoot nilghai, and prevented by his religion from killing a cow, corrected their name in his state from blue cow to blue antelope. There was then no further bar to his sport.

TWENTY-EIGHT

End of an Era

One day in November 1918, just as we were starting lessons, the runner arrived with the mail. He had been a week on the way, and he brought the news that the war was over. So the Burke family celebrated the Armistice a week late.

There were no more lessons that day. Instead, Harry and I built a bonfire for the evening, choosing a safe spot for it, and piling it high with dry grass and branches from the jungle. When we had done, I sat on the verandah in the shade, gazing out into the sun-dazzle, and contemplated it with satisfaction. It was going to be a fine blaze.

Just then a hawk dived out of the deep blue sky in pursuit of one of our chickens, and the hen fled shrieking for her life under the trees—always under something if they could, poor things—and towards the unlit bonfire. If she could have reached it, she might have escaped into it, but he killed her.

I rushed out to save her life, yelling and waving, but I was too late, she was dead, and I could only carry the carcass with feathers floating off it to the cook. The hawk had killed, and he was still hungry. He climbed back into the sky.

That night we had the bonfire.

We also, a week late in the jungle, celebrated the end of the Kaiser's war, and his flight to Holland.

As I built that bonfire—as I saw the hawk kill that chicken —as I danced about the blaze that night—I had no idea that my whole life was now to be altered.

Now the war was over, the seas were safe, we could at last be taken home to school in England.

Now was the end of our life in the jungle. This was the end of camping and fishing and childhood, and all the magical beginnings of life, lit by a special light for everyone, no matter where those beginnings may be.

Now there opened new horizons. Now we were to leave the jungle, and all the trees and all the animals who had surrounded us in friendly fright for as long as we could remember.

Now a new life opened—England, school, Auberies, London, Paris, Switzerland. Things I had never even imagined were in store for me.

All the time I was a jungle child, I used to hanker for school and the normal life of a ten-or-twelve-year-old English girl. I loved the jungle, but also I used to long for companions of my own age. Not realising that the life I was living was unique and after a few years would never happen again in the whole world for anyone, I wanted girl-friends and school and games and—yes, even lessons. To pit my brains against theirs and try for the top of the class. To struggle for a place in the first eleven. To have girl-friends. I thought with ardour of the life of an ordinary girl.

And yet at the same time I knew first of all when I said goodbye to Squinch that something was going from me for ever.

We were to go home to England.

It was the following year. Our Lansdowne home was

already broken up and packed. I saw the furniture taken out. I saw mountains of things being divided into heaps and distributed by lot among the Indian staff. This was when Gwala Ram won the elephant's trunk. But still, though I saw, I had not perceived.

The dogs were to be looked after by others until my parents' return after depositing us at home.

Now we were at Kotdwara. Railhead. Where Father previously shot the rogue elephant.

Squinch lay under the dining-room table, and I crawled in on hands and knees to kiss him goodbye. I had no idea why there were tears streaming down my face. How could I, at twelve years old, know that I should never see him again? I loved him as we all love our dogs, with all our hearts, and the time comes when they must go for ever.

I kissed him goodbye, under the table, and then I came out, and presently we were setting off for the station.

It was dark when we left the bungalow. By the light of hurricane lanterns we mounted the elephants and then they walked us down to the station. It never occurred to me that this was the very last, last time I should ever climb upon an elephant as a natural daily act and be transported in the usual amiable style at about 3 m.p.h., to my destination.

I had not known why I wept when I kissed Squinch goodbye. I did not realise at all that it was goodbye also to our dear friends, Ayah and Gwala Ram and Rags and Ponko, and everything that had made the solid land under my feet.

We were never to see any of it again. The dolls were already packed in their boxes and in the crates. White Swan and May Blue and Melinette and Jappy and Grey Hen and Mr. Brown and all the rest. They too were all on their way to England. The sun of India would not again bleach their glued hair or satin robes. Nor would I sit on verandahs, stringing the dazzling beads to make them yet more gorgeous. They would never again hear the roar of tigers nor the trill of rapids full of trout.

The Gujars who inhabited our jungles, with the women wearing trousers long before white women did, and all their wealth stored in silver jewelry at ear and nose and wrist and ankle—they would live their life on in the green glades of the forest, grazing their buffaloes, fearing the tiger, making the white butter, without once knowing who owned India, who was come into the thrones, or who was gone from them; in whose crown the Koh-i-Noor.

The mehta's daughter—that child of poverty in whom the basic passions of the human female yet flowered—would know other masters. I can see her now. She had never owned anything in her life, not a bead, not a yard of cloth. She was dressed in stolen rags. She took one of my brother's castaway shirts from the rubbish heap and put it on and danced in the strong sunlight, watching her shadow. These were the nearest to a mirror and a new dress she had ever had in her life.

" 'Gar!" shouted our baby brother Peter to the khitmatghar on that last evening, as if he had been a prince clapping his hands. " 'Gar! Toast!"

The willing and beaming 'Gar brought it. It amused them to serve a small white autocrat. In affectionate teasing, they obeyed him as if he were a grown Sahib.

But that was the end of a life.

No more the elephants and tigers. No more turtles and mahseer.

We were going home to England, and had got to adjust ourselves, savages, to the life of a different planet. Quite tremendous changes, such as we had never dreamt of, lay ahead.

TWENTY-NINE

Then the Ship

The journey home was packed with interest.

First of all there were days and nights in the train to reach Bombay.

We crossed the Thar desert. Mile after mile of dead land streamed past the windows, grey and brown, with an occasional dried stump where something had tried to grow. All the windows had to be kept shut, in spite of the heat, and even then a fine dust covered everything. We ate dust. We breathed dust.

Mother had brought boiled drinking water with her for her children, but there were other babies on the train whose mothers had not thought of this, so Harry and I had soda-water while the babies rationed the drinking water between them. It became warm and sandy, and they all said so at the top of their voices.

Suddenly there was the first sight of the sea—a grey triangle in a V of sandhills. My heart leaped with excitement. The sea! Soon we would be on it.

But first of all there was Bombay and a hotel—a *palace*, lit

by electric light. We were allowed to switch ours on and off
if we were good.

The place swarmed. The passages were like streets,
with all sorts of people going and coming that we didn't
know and weren't particularly supposed to smile at. Up till
now we used to know almost everyone we met. But not
now. We had never seen such a place. Other people used
our bathroom. I don't mean just our parents, which would
have been odd enough, but total strangers. We had to wait
till they'd finished. And then there was no bhisti with his
goat skin. The water came from taps.

Suddenly in the passage I caught sight of a cousin of mine,
a girl my own age, with whom we had once spent Christmas
at Lahore or Gwalior. We talked and parted without thinking anything of if. I was puzzled by my parents' surprise
when I mentioned this meeting. In all of India, they said,
fancy finding her here. They were surprised at seeing one
person I knew. I was surprised at seeing so many I didn't.

Then the ship. This was a P. & O. liner. Later she sank
under the waters of the Mediterranean with treasure in her
hold.

But she was then, at any rate to one pair of eyes, the
most wonderful dream-ship ever to sail the sea. The grownups
spoke of her as slow and rolling. They were wrong. She was
even more wonderful than the hotel. There were passages
and steps and ladders to run up and down. There were
ventilators that were warm to touch, and out of which
wafted the smell of engine rooms. There were clanging bells,
and hooters, and all the ship throbbed like a heart.

Everything was white and gold and scrubbed. In the
mornings the sailors broomed the decks with sand and
water, and then hosed them down. Those who were up
early enough could paddle about barefoot in all the sluicing
water, and scrunch the sand under prehensile toes, and

pick up pink shells and collect them in the cabin where, for some reason, they were not popular. We washed in sticky salt water and rinsed in fresh. Sometimes the stewards clamped wooden things onto the tables to stop the plates crashing about. There were even the smartest possible grey-and-scarlet cardboard boxes to be sick in.

We moved majestically out of Bombay harbour, and set course across the Indian Ocean. I stood alone at the deck-rail and watched India disappearing until only a single dome was visible, like a pearl in the blue-and-silver haze of the horizon. I did not understand what I was feeling. Everything around me was so exciting, and further wonders were in store, but a thousand miles behind the pearl and blue-and-silver were Ayah and Gwala Ram and Bunty and Squinch and everything I had ever known.

A man came up and stood beside me. He was brown and nice, he looked as nice as Father, and he smiled.

"What's the matter?" he asked.

"Nothing."

"What's your name?"

"Norah."

"Hullo, Norah. How old are you?"

"I'll soon be twelve."

"And going home to school? Are you excited?"

"Oh *yes!* But I know a lot already. I like writing stories."

"Will you let me read them?"

"Yes." And I said "I'm feeling funny because that's the very last bit of India that I can see, and we've left Squinch behind."

"Come for a walk with me," he replied at once, not noticing the tears in my eyes, and he put an arm round me and walked me briskly round the deck, round and round the ship while he talked hard all the time and joked and laughed.

We passed my parents in their deck chairs, and I smiled at them proudly as I went by.

Later, when I met them in the cabin—"Look here!" said Father. "Before you get officially engaged, I expect to be consulted first!"

I was too shy to ask my new friend's name, not even his surname, and he did not mention it, but I noticed that passengers' names were painted on their deck chairs. The stewards could thus find the ones they wanted every morning, and set them in the right place. So I found out his surname. I never knew anything more, not his Christian name nor rank—nothing, although the ship took four weeks to get us home, and we were friends all that time.

But I fell in love with him. He was my first love. Up till then, although I was married to Geoff, the only men I had really been in love with were, as I say, the heroes of those adventure serials in the *Boy's Own Paper*. Mr. C. was the first flesh-and-blood man that I loved, and I loved him for two years after we parted, although we never met again and I didn't know his address and never heard from him.

But the voyage, even apart from my shipboard flirtation, was beautiful and exciting. All across the Indian ocean, the sea was phosphorescent. At night, where it curled over at the bows—where it tossed and plaited along the sides and foamed away behind us in a broad wake, everywhere the touchy water quaked with light.

Then at Aden appeared the swarms of boats and the men who dive for coins. I threw mine in, a silver one, I forget what, and the nearest Arab was overboard at once. In the clear green water, I could see his shape wobbling down—down—till he turned, shot upwards again and broke surface, shaking the water from his hair and grinning up at me, his white teeth shining in his brown face, and the silver coin held between them.

The Red Sea was hot, and the Canal sweltering. We moved on glass between sand that ran with heat wobbles. Occasional strings of camels strolled along the banks.

At Port Said, Harry and I were taken ashore and ate the very first ices we had ever had in our lives. They were enormous water ices, and you could have a pink or a yellow one. We ate them reverently. We had éclairs too, and meringues.

At the waterfront we were rowed back to the ship by an Arab hurling imprecations at all his fellow boatmen who had tried to steal us from him. Harry and I were puzzled because we could not understand him. He looked like an Indian and yet we did not know what he was saying.

I think it was at Port Said—somewhere around there—that we took on hundreds of troops going home from Mespot and places after the war. Half the ship was given to them, and the passengers doubled up in the other half. All one side of the deck was roped off for the soldiers, so Mr. C. and I had to go up and down on our walks, instead of round and round.

There were lots of other children on board, all going home from India, and I was able to find plenty of friends of my own age at last. Girls, even. Not only boys. The mother of one of them was badly marked by smallpox, which she had caught in India, poor thing. I decided that it was right, after all, to vaccinate babies, even if it hurt them. Then there was one small girl, aged two, who smoked cigarettes. Her parents had taught her, so as to show her off to their friends for a joke.

One way and another, the voyage was a joy to Harry and me. Not so to my mother. I have not the slightest doubt that, during that month on board, we three children helped to turn her hair grey before its time, even though Father was at hand. What with keeping us away from the rails and from irritating other people, and looking after us when we were sea-sick, and making us quiet when we were noisy, and wondering where on earth we were when we were too quiet, and getting us to wash and eat and behave and—well, all of it, and no ayah or governess now to help her, and never a moment in which to feel peacefully ill herself, Mother must have had a horrible time.

Two American friends of mine, a man and a woman, were discussing an identical voyage which each had made to England from the Pacific just after Hitler's war.

"It was six weeks' hell," said the mother.

"Oh I enjoyed it," replied the bachelor. "Nice lazy time."

"But you didn't have children to look after," she pointed out.

"Oh there were plenty of children on board," he replied. "They were no trouble at all. Except when they came in the lounge."

For all the grownups on our boat, especially the parents, there was anxiety about mines left over from the war. We had boat drill and lifebelts of course, and nothing happened.

After Port Said, we threw away our topees. They had been our daily companions all our lives, always at hand like a handkerchief, and it was going to feel odd without them. But now the sun was no longer dangerous. We could go hatless. It felt peculiar, but also very nice.

Harry and I hacked the rims off our topees and hurled them like quoits into the wake of the ship, where they floated further and further behind till they were out of sight. We made masks out of the crowns and painted them fearful colours to frighten people with, and finally threw them away too. It was rather nice to destroy and throw away a perfectly good thing. I don't know why. Probably a sign of some grave moral disorder.

It was also great fun to hang through a hatch over a companionway and hook off the sailors' caps as they passed below and throw them to the bottom of the steps, so they had to go down and get them again. I hope we got smacked for this, but I don't seem to remember it.

Everyone's thoughts were now turned to England. All the hopes and longings of people who had been exiled for years in the heat and dust and fever of a foreign land; who had devoted their lives to India, and given her their health; who had parted from their children and all they loved for her sake—the dreams of all these people were centred on the promised land, now so rapidly approaching.

All our lives we had learned that the best of everything came from England. In India, the chickens were like bantams, and the grass worn and brown.

"In England, the grass will be green, the eggs will be large——"

In England. . . . In England. . . .

Somewhere in England was Auberies, the old grey house set among its cedars and parkland and all its farms and coverts. It belonged to Father now, it was our home. We hardly remembered it, but we knew it by talk and imagination. Somewhere in its many rooms and vast cupboards lay Harry's magnificent clockwork boat and that blue cushion of mine that squeaked and which I had never been allowed to put underneath Grandfather as he sat down.

Grandfather had died some years ago now. After weeks of grave suffering, he had passed away. That night there was a storm such as people speak of for years afterwards. It levelled the whole plantation below the lake, every tree went down, giants fell everywhere, and Grandfather fell too. He died in the great four-poster bed of pale golden oak in which Father also died, more than thirty years later.

The devastated plantation was set out again after Grandfather's death, with poplar and willow and fir and spruce. We used to get our Christmas trees there, and the trees for my children too. Whenever I see that plantation, now grown sky-high and all the trees pencil-slim because there was no money after the war and they were never thinned, I think of Grandfather.

But as that P. & O. liner chugged her way through the Straits of Gibraltar and the Bay of Biscay in 1919 all this was yet to come. England, the land of ice-creams and Auberies and school and green grass was now approaching.

And then suddenly it was there, the white cliffs. There they were, snow white, and crowned as everyone had promised us with pure emerald green.

THIRTY

England!

As we moved to the gangway, Mr. C. said to me "Well, goodbye, Norah," and he bent and kissed me.

"Goodbye," I said, and kissed him back. It was the first kiss I had from a man I loved. He disappeared in the crowd and I never saw him again.

Meanwhile there were other matters to occupy us.

The first thing that really astonished me in England was that somebody on the platform asked Father the time. To begin with, up to now, people round me had not bothered much about time. The parents were very punctual of course, and took count of it for things like our lessons and sending us to bed; but for us the day had been roughly lesson-time, marching time (to the next camp), tiffin time, bedtime, etc. Certainly none of our Indian friends cared two hoots if it were eight or nine or ten, or Monday or Saturday, for that matter. If they were to go by train, they repaired to the station and camped there for days if need be, until there happened to be a train going in the direction they wanted.

Now here was a total stranger who wanted to know the time. But that wasn't the whole of it. Father told her "Nine o'clock." This was in the evening.

Nine? I looked about me. It was still broad daylight. It couldn't be nine o'clock. Nine o'clock at night was dark, with panthers and jackals on the move. But now the daylight went on and on, and it took ages to *get* dark too, as if it couldn't make up its mind. The world was full of surprises.

Another one was that there was apparently no such real person as Sherlock Holmes. I had planned to consult him if need be—if, for instance, I should have the great good fortune to come upon a body—but now I was told he existed only in books. This was a keen blow.

But the temperature of England in the summer and India in the winter seemed to be much about the same. We had arrived in England in May or June, so that though we had come through some real heat on the way, we did not yet realise how cold this new country could be. As a matter of fact, I didn't begin to feel the cold for several years, even in the winter, and other people who have lived in warm climates say the same. It takes time for even English mist and chill to penetrate sun-soaked bones. After that, you probably notice the cold rather a lot. But at the moment the temperature seemed much the same as the cold weather in India.

We went to stay in Bedford, where Aunt Jessie was living with some other old ladies. One of them was the widow of an Assamese tea-planter, and she still had his magnificent collection of moths and beetles. These were all the ones we had known in India as well as many others. But instead of being folded into triangles in pages of the *Pioneer*, as ours were, they were superbly mounted, and displayed in glass-topped trays in polished mahogany cabinets such as you never see nowadays. Master craftsmen made those cabinets. The trays slipped in and out as if cushioned on air, so that it was a pleasure to open and shut them, simply to experience this silken perfection. And when they slipped shut, they blew out at you a breath of cedar or sandalwood—the linings of cigar boxes. Kept thus, in exactly the right conditions, all those frail colours which, in Creation, were never intended to be seen and were given to creatures whose lives are lived in darkness—all those frail colours of the moths, and all their invisible feathers dusted with white and pale green and marigold pollen, were there undamaged. The lady who owned this collection used to read four novels a day. As a writer, I think of her with gratitude.

In Bedford there were cinemas. When I quarrelled with the family, I did not now stick a half-anna stamp over Father's photo in the silver frame in the drawing room. I took eightpence of my pocket money and went and watched Mary Pickford by myself instead, hoping the family would get frantic about my absence. They took it with heartless calm.

But Mother decided it was high time I began school, even though it was the middle of a term. After four weeks in cramped quarters on the ship, keeping us safe, keeping us occupied, keeping us from annoying people, she must have been at the end of even her tether, which never gave out. Anyway, I was to start school at once.

With this plan I wholeheartedly agreed. Bedford is a town of schools, and I had often gazed shyly at the girls in their uniforms. They all seemed to know each other as they bicycled along the smooth grey roads with their satchels and tennis racquets, or their towels and bathing suits. I longed to be one of them.

But I did not go to one of the Bedford schools, as I expected, already seeing myself in a gym-tunic, with a hockey stick, walking in crocodile, and the uniform hat on my head. "Don't keep looking at your feet, Norah. Everyone'll know you've got new shoes."

The school chosen for me was in Devonshire. It was run by a friend of one of the Bedford old ladies who recommended it in glowing terms, and she was right. It was a small school in the country, with only about twenty boarders and twenty day-girls, and so more suitable than a big high school for a child straight from the jungle. Parents thought so highly of it that one girl used to come to it from Lancashire, a two-day journey.

Almost at once Mother took me down to it as a boarder. Many surprises were waiting for that little girl from the jungle. I was a thin, odd child, yellow from too many years in India. I did not yet know how to behave in a crowd of other girls. I had never really been teased. I looked forward eagerly to school.

We arrived in Bideford, the town of Sir Richard Grenville and the Rose of Torridge. Four centuries ago, down this broad glittering river, famous sailors put out for America, and sailed back too to Bideford, bringing with them the dried leaves of the tobacco plant. These were waters familiar to Sir Francis Drake, Sir Walter Raleigh, and all the great golden-bearded Elizabethan adventurers.

Mother and I walked up to the school.

It was called Nilgala, and it was built somewhat in the shape of a Burmese pagoda at the top of Raleigh Hill. It had a verandah, which seemed perfectly natural to me, and on this verandah stood two girls eating oranges. They threw the skins at us. Had they been seen, they would have been punished, but they escaped, bless them! Both afterwards became close friends of mine, and one of them was one of my bridesmaids.

She was the prettiest girl I had so far ever seen, and I was a great admirer of beauty. My own hair was long and straight and dark. Hers was sunshine gold, naturally curly, and cut short. That was 1919, the era of the Bob. There was no permanent-waving yet, not even for grownups, and most certainly not for girls, who must never be encouraged to think too much of their looks, thus becoming vain and value-less. None of us at school, even up to seventeen, used any make-up whatever, not even powder. So Peggy's deep lolloping natural wave and bright curls received their due of admiration. She had a perfect fair skin and large blue eyes to go with the hair, but she never ever got a swelled head about her looks. Peggy's mother was the first person ever to present me with a prize for literature. She offered it later, for competition in the school, and I had the good fortune to win it.

But that was later. On that first day, Mother and I were shown into the drawing room and received by Miss Ethel and Miss Ada Dawson, the sisters who ran the school.

How sweet the two old ladies were, in their drawing room of porcelain ornaments and maidenhair and bulbs, the flowerpots hidden in china containers; and old-fashioned prints on the wall, of Hope and other similar romantic female figures, some printed in terra cotta, and all dressed in swathes of white georgette. The conservatory, off the drawing room, was full of ferns and flowers; and Miss Ethel's davenport was stacked with letters from parents, which she kept in tidy but very tall columns permanently on the bureau.

I did not then know how much was going to happen to me in this room—the results of exams, advice about life and writing stories, comfort, admonition. How well I should get to know it, with its firelight playing quietly upon well-polished steel and brass, and its fragrance of damp earth if the pot-plants had been recently watered.

In this setting moved Miss Ethel, the elder sister, in her mauves and greys and blacks, with her long necklace of cowrie shells which she would twist upon one finger, round and round, and then trickle off again; and Miss Ada, the younger one, in her pinks and browns.

Miss Ethel was the head of the school—a tiny gentle old lady, getting bent even smaller as the years went on. Her white hair was parted peacefully in the centre and done up in two cream cocoons above each temple, and in a bun at the back. Her greatest interest in life was literature. During the five years I was at Nilgala, she read many of the classics to us in that drawing room, while we did our embroidery or other work. At the end of each reading, she would put the book down and discuss with us what she had read. She wrote stories herself, though she had not published any, and she took the keenest interest in mine.

One term she read *Adam Bede* to us, and we came to the chapter where Mr. Irwine calls upon Adam to tell him that the girl he loves, Miss Hetty Sorrel, has been arrested.

"For what?"

"For a great crime—the murder of her child."

Miss Ethel closed the book.

"And that," she said gently, "you see, is what comes of playing at being married."

She sat there in silence, the lamplight on her white hair and on her pale fingers folded upon the book—the dark-red leather and the gilt-edged pages of a classic.

Miss Ada was so definitely a younger sister. Her hair was still partly brown and her step light and brisk. She had a light, quick lift to her head too, like a bird. Geography was her great subject, and under her guidance we travelled about the maps of the world with intense interest.

There was always a Mademoiselle in residence as well, to teach French; and one other teacher living in the house. Besides these, there were visiting tutors from Bideford and Barnstaple for such subjects as music, maths, and dancing. Those of us who learned drawing and painting walked into Bideford to the School of Art for lessons. Miss Grace Dawson, a third sister, living in the town, took us for what was called gym but was really physical exercises without apparatus, and she gave massage and exercise to one or two who had curvature of the spine, and so on.

This, then, was the school to which my mother had brought me, and on that first day it was all exciting but also a bit frightening too. Mother left. I don't remember her going. One minute she was there, and the next she was gone. I was alone in the world for the first time.

But the girls were kind. A patch of severe teasing came later; I weathered it, and it never came again. But at the beginning they had been told that a new girl was arriving from India, that she would feel strange and homesick without her mother for the first time, so naturally they were nice to me.

The very next morning I had a letter from Mother, and it was one of those letters you never forget. *I am thinking of you*, she wrote, *and I am sending you this black cat brooch for luck*. I still have it.

Nilgala was an unusual school, I suppose. It was small and individual. We did not wear uniform. We never walked in croc. No great attention was paid to games. Those of us who were keen to play well had to struggle along untaught as best we could, losing every match to bigger and better-coached schools. I daresay it was very good for us. I still remember the only few matches we ever won the whole five years I was there, and how I lay in bed rigid with excitement, re-living every stroke. Games were not considered so important as writing stories and plays and producing them, and painting pictures and playing the piano well and learning ballet and design and all those things.

Nilgala stood on a hill, with the lawn at such a slope that when we played croquet on it we had to have a rule that you could stop your ball at the top of its trajectory, before it began to roll downhill again.

But let me hasten to add that croquet was not our idea of fun and games. The belles of St. Trinians preferred Red Indians and Scalping. Most of us had plaits in those days, and when we were fighting, a good old pull on a plait was most effective.

One very cold night my neighbour's eiderdown slipped off her bed onto the floor between us. Thinking I had stolen it, she leant over and, as she thought, drew it back again. I saw the theft of my eiderdown. I felt it too, for it left me freezing. I rose immediately and gave her one of the best. Her nose bled for an hour.

THIRTY-ONE

Nilgala

Nilgala was attractively placed. All around us lay the rich red Devon earth that grows the grass that fattens the cows to give that world-famous cream. You can scald cream anywhere in the world, and it's still not Devonshire cream. In Bideford market, the country women would come in and sit down with their things for sale—beetroot and apples and a clutch of turkey eggs, perhaps, and a wallop of cream in a great brown earthenware farmhouse dish, piled up high like a loaf of bread.

And all this red land with its high banks that hunters jump in a special way, and its beech hedges and evergreens, its meadows and mushrooms and cows, was interlaced with those deep Devonshire lanes. I have walked miles and miles in them, with earth and tree-roots each side. We played games only twice a week, and on the other days we went for walks.

During the time the heavy teasing was going on, I walked alone. Apparently I was different from the others. I used long words which I had got from books, not people. "Your eyes are always dreaming, miles away," they said. "Wake *up!*"

There was this and more. But everyone has to learn to be teased—your stamp collection snatched away and thrown out into the rain, your book slammed shut, your plaits pulled—and I soon learned to take it, and it passed. At the end of my sons' first terms at school, I said to each of them "Remember what it feels like to be a new boy, and always be nice to new boys yourself." One of them replied "I was only homesick once, and then one of the prefects took me to Mrs. Vass's room. I'm working up to be a prefect, Mum, and when I'm a prefect I'll be the kind of prefect who takes homesick new boys to Mrs. Vass's room."

But now at Nilgala the girls walked with me. They walked each side of me, and there was competition to be there, to listen to my stories. This was most excellent practice for any story-teller. I had an appreciative but critical audience always to hand. I had to invent and tell a good tale, making it up as I went along. When we are grown-up it is not easy always to find an audience for our work. We can write and write, and it may all be wasted. We are denied that absolutely elemental thing, audience reaction, from which one learns things which can be learned in no other way.

The girls listened to my stories. They wanted plays from me which they could act. The editor of the school magazine *The Golden Goblet* asked me for a contribution. This was a step forward. It was the first time I had contributed to a magazine of which I was not myself the editor. I think I gave her a poem.

Now the walks instead of games did not seem so bad after all. I grew to love the scented lanes, all scrambled over with honeysuckle and wild rose, and the carmine earth. There were still wild creatures for me. Much smaller, and mostly birds, but still wild. In the hedges high above us nested whitethroats and finches, the whitethroat nests so thin you could see through them. Deep in the thorny cushions of furze in the sweet thick yellow-honey smell of gorse, nested goldfinches. On rock ledges over the ocean, where sea-pinks strained in the wind, were the eggs of gulls and terns. Rare birds inhabited this coast of rock and whin, of sand dunes and woods and great hedges and wind-bent trees.

There were new names to be learned, of trees and flowers. Thousands of wild flowers. Wild strawberries, too. Fuchsias hung from above grey stone walls over the roads. In the spring, in cups of pale sunlight, warm early after a mild Devon winter, the first primroses opened. Daffodils grew wild.

Sometimes we walked to Westward Ho, where there was a big dead building with glassy grey windows, and nobody inside—the United Services College. Killed, so they said, by Rudyard Kipling's book *Stalky and Co.*

At Westward Ho there was the Pebble Ridge, between the famous golf course and the Atlantic. There was a stretch of sand for gallops, the mouths of the Taw and the Torridge and, away in the mist, Lundy Island. If you could see Lundy it would be fine. If not, wet.

It was always for me only a smudge on the horizon, but I planned to go there one day, because of the millions of sea birds that nest there, guillemots specially. Their eggs fascinated me, so big, and all dashed with marks and wriggles; and tapered one end, so that when they roll, they revolve around their pointed end instead of tumbling off the sea-ledges onto rocks hundreds of feet below. There were puffins on Lundy too, nesting in rabbit-burrows. We saw them flying level over the jumbled waves, sometimes, their great striped beaks crammed full of sand-eels.

Sand-eels were to be seen too, stranded in the bigger rock pools by the tide. But we never caught one. They were too fast, like a dart of electricity. The pools had shrimps in them, though, quite transparent to match the pools they lived in, which looked solid as glass until they gave a shiver in the wind. You could touch a finger to the rose petals of anemone in these pools, and feel them close on your flesh and not want to let go.

At Westward Ho we bathed, but not in the sea. Miss Ethel and Miss Ada were responsible for us and too nervous to let us do that. Who can blame them? We bathed in an artificial rock pool, probably still there, and in this pool I accomplished an ambition; I learned to swim. All the time in the jungle, among the deep rivers and the big pools where I might have become a fish, we were not allowed to bathe. The danger from crocodiles, strong currents, pythons, fever, typhoid, and the rest were too great. At twelve I still could not swim.

We walked down to this rock pool and undressed in the row of bathing huts. I don't know what they're like now, but in those days they were individualists. The best was Jonah, an old carriage. In these huts we arrayed ourselves in our navy-blue cotton-stockingette swim suits, and stuffed our long hair into bulging gathered caps of reddish rubber. We looked terrible. Some of the girls put on gym shoes to go down over the rough rocks, but my feet were hard. I ran.

The pool was shallow. There was nowhere where you could jump in and just *have* to swim or drown, and thus learn how to do it. So I had to use my imagination. I told myself it was deep, and I smacked in from a rock at the deepest part and struck out. Suddenly, between one second and the next, I knew how to swim.

It was a pity no one taught us. We had to teach ourselves, and the result was that our styles were unorthodox, and consequently not very good. We might keep afloat, but we would never win races. The girls who had lived in China, though, and bathed from hot beaches all day long in warm water, were all excellent swimmers.

Still, we had fun. Inventing sidestroke and crawl for ourselves, me confident I was fast and splendid when really I looked like a turtle. Floating, trying hard to keep my feet up, and feeling the water trickling into my cap at the back and soaking my wretched plaits. Then coming out, blue and shivering, but trying not to let Miss Syrett hear my teeth or she'd know I'd been in too long and must come out sooner next time. She timed us all, and some—the ones who went blue easily—had to come out sooner than others.

After bathing, we all went along to a beach kiosk to buy twopenny packets of biscuits and eat them as we walked home.

It was either in Westward Ho or Bideford that I went into a sweet shop for the first time in my life, never having been allowed to buy those dusty flyblown sweets in the Hardwar and Lansdowne bazaars. But here they kept their edible jewels in glass jars. You could buy hundreds-and-thousands, all running about and all colours, poured into a cone-shaped paper bag. You could buy satin cushions and marshmallows and fondants, of which the mauve ones always had a special taste. Turkish Delight: I used to wonder what happened to all the loose sugar left behind in the box out of which we bought it by the ounce. I presumed the shopkeeper ate it. We all pretended to dislike liquorice—ugh! So much so that I never even tasted it once. There was marzipan. There were jars of barley sugar. Each jar had a coupon on the bottom with a letter on it. When you had collected the right letters to spell the name of the barley sugar with these coupons, you could send them in and get a free jar. Try as one might, it was impossible to see from the outside, before buying it, what the letter on the folded coupon was. Sweet-buying was always a bit of an orgy, because we all handed our purchases around to everyone as we walked home.

We had midnight feasts too, of course, generally about ten

o'clock because we couldn't keep awake any longer. I regret to say I was always able to eat my whole share as well as what the others were leaving because they'd had enough.

It was not difficult in a school of only forty to fifty girls, many of them little ones, to get into all the teams. Maybe this helped me to enjoy my time at school so much. Once I'd learned how to behave myself, all my dreams came true, and I loved every minute of it.

When I first went there, I was naturally put in the lowest class, because I'd never been to school before and could be expected to know nothing. But I'd had the good fortune, in spite of living in the jungle, to receive top-quality intensive tuition from my mother and governesses, who'd had only two children to teach at a time, not ten or twenty. Also Father had always read and corrected my stories; and I had read voraciously. The only thing they had not taught me was French. During my first term at Nilgala there was a prize offered for French, to be competed for by the whole school. It was for the girl who had made the most progress in French during the term. As I began by not knowing one single word, it was easy to be the one to make the most progress, so I went home after six weeks with a move and a prize, very full of myself, I'm afraid, and absolutely delighted with school.

The favourite books for prizes at Nilgala were, of course, *Lorna Doone* and *Westward Ho!* because they were famous stories about Devonshire. I won them both in time. I'm afraid I liked lessons. It is a terrible confession to make, and I'd never have dared make it at the time, but now I feel brave enough to do so.

A wave of literary enthusiasm went over the school. Everyone was writing novels and poems, sketches for our shows, and whole plays. My plays were now all about Rajahs and treasure. I erred with the gods: like Shakespeare, I did not hesitate over scenery. An encounter in the jungle might last a bare two minutes, but I expected whole trees for it. I did not pause over caves of jewels nor love scenes. Everything went in. Like Shakespeare, too, I expected to act in my own plays, but unlike him I demanded a lead. What I wanted was to play the heroine with my hair loose and some red make-up on my mouth. The best I ever was given was the hero, when the hair had to be hidden and I was not expected to beautify myself. It was a blow. Especially when they chose a very pretty but very tall girl as heroine. When I gazed up at her and spoke my own love-lines—"Bless you, little woman"— there were one or two snorts from the audience, I am sorry to say. When the lovers hid in the wood, there was but one laurel bush where they could hide, but the villain stamped about the stage shouting, "Where can they be? Where can they be?" Then there was the Rajah who crouched behind the piano and thus overheard a plot about his jewels. As she hid there, the Rajah leant her whole arm heavily on several octaves. The plotters played on like troupers, hearing nothing.

THIRTY-TWO

The Parting

Very soon after I began school, it came time for my parents and the baby brother Peter to return to India. Father's leave was up, and it would be at least two more years before he retired from the Forest Service. When my mother saw me off on the school train at Waterloo that time, she knew that it was goodbye for years. For her also, as for all other mothers from India in those days, before the era of air travel, this was goodbye for ever to the small child she had known. When we met again, I would be a different person.

I did not know this. For me it was just the beginning of another term, and I was looking forward to it.

I got into the carriage, and began chattering to my friends. When I looked at Mother, I saw to my amazement that there were tears in her eyes.

Suddenly she walked away. When she came back she'd got a box of chocolates for me. Her eyes were dry.

The train pulled out.

I did not see Mother again for two years.

After a while it dawned on me that she was very far away. My heart began to ache.

While the parents were abroad, Harry and I spent our holidays in Bedford, partly with Aunt Jessie, partly in another house where they catered to children like us, whose parents were in India. Harry was at school at Temple Grove in Eastbourne, the prep school where my father had been, and he found Father's name there too, carved on a desk.

Harry and I met for holidays. Sometimes, if we both broke up on the same day, he met my train at Waterloo and escorted me across London to our Bedford train.

I never could understand why he was allowed on the railway alone and I was not. I was more than two years older than he was, yet I must never speak to strangers, I must never travel alone. Why ever not? All the world was kind and good.

Every week we had letters from India, and often photos, too. Father was transferred from the Lansdowne division to Kumaon, of man-eater fame. Their hill station was not Lansdowne any more, but Naini Tal. Mother described it all to us with photos and letters. She had to tell us, too, that Father had had to shoot Squinch after that accident.

We had one or two letters also from Gwala Ram—Pundit Gwala Ram Bahadur, the wise, the brave. I valued these highly. I knew that, in order to send me a letter, he had to go to a professional letter-writer in the bazaar and dictate his letter and pay for it, too, out of his small wages. I wish I could tell him again now how much his letters meant to me, and that I never threw them away.

My own letters to the parents became longer and longer, and more and more boring. In the fever of literary enthusiasm at Nilgala, we all saw ourselves as famous authors of the future, and admired anyone who could write twelve and fourteen pages home. Father gave up the struggle with my letters, but Mother always toiled through them, all fourteen pages, I believe.

Her own to me were thrilling, every line packed with news

and interest. I sent them my stories for Father to correct and criticise. How much an Indian stamp on a grey envelope meant to Harry and me then. I kept the letters in my pocket and read them again and again.

Now we realised what the Indian parting meant. Up to now we had lived always with our own father and mother, a single unit, a family, surrounded by love and strict rules of behaviour, and by the unique light of home. Now things were different. Although Aunt Jessie treated us always with kindness and affection, and bore cheerfully this burden of children again on her hands, something was not there. All children from India, now grown up, will know exactly what I mean. I think I know, partly, what it must be like to be an orphan or the child of a broken home.

Nowadays, with air travel, parents living abroad do often have their children visit them for the holidays. This was impossible for us. It would have been impossible anyway, because of the expense. My parents were facing the heavy duty of three children to educate. Although Father had inherited Auberies, there was little enough to go with it. He was the eldest son, but he was one of ten children. Death often wrecks an estate. What with war, death duties, taxes, and division of money, the stately homes were now beginning their slide into ruin. The era of the great estates was already over, and repairs beginning to accumulate in the great houses. But even among the many difficulties which beset my parents, Father now began insurance schemes for his children, and paid them as well as school fees, he and Mother denying themselves much in order to do so.

But now Harry and I realised what had happened to us. Not only everyone in India, but the parents, too, were thousands of miles away. Peter too. We had no idea when we should see them again. There was a great aching gap, and we did not know when it was coming to an end. Most of the time we had plenty to occupy us, and anyway it was no use brooding. We were happy, too. But sometimes it would come on you suddenly at night, and you had to turn your face so no one heard you, and the tears ran into the pillow which soaked them up. After a bit, the accumulated ache was washed out of you, you turned the pillow over, and went to sleep, and weren't so feeble again for a long time.

I was puzzled by what one old lady said of us to another one. They were unmarried, they had never had children, nor been asked to part from them. I knew my parents could not afford luxuries, and yet I heard this old lady say "The Burkes must be very rich. Mrs. Burke says that while she is away in India, Harry and Norah must want for nothing. If they are ill, they are to have the best doctors and the best of everything that money can buy."

I was much comforted by this. The parents were still *there*, however far away, and looking after us still.

While they were still away, I had measles, and rather badly. Poor Aunt Jessie—I had it in her house. She was getting old by then, and to have an irritable young patient lying in the dark in one of the top rooms and always wanting something, must have been a great burden. There was no radio. I was not allowed to read for fear of damaging my eyes. I lay in the dark, feeling ill, with nothing to do. I must have been a frightful nuisance in that house of old ladies, with all the steep stairs and trays and things.

Finally they got a nurse for me. Miss Everitt had the patience of Job. One day she gave me all clean sheets, and when she had done, she put a little iridescent bowl of violets on the table beside me. "Now, don't upset that," she said.

What pretty colours moved in the green opal glass. I picked it up to look at them. I tilted it to make the colours run. . . .

Miss Everitt came back and changed the sheets again without a word of scolding. It was a lesson in patience and goodness which I have never forgotten, but which I have also never learnt.

Presently Miss Everitt left to marry one of her patients, also called Everett. She just had to learn to spell her name differently.

Meanwhile I was getting better, and was allowed downstairs. All day long I wrote stories. The sight of this pale sniffly girl, forever bent over an exercise book, got on the old ladies' nerves.

"That child mustn't be allowed to write so much," snapped one of them.

I gave her a look of pure poison. It was the last straw. If I got on their nerves, so did they on mine. All feelings of gratitude, alas, vanished. All day long, criticised and corrected by old ladies—*picked* at, never let alone. Do this. Do that. Sit up. Don't sniff. And now sent for deadly walks instead of writing. I got to hate all old ladies. It was shameful of me, but I did, and now I am fast becoming one myself. Please Heaven, I'll try and remember not to. . .

But the family assures me that, no matter what resolutions I make, I shall be both eccentric and troublesome.

Measles left me very deaf. I returned to school still unable to hear. For half a term it never occurred to anyone to take this deaf child to a doctor. I remember even one of the mistresses jeering at me because I couldn't hear her. But at last I was taken. Fortunately the damage was not yet irreparable. I got back the hearing in one ear. The other remains very deaf. This, however, has its advantages, like Nelson's blind eye. I need not hear things I don't want to. Also, although I contemplate with regret all the sweet asides I must have missed because they were whispered into the wrong ear, I am able to lie on my good ear and turn the deaf one up to any noise when I want to sleep. How many times, though, must some dashing suggestion have been met with nothing but a dull stare from me. Perhaps I've had some narrow squeaks in my time? I can only hope so.

Had the parents been at home, I should naturally not have been left deaf and unattended for so long. They were still in India. The months went on and on.

But the time must pass. That simple thought has got me through many a sticky patch. However bad this is, there will come a time when it is over.

The parents were coming home!

I swallowed and blinked when I got the news. They were coming home. Mother and Peter first. Then, later, Father.

Harry got his letter just before class at school. It was from Father, and the twelve-year-old boy had only time to read "Mum and Peter are coming home. . . ." when the master rapped out "Come along now. You can read your letters later. No, Burke, you may not just read to the end of the page."

Harry put the letter in his pocket. You can imagine just how much attention he paid to that lesson.

But now Mother and Peter were coming home—*were home!*

Mother met my train.

I walked towards her.

"Hullo, Mum," I said.

We returned first to Bedford where Mother had taken rooms, and we got there in the evening. I was longing to see my baby brother again too, but for one moment there was no one I knew in the room.

A little boy of four was running about in his dressing gown. It couldn't be—? It *was!*

"*Peter!*"

He gave me the most delightful smile. "Look," he said shyly, "if I throw this ball up, it comes down again."

Suddenly he hugged me.

I laughed and laughed.

We were to travel to Auberies and wait there for Father to join us. Now we were going to live at Auberies, all of us together again as before. Times having changed since my grandparents' day, there was as I say very little money to meet the needs of a big estate; but naturally the eldest son, on whom the lot had fallen, would do his duty to the family, his ancestors, and our home. In spite of the difficulties, he would try to keep it going.

We travelled to Sudbury in Suffolk, the town of Gainsborough. The great painter walked these streets. These landscapes were the background to his portraits. In the big houses of Suffolk and Essex glow his paintings, part of our national treasure. Robert Andrews and his wife posed for him under that oak tree in Auberies park.

This slow river, the Stour, green and golden with waterweed, the haunt of moorhen, easily flooding its low meadows in winter, and wisped with fog; but set about with the silver-green of willow and the long brush-strokes of lombardy poplar—this river where gentle cows drink and the heron fishes, flows down from Sudbury into Constable's country. In its tranquil waters are reflected the bridge at Flatford, Willie Lott's cottage and, once, a haywain.

Within the Stour valley, close to Sudbury and Auberies, lies the hamlet of Borley, and in Borley at that time stood a big but unremarkable house, the Rectory. It was a great old-fashioned cold and difficult place, like Auberies itself, with nothing specially to distinguish it. It was a happy home. Pleasant tennis parties took place on its charming lawns. I have played tennis there. I have danced in it. We did not know that it would presently become world-famous as the most haunted house in England, or that all the nice people we knew there would be part of its strange history.

From Sudbury station, that first day, we drove up to Auberies in a hired cab. *Cloppety-clop* went the horse's hooves

as he trotted cheerfully through Sudbury streets, and then
clop, clop as he walked slowly up Ballingdon Hill.

At the top of Ballingdon Hill, almost out of sight among its
trees and park, stood Auberies, the great shabby old loved
house, now to be our home. Dead since Grandfather died—
all its many rooms and passages cold with height and disuse,
now to come alive again.

Here we'd get to know each other, make the perhaps difficult adjustments that must follow long separation. Here we
were to become a family again, and build the invisible but
concrete walls of home.

THIRTY-THREE

Auberies

I remembered Auberies from an earlier visit, as a child of four, when my grandparents were alive, but what I remembered was a different house.

Then it had been full of people—family and staff and guests. There was always something going on. I remembered the school treats given by my grandparents for the children of Bulmer School, and much enjoyed by everyone, grandparents included. Boys and girls ran screaming on the lawns, as we did also in our time. At tea they did not choose jam, because they got that at home, nor even cake, but bread-and-butter by itself as a treat. During the afternoon Gran-Gran distributed presents, one to each child, and a bag of sweets. The presents were laid on trays at the long windows of the dining room, which opened on to the terrace; and the children came forward, one by one, to choose what they'd have. All the shut-knives, as they called them, were removed before the smaller boys came up to make their choice. I think this showed the same charming good sense as prompted one lady I knew in her gift of wedding presents to her maids.

261

She gave wonderful presents, but not until nine months after the marriage and no baby.

At four and two, Harry and I had been in England on a visit from India, and we had been trainbearers to my Aunt Evelyn when she got married from Auberies. What an unforgettable wedding that was, the bride so lovely and all the guests too. It was the time of very large hats. I saw one lady put her head right on one side in order to get a huge brim in through the carriage door. My mother's hat was gigantic, pale blue, and round it lay coiled a single great perfect pale-blue ostrich feather. With her black hair, she was quite ravishing.

Yes, that was a different Auberies from the one to which we now came. My Aunt Audrey tells me that her earliest recollection of the house is of the footmen chasing the housemaids round the kitchen table. She, who has known Auberies in the time of her father, her brother and her nephew, says that it has been like living in three incarnations.

For me too, my own earliest recollection of the house is also of one of the footmen. He used to vault the gate in the nursery passage for us, and twirl a chair round by its leg balanced on the point of his finger. The lesser members of the staff were often young and giddy and not so many years older than the children of the family who loved and admired them so much.

But now as we drove up to Auberies, and in through the gates with the Burke cat in stone on top, each side; and down the half-mile drive and the elm avenue and the laurels and ornamental shrubs and trees, a new era was opening.

The house had stood unused for several years, and there had been a war. Such things damage a place. Even the Kaiser's war, without bombs to shake the plaster, or an army to occupy half the house as in Hitler's time—even that war helped to take the polish off the house and grounds. As I say, a death always changes an estate. All the arteries of organisation and income are cut. There are death duties to be paid, the will divides the money. Everything is pulled apart, and something new has to be built up in its place.

Auberies is not yet a really old family seat, it has belonged to the Burkes now for only about 125 years, but these things take time to put together, and we were part of it. When we came to Auberies, my parents did not know if they could carry on, but they meant to try.

The task was a heavy one. The house had been built to accommodate a great many people. Sixty to be fed was not unknown. A family could be expected to number ten or twelve at the very least, and the staff about the same. All these people needed bedrooms and living rooms. There had to be guest rooms and reception rooms, and rooms for the nursery and schoolroom hierarchies, to say nothing of housekeeper's room and sewing room and gun room and study and pantries and larders and dairy and laundry and all the rest. But all this great long house with all these rooms had, as I've said, *no modern conveniences of any kind.* There was no proper bathroom, no piped water. The place was lit by oil lamps. Cooking was done on a kitchen range lit afresh each day with sticks and paper, and fed by coal. On January mornings you could sometimes actually smell frost inside the house.

In some earlier epoch, there had been an attempt to heat the place by a hot-air system, and the grids are still there. It had also at one time been lit by gaslight, but this had apparently not been a success. Up at the Home Farm was the old gas-yard, where the private gas plant, complete with gasometer, used to manufacture the stuff for the house. But it had fallen into disuse, and the place was now a crop of nettles where people threw things they didn't know how to get rid of, like old bike tyres and paintpots half full of stone-hard paint. Through all the rubbish and nettles went well-worn rat-runs. In the house, some of the bedrooms still had jointed

gas-fittings each side of the mantelpiece; and there were
boxes and boxes of mantles and glass gas-shades that nobody
quite liked to throw away.

But now, wherever heat was wanted in these acres of
house, you lit a coal fire. When hot water was wanted, you
carried it in brass cans. When light was wanted, you went to
the lamp room, and you could smell from outside with the
door shut that this was where the lamps and paraffin were
kept. Inside, the table was saturated with the oil of years,
there were special-shaped scissors for trimming wicks, and
lots of oily rag. You chose a lamp which had been previously
filled and polished and trimmed, and of which the chimney
had been either blown on and rubbed up, or washed, and
very thoroughly dried or it would crack when lit. You lit it,
not turning up the flame too much at first, and keeping an
eye on it all the time, so it didn't smoke and smell and black
the place out. Then you carried this lamp to the place where
you wanted a light. The illumination was poor, and if there
was a window open, there'd be moths banging round the
chimney all the evening. Sometimes the ting of a cracked
chimney too, and sometimes the smell of oily black smoke.
Filling, wiping, polishing—all had to be done for each lamp
every day.

In the time of large leisured staffs, with plenty of hands to
do everything at their own pace, all this hardly mattered. It
made employment, there was no rush or overwork, and everyone ambled along in unplanned peace.

But now, with very little money and only a skeleton staff,
the parents had got to try and keep up a place which had
been made for quite other circumstances. They began by
putting in an electric-light plant and a bath, not only to make
the house habitable but to cut the work. Water still came—
and still does—from the well in the courtyard; but now, instead of this being got up by a yoked pony going round and

round, in the ancient way, a small engine was installed, chugging away manfully every day. The circle of special non-slip bricks for the pony's feet, however, remained in the courtyard until yet another era began at Auberies, thirty years later.

But all these things had not yet been done when we drove up to begin our life there in 1921.

A green woodpecker flew, laughing, from the lawn of the deserted house. The place was cold and shabby. Repairs had accumulated. It seemed as if every room wanted doing up at the same moment, but had to wait its turn.

The repairs got done bit by bit—most of them, anyway—but it was no use looking at the twelve-foot-tall windows of drawing room, dining room, library, and billiard room and noticing that the sun had split the curtains, top to toe, and yellowed the chintz, and changed the crimson velvet to brown, the emerald velvet to a lovely old faded green that you can never get in any other way. Re-curtaining of these rooms alone would cost several hundred pounds. It was no use pudging the dead billiard cushions and wishing the table could be recushioned and re-covered. It must wait.

Big hard old-fashioned furniture filled the large cold rooms. Only bit by bit could it be done up or replaced. Much of it was Victorian, then despised, but now sought.

"We're too near to the Victorian age to admire these things," said Father. "They're hideous. Look at them. But in years to come they'll turn into antiques and be worth a lot."

Whether things were ugly or beautiful did not bother him in the least, so long as they served their purpose. Usefulness and efficiency were everything to him. He saw nothing odd in keeping a little bedside butterfly net with which to deal with any mosquito that might trouble him in the night.

There were good things in Auberies, as well as rubbish. In the kitchen were solid old implements that had mashed potatoes and whipped eggs for three and four generations of the family instead of bending or melting away at the first touch. There were Victorian four-poster beds in the best bedrooms, with linen sheets measuring twelve feet by ten to cover them. In some of the other rooms were iron bedsteads with brass knobs that unscrewed and got lost, and no springs but only things like metal rulers hooked across. Even a straw palliasse or two!

But to Harry and me—as indeed to all other children before and after—Auberies was a heavenly place. We never found his boat or my squeaking cushion, which we had remembered all the time we were in India, they were gone, but other joys crowded to take their place.

There were several staircases to tear up and down and play catch on, and squeal when you sighted danger and leaped away from it down ten echoing steps in one jump. There were staircases that led to nowhere in this house of many alterations, and you could leave one person to tap the wall while the other went round miles to listen in other rooms for the tapping, and then both be astonished to find where that staircase once used to lead. There were dozens of unused rooms holding boxes and cupboards in which you might find anything from an ostrich egg to an old evening dress and train, and the Prince of Wales's feathers under which some bediamonded beauty had made her curtsey to the Throne. There were swords, and cockades of white cock plumes. There was an opera hat, flat as a pancake, and it jumped out at us when we touched it. There were egg collections and fossils, and all sorts of peculiar things used by invalids. Trunks with dead peoples' names on them.

In the stables where the carriages used to stand was Gran-Gran's Fiat, waiting to be sold. It was a beauty. A great deal more magnificent than the upright bath-chair kind of car in which I had travelled, in India. We never went in it, but we played in it. Harry was chauffeur, and I sat at the back like a lady, and gave orders through the speaking tube.

Also in the stables, in a loose box, was a real bath chair. Two generations ago there had been a pale beautiful invalid to be wheeled about the lawns and under the cedars, wrapped in her dark-blue-and-green tartan rug.

The billiard table was so far gone we raced our white mice on it. Underneath, the parents spread one of their tiger skins. They had brought home all their shikar trophies from India, but this was the only one they ever put out. Suddenly, somehow, the trophies seemed wrong. This English country house was not the place for barbarism. Years later, another little girl, Marilyn Burke, looked at that tiger skin and asked "Do they always go about flat?"

All the house held reminders of those who had gone before. I had been named for an aunt of mine, another Norah Burke, so when I took a billiard chalk and crawled under the table to write my name on the slate slabs above me, I was much surprised to find it already there.

Above the sink in the butler's pantry were places for six or eight decanters to hang upside down and drain, after those terrific dinner parties. Heaps of glass stoppers too, left from decanters that had got broken by the hasty young fingers of pantry boys, no doubt. Each one of those stoppers had probably heard a sharp reprimand from the butler, who'd had to enter it in his list of breakages.

The very top rooms of the house, the tent rooms, had not been repapered for a great many years. Among the roses and vines of the old wallpaper there still climbed dozens of little figures and caricatures exquisitely drawn on the paper itself and coloured with water colour by an artist great-uncle when this had been his boyhood bedroom, more than half a century ago.

We, too—we added to the house the print of our lives and

personalities: a penknife, a painting, a letter, a list. When the house was being cleared recently, prior to being partly pulled down and turned into a smaller, more easily run home for these modern times by my brother Pete when he inherited it, I found *Reading Without Tears,* and on the fly-leaf, *Norah from Mummy 1911, hoping she will learn to read without tears.*

At one time, a cousin of mine was agent at Chatsworth, the famous Derbyshire seat of the Dukes of Devonshire. Later, Auberies and Chatsworth slid together in my mind, and came into focus as the fictional house of Hazelwood, in my novel of that name. The decline and fall of the stately homes of England has been as majestic as the fall of Rome.

There was no end to the delights of the large neglected house for Harry and me. It did not matter in the slightest to us if colour were chipped or a hand-painted ceiling stained because snow had piled up above the lead coping on the roof and then melted while the house was empty and no one here to send a man up to shovel it off. It did not matter to us that the whole place was cold as ice, that you could never change the pictures because each had a dark square under it where you could see what the colour of the wallpaper had once been.

There was all the house to explore, from the complicated roof where you could walk about among the slates and lead and odd water tanks and chimneys, to the cellars where frogs hopped and champagne bottles lay in a lace of cobweb.

There were miles of lawn to run on, and dark exciting shrubberies, and those great cedar trees scenting the air and full of secrets. Red squirrels still ran on the dark sweeping branches, from one tree to the next.

Down through woods and evergreens went the path to the lake. A cobbled gutter had once taken off the rainwater from this path, but now the gravel was so much worn down that the gutter stood up higher than the path. At the lake were boat and boathouse, as well as a folly called The Temple in which pigeons had, over the years, collected a mountain of sticks in the top storey. If you climbed up to it—and this had to be on a rope—you could always find white eggs there, in twos, on the pile of smelly sticks.

The boathouse is burrowed into the hillside that meets the lake. We opened the ivy fringe that curtained it, and there was the boat on black glass inside, the oars shipped along walls of brick that were already parted by roots. You could hear the dribble of the spring that feeds the lake and that enters it here at the back of the boathouse, behind cobweb.

At the lake we could bathe, pull up weeds, boat, fish, collect blackberries from the boat, or go skating, according to season.

Blackberries hung in rich black folds of material over the water. You can fill a basket in no time, even if you eat as well; and the fruit is fat and ripe, so of course we kept on popping the sweet, seedy berries into our mouths. Drunken wasps clung to them, and stung us sometimes, or fell off into the water, too full to care. There were bluebottles coloured like witch-balls, millions of them, eating the overripe parts of the berries, so we had to be careful which we picked, choosing only whole ones.

Moorhens and coots nest at the lake, and sometimes a podge of waterweed is really a dabchick nest, with the eggs hot inside the rotting weed. Part of an old duck decoy still lies at the other end of the lake from the boathouse. It's a brick tunnel, one or two hundred years old, I daresay, and not used within living memory, but wild mallard still drop down out of winter skies to feed on this water, which was made on purpose to be attractive to ducks. The lake is visited also by kingfisher and otter and heron. Once, when it was cleaned out, sixty or seventy years ago, they caught a five-foot eel in it.

Now Harry and I caught rudd and perch, instead of trout and mahseer. They are either so muddy or so full of bones that they are really uneatable, although they look so glorious when first you pull them out, all throbbing with rainbows, but of course we always had them for breakfast next day, because it's so important to eat what you catch, isn't it?

Weeding was fun. You rowed into a good patch of weed, and stuck the oar in and twisted it round like a fork in spaghetti, then heaved out the result. It came up sizzling, full of water snails and leeches and things, and smelling of pond. It was frightfully heavy, we let it drain and dumped it in the boat. When the boat was full we transferred the weed to the shore, where it lay and rotted, and stunk to high heaven too. Sometimes we did our weeding in bathing suits, and then the bubbles from the disturbed mud ran up our legs like spiders and burst round us, and we could smell the gases that form in mud made of dead weed and dead conkers and leaves. When we swam in the clear water, we had to be careful not to get a mouthful. It tasted soft as rain water, and clean too, but of course it was full of Heaven knows what.

From the boat, Harry lost his best penknife, with all its gadgets, when we were weeding. We dredged and dredged but never found it. And what is a replacement compared with the favourite that is gone?

"I droped my knife in the lake," he wrote to Father, still in India. "It is lost. These sploges that you see are not sploges. Tha are tears."

Mother had brought us three children to Auberies before Father came home from India. She was to blaze the trail into the great cold dead house, try to get it going, and to begin the chicken farm by which they hoped to make enough money to keep Auberies alive. She used to get up at six each morning to do the chickens. It was a hard and rough beginning, but in the years to come she built up a big industry, covering many acres, employing a large expert staff, and raising hundreds of thousands of birds.

There were other tasks for her too. That was still the time of formal afternoon calls. The Fiat was not licensed, it was not ours, and anyway at that time Mother could not yet drive a car, so though she had no conveyance but a bicycle, she was obliged—strictly at the correct time—to return the calls of those people who in their turn had been obliged to call on her, whether they wanted to do so or not. As a first call must take place only between three and three-thirty in the afternoon, my poor mother bicycled miles and miles every day, since she could not do more than one or two calls at a time, and it would be rude not to return a call within the prescribed time.

Although this was 1921, there were still people who used carriages. My great-aunt Alice, then living at the dower house in Bulmer, used to drive up sometimes in her open landau to make an afternoon call. She was completely out of a bygone era. She wore skirts to the ground, and waited for the man to take the carriage rug off her knees before she got out.

So though Mother was so busy in the house and on the chicken farm, and began her day in gum boots, she had to be ready in the afternoon for these calls.

Still, she was never too busy for us, and Harry and I got to know her and our small brother again during this early time at Auberies. Soon it seemed as if we had never been parted.

THIRTY-FOUR

Father Begins His Reign

Now Father was coming home, too.

We counted the days. Excitement knew no bounds. Harry and I were on the terrace of Auberies when we heard the sound of carriage wheels on the gravel of the drive. We stopped dead and looked at each other. *Father?*

We dropped everything and raced round the house, slowing up at the end, suddenly shy.

Yes, there he was on the front doorstep, paying the driver of the hired cab which had brought him up from the station.

"Hullo, Dad."

"Good gracious, how you've grown!"

We all walked into Auberies together, the master of Auberies and his children at the beginning of his reign. It was thirty years later before he left it for ever by this same door.

As bricks absorb heat, so an old house draws into its walls the essence of things that have happened there. How much must have happened on these front steps of Auberies—brides ducking through rice, sons going off to the war, the old lord carried out. Silk and jewels, trunks, campaign kit, orange blossom, crêpe—all have passed in and out of this door. That's

272

why old houses mean so much more than new ones. In this room I dressed for my wedding. In this, I saw my father for the last time. Up these steps I carried my first-born son, in a shawl twinkling with snow-flakes, on his first visit to the home of his fathers.

When Gran-Gran, a tiny old lady of eighty, still brilliantly alive, paused by the gate into the park, and gazed down across green rolling pasture to the limes and the Gainsborough Oak and the lake, what was she seeing?

Gran-Gran lived to watch her great grandchildren at Auberies—to be four generations under one roof during Hitler's war.

But now Father was home, we could make real plans again. First we thought we'd use just a corner of the big house and shut up the rest. But then another idea came. There was plenty of room, so why not give a home to children of friends still in India? Many such boys and girls had nowhere to go for their holidays.

It was heavy work for Mother, added responsibility for Father, but great fun for all of us. The child population of Auberies in the school holidays was now anything up to fourteen, all boys except me, though once, for a while, there was one other girl. How lucky I was. It was like having ten or twelve brothers, and almost all of them from India, as we were. Peter was the baby by several years, but he would carry things into the house and give them to people, such as a sprig of holly to the cook for the Christmas pudding. Dusting off his hands, he would observe, "The children might like it," and go his way.

There was space for our energies and adventures. We bicycled everywhere, ripping down Ballingdon Hill to Sudbury with the wind freezing our ears, and then toiling back up again. We even biked from one fruit tree to the next in the big walled garden with its little clipped box hedges and its nectarines and golden plums. There was always a blackbird caught in the fruit nets to be let out, and fallen apples to be picked up—but taking care there were no wasps inside—and fed to pigs. We went sugaring for moths, and trapping moles and ratting up the farmyard.

We were paid a penny for each rat we killed, and we had our own ratting sticks, with our initials on them. Mine was hazel, curled over in the proper way, like a hockey stick, and well-seasoned. There was a loop of string to attach the straight end to my wrist, and I spent hours making sure I'd got the stick the exact right length. Every rat I killed, I cut a notch in the handle till I'd almost chipped the stick away.

Up the farmyard, mud glistened in the moonlight, and you could see the rat-runs going along through it and around the edges of sheds and manure heaps. We tiptoed in gym shoes, not caring how dirty we got, and listened outside the pig-meal house. Inside, there'd be the exciting squeal and slither of rats. Some of us took up positions at the various exits, and then one of us rushed in with a torch and a hullaba-loo, so all the rats fled, and some got killed on the way.

We were terribly bloodthirsty. On threshing days we'd be at the stack with our sticks all day. Each rat still rated a penny, each mouse a farthing, so if it was an old stack, there was real money to be made. As the sheaves were spiked on the prongs of hayforks well-polished by work, and the man dug in twice to get a good grip and lifted the sheaf and tossed it into the thresher, mice might fly out in all directions.

Geoff from India, my ex-husband of two or three years ago, was one of us, and as he bent to kill a mouse, he caught the blow that I had aimed at it. This was a good lusty hit and he took it on the head. He staggered back, white but silent.

I thought I'd killed him.

"Oh Geoff, what have I done? Oh I'm sorry—sorry—"

"It's nothing," he replied politely. "Don't worry. I like it."

He recovered, and we carried on. Chug-chug went the rocking noise of the engine, and the broad shiny belt flew round, and the machine ate away mouthful after untidy mouthful of corn, and the grain poured into bags, and the straw went up on the travelling spikes of the elevator to the men making the straw stack with the inherited skill of generations of farm workers. All the air was golden with dust. You could smell it was threshing dust, and when we blew our noses, the hanky was dirty, like after a day in London. Mice darted out, sometimes a rat or two, and once or twice a stoat. It got really exciting as we worked down to the bottom of the stack where the rotted straw was, and the pieces of wood laid across to keep the corn up a bit. You could see the whole shape of well-used rat-highways in the débris, and there was plenty for us to do, because rats and mice had accumulated in this last bit of cover. Everyone got results.

All those boys now, they are Colonels and Air Vice-Marshals. The Battle of Britain was waiting for some of them, and some died in submarines. And Auberies, like other stately homes, had to be half pulled down, before a new Auberies could rise like a phoenix, fresh and beautiful, from the rubble of the old. Only young, brave people could have tackled it. Luckily they were there.

When we were children, moles were worth even more than rats. Dealers in moleskins advertised that they would pay a shilling a skin for clean winter pelts, which meant you could expect sixpence or ninepence each for anything you could trap during the Christmas holidays. We had lots of practice skinning them, and tried to get faster and faster at the job, until at last I could do a freshly killed one, still warm, in one minute flat. Just like the tiger skins, they were tiresome around the ears and feet. Then we'd tack them out on boards to dry, trying to get them as square as possible.

Once, on the last day of the holidays, I went to skin the last mole I'd caught, and could not find it. Now where on earth could it be? I'm sure I put it in my pocket yesterday and—ah yes, and that coat is packed in my trunk and it's gone to school. Oh well.

Rabbits, rats, moles, mice, stoats, weasels, sparrows, and jackdaws were the things the boys killed, and I followed suit, though I could never get to using a gun or rifle for fear of wounding anything. A blow with a stick was the cleanest death a rat could hope to die; and I believed that the mole traps which I set with such care and, I hope, skill, were humane. Every mole was dead when we came to it, of course, but I now doubt if these traps were merciful, though I thought so then.

When we went birds'-nesting we never took more than one egg from a nest, and it was a point of shame to us if we caused a bird to desert. The nest must hatch out after we had had our one egg from it, and it must therefore be approached quietly so the bird would leave it in a precautionary frame of mind, not a startled one. Fortunately fashions change: birds'-nesting is now quite out of date; bird-watching and photography have taken its place.

There is a cuckoo on the Auberies terrace every year. Its egg goes into the wagtail's nest, which is always made on a window sill behind one or another of the shutters. I imagine these birds all inhabit the place, generation after generation, as we do. One year the wagtails came into the house and built on a ledge inside the schoolroom. The cuckoo followed, right indoors. You can destroy the cuckoo egg if you like, or let it hatch and give the wagtails immense pride in having reared this enormous child with the bright orange mouth.

It was fortunate that, though we knew no better than to birds'-nest, we at least did so in a proper way without harming the bird population, because uncommon species, including nuthatches and goldcrest wrens, nest in the quiet coverts round Auberies. Even crossbills have been seen; and once a Patagonian Goose came down to the weed and vegetation of the lake.

How near we came to tragedy at that lake. I sweat even now when I think of it. All of us young people were there for a picnic, and Peter, still only four, wandered off by himself to fill his water pistol. He walked along the plank going out to the boathouse. No one saw him fall in.

Suddenly one of the boys stood up from the campfire we had.

"What's that funny noise?" he said.

We looked around.

Through the bushes we caught sight of Peter's white cotton hat on the water.

We tore round to the boathouse, and there he was, still attached to the hat, and still held up by weed. I happened to be leading, so I took a flying leap off the end of the plank. While I was in the air I had time to think "My new blue dress —oh dear!" It had pants to match, and this was the very first day I'd worn the outfit.

I reached Peter and got him back to the plank where others helped us out.

He drew a great gasp of breath.

"Thanks," he said.

"How did you get into the water?"

"I was filling my pistol." He'd still got it tight in his hand. This gave him an idea. He fired it at us.

We all set off for the house, Peter walking, but halfway home he could suddenly go no further. I carried him. I took him upstairs and put him into a hot bath. Then, in a cowardly way, I sent one of the others to confess the accident to my parents.

I was a bit scared what they'd say to me for letting this happen, and my new dress too, but it was all right, as it turned out.

About this time I began to realise how the years were adding up and how old I was getting. What a lot I knew. What a lot had happened to me. Tempus fugit.

On August 2, 1921, I opened my diary and wrote in it *"Fourteen!* What an age."